Computer Networking: The Complete Guide

Computer Networking: The Complete Guide

Benjamin Murray

MURPHY & MOORE
www.murphy-moorepublishing.com

Computer Networking: The Complete Guide
Benjamin Murray
ISBN: 978-1-63987-125-4 (Hardback)

MURPHY & MOORE

Published by Murphy & Moore Publishing,
1 Rockefeller Plaza,
New York City, NY 10020, USA

Cataloging-in-Publication Data

Computer networking : the complete guide / Benjamin Murray.
     p. cm.
Includes bibliographical references and index.
ISBN 978-1-63987-125-4
1. Computer networks. 2. Network computers. 3. Electronic data processing--Distributed processing.
4. Cyberinfrastructure. I. Murray, Benjamin.
TK5105.5 .C66 2022
004.6--dc23

For more information regarding Murphy & Moore Publishing and its products, please visit the publisher's website www.murphy-moorepublishing.com

Table of Contents

Preface

A computer network is defined as a digital communications network which allows sharing of information and resources between nodes. The network between these nodes could be either wired, optical, wireless or a combination of them. The nodes could include a variety of devices such as servers, personal computers, networking hardware, etc. Depending upon the size of the networks or the number of devices connected, they can be classified into four categories, namely, personal area network (PAN), local area network (LAN), metropolitan area network (MAN) and wide area network (WAN). They can also be classified on the basis of the layout arrangements into bus, star, ring, mesh and tree topology. Computer networks have many applications such as access to World Wide Web, instant messaging, e-mail and shared use of devices like fax machines, printers, storage servers, etc. The topics included in this book on computer networking are of utmost significance and bound to provide incredible insights to readers. It explores all the important aspects of computer networking in the present day scenario. Those in search of information to further their knowledge will be greatly assisted by this book.

A foreword of all chapters of the book is provided below:

Chapter 1 - A computer network is a set of computers connected together for the purpose of transmitting, receiving and exchanging data, voice and video traffic. They can be wireless or connected with cables. This is an introductory chapter which will briefly introduce all the significant aspects of computer networking; **Chapter 2** - Network protocol refers to the set of rules that determine how data is transmitted between different devices on the same network. Hypertext transfer protocol, domain name system, transmission control protocol, etc. are some network protocols. Internet protocol is the method by which data is shared between devices on the internet. This chapter deals with network and internet protocol and their different types in an in-depth manner; **Chapter 3** - Routing is the process in which data packets are transferred from the source to the destination through the optimal path from one network to the other. Routing protocol is the formula used by routers to determine the optimal network transfer and the appropriate path between the networks. This chapter sheds light on routing and its related topics for a thorough understanding of the subject; **Chapter 4** - Network topology refers to the manner in which the links and nodes of a network are arranged physically or logically in relation to one another. It defines the way different nodes are placed and interconnected with each other. Network topology and its different types like ring network, bus network, star network and mesh network are discussed in detail in this chapter; **Chapter 5** - Data transmission is the process of sending data over a communication medium to one or more digital devices. A data link control is a service that ensures reliable data transfer by managing error detection and flow control. This chapter closely examines the process of data transmission and link control in computer networks to provide an easy understanding of the topic; **Chapter 6 -** Network security is a broad term that covers a multitude of processes designed to protect the integrity and confidentiality of computer networks and data, using both software and hardware technologies. Internet security comprises of the various means used to ensure the security of data transmission and transactions online. Network and internet security along with the various methods employed by then are examined and explained in an easy to understand manner in this chapter.

At the end, I would like to thank all the people associated with this book devoting their precious time and providing their valuable contributions to this book. I would also like to express my gratitude to my fellow colleagues who encouraged me throughout the process.

Benjamin Murray

Introduction to Computer Network

A computer network is a set of computers connected together for the purpose of transmitting, receiving and exchanging data, voice and video traffic. They can be wireless or connected with cables. This is an introductory chapter which will briefly introduce all the significant aspects of computer networking.

Computer networks are the basis of communication in IT. They are used in a huge variety of ways and can include many different types of network. A computer network is a set of computers that are connected together so that they can share information. The earliest examples of computer networks are from the 1960s, but they have come a long way in the half-century since then.

What Do Networks Do?

Computer networks are used to carry out a large number of tasks through the sharing of information. Some of the things that networks are used for include:

- Communicating using email, video, instant messaging and other methods.

- Sharing devices such as printers, scanners and photocopiers.

- Sharing files.

- Sharing software and operating programs on remote systems.

- Allowing network users to easily access and maintain information.

Types of Network

There are many different types of network, which can be used for different purposes and by different types of people and organization. Here are some of the network types that you might come across:

- Local Area Networks (LAN): A local area network or LAN is a network that connects computers within a limited area. This might be in a school, an office or even a home.

- Personal Area Networks (PAN): A personal area network is a network that is based on an individual's workspace. The individual's device is the center of the network, with other devices connected to it. There are also wireless personal area networks.

- Home Area Networks (HAN): A home area network connects devices within a home environment. It might include personal computers, tablets, smartphones, printers, TVs and other devices.

- Wide Area Networks (WAN): A wide area network is a network that covers a larger geographical area, usually with a radius of more than a kilometer.

- Campus Networks: A campus network is a LAN or set of connected LANs which is used by a government agency, university, corporation or similar organization and is typically a network across a set of buildings that are close together.

- Metropolitan Area Networks (MAN): Metropolitan area networks are networks that stretch across a region the size of a metropolitan area. A MAN is a series of connected LANs in a city, which might also connect to a WAN.

- Enterprise Private Networks: An enterprise private network is used by a company to connect its various sites so that the different locations can share resources.

- Internetworks: Internetworks connect different networks together to build a larger network. Internetworking is often used to describe building a large, global network.

- Backbone Networks (BBN): A backbone is a part of a network that connects different pieces and provides a path for information to be exchanged.

- Global Area Networks (GAN): A global area network is a worldwide network that connects networks all over the globe, such as the internet.

Network Design

Computer networks can have different designs, with the two basic forms being client/server and peer-to-peer networks. Client/server networks have centralized servers for storage, which are accessed by client computers and devices. Peer-to-peer networks tend to have devices that support the same functions. They are more common in homes, while client/server networks are more likely to be used by businesses.

Types of Network Connections

There are also different types of network connections that concern how elements in a network are connected to each other. Topologies are used to connect computers, with a collapsed ring being the most common type due to the Ethernet supporting the internet, local area networks and wide area networks. Here are some of the topologies that are used to create networks:

Star Topology

A central node connects a cable to each computer in the network in a star topology. Each computer in the network has an independent connection to the center of the network, and one connection breaking won't affect the rest of the network. However, one downside is that many cables are required to form this kind of network.

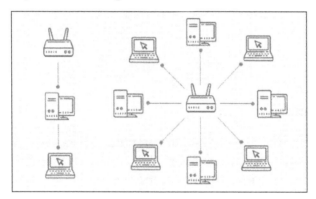

Bus Topology

In a bus topology network connection, one cable connects the computer. The information for the last node on the network has to run through each connected computer. There is less cabling required, but if the cable breaks it means that none of the computers can reach the network.

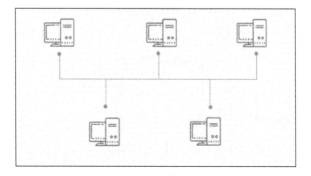

Ring Topology

A ring topology is similar to a bus topology. It uses a single cable with the end nodes connected to each other so the signal can circle through the network to find its recipient. The signal will try several times to find its destination even when the network node is not working properly. A collapsed ring has a central node which is a hub, router or switch. The device has an internal ring topology and has places for cable to plug in. Every computer in the network has its own cable to plug into the device. In an office, this probably means having a cabling closet, where all computers are connected to the closet and the switch.

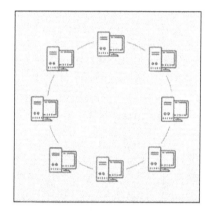

Network Protocols

Network protocols are the languages that computer devices use to communicate. The protocols that computer networks support offer another way to define and group them. Networks can have more than one protocol and each can support different applications. Protocols that are often used include TCP/IP, which is most common on the internet and in home networks.

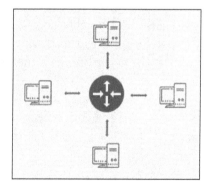

Wired and Wireless Networks

Many protocols can work with both wired and wireless networks. In recent years, however, wireless technologies have grown and become much more popular. Wi-Fi and other wireless technologies have become the favorite option for building computer networks. One of the reasons for this is that wireless networks can easily support different types of wireless gadgets that have become popular over the years, such as smartphones and tablets. Mobile networking is now an important thing to consider because it's not going to go away anytime soon.

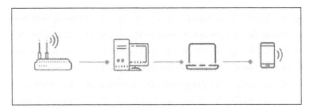

Advantages and Disadvantages of Computer Networking

We use computers of all shapes and sizes to communicate with one another every day. These tools help us to be more productive at work, play games at home, or scroll through our Facebook feeds.

There are several ways that we use them without thinking about their presence in our lives. Modern automobiles use sophisticated computing to maximize fuel economy, response times, and many aspects of the driving experience. Smart technologies use networking capabilities to tackle a variety of needs, ranging from thermostat management to the locks on your home's front door.

Computers help us to find new resources. They are responsible for showing us the secrets of what lie beyond our solar system. We also use them to explore how certain cells contribute to our health. This technology makes the macro- and micro-worlds come alive for us in a variety of ways.

When we consider the advantages and disadvantages of computer networking, there is an opportunity to link the power of individual units to create even more possibilities.

Advantages of Computer Networking

Computer networks create more opportunities for information security: A single computer can be a powerful tool to protect personal information. If you have that unit offline, then there is no way to access it unless you're local and have the password for it. When you have an online network of computers, you can experience the same benefits, even if you are connected to the Internet. In this era of data breaches that happen on a massive scale, we can all use this technology to improve our standard of living and increase productivity without compromising our privacy.

Almost everyone can afford the benefits of a computer network: Computers are remarkably affordable tools. Families can purchase a brand-new unit for less than $200 and still receive the powerful benefits of a network. You can even build computers to take advantage of what this technology provides for under $100 for basic models. Humanity discovered more than 30 years ago that when we can use this tech to communicate with each other and make better decisions that life becomes better.

Even when computer networks have artificial limitations placed on them, the benefits of their presence still exist. You can even find them in some of the most restrictive countries in the world today, like North Korea. Even premium products, like an Apple Mac, have come down in price by 50% or more since their introduction in the 1980s.

A computer network offers a personalized experience: The first computers suitable for home use required individuals to follow specialized processes if they wanted to be more productive. If you didn't input the correct commands at the right time, then you had to start over from the beginning. Games were few and far between – unless you liked chess or Battleship.

Modern computers provide a very different user experience. It's no longer a system that requires you to take what is offered or look for something else. You have more computing power in your pocket than what the astronauts used to fly to the moon. This personalization of our networking potential allows us to have information however and whenever we want it.

You can expand the potential of computer networks: If you have two computers at home, then you can link them together to create a personal network. The Internet of Things system links tools together to create benefits in a similar way. What makes this technology such a fantastic addition to our lives is that it can also incorporate new units at any time. If you purchase a third computer, then you can add it to your personal network to create even more rewards.

You can continue expanding this potential by adding external storage and additional user features over time. People today think that the 5 GB of storage you get for free from many cloud-based providers is limiting. When IBM introduced the first 1 GB hard drive in 1980, it weighed 550 pounds and was the size of a refrigerator. Buying it would have set you back $40,000. When you incorporate inflation into the mix, that's like spending over $124,000 in 2019 dollars on that product.

Almost anyone can use a computer to create networking experiences: When you purchase a modern computer, what you see is what you get (WYSIWYG). If you can press the power button on the unit, then it is pretty easy to figure out what you'll need to do afterward. Most people can set up computer networks in a few minutes to start taking advantage of its benefits. Even if you have no experience, you're only a few clicks away from receiving the assistance you need to get going.

Computer networks make it easier to collaborate on projects: There are several different ways that computers make it easier to work with others on projects. Most companies use this technology to connect teams so that they can share documents, work on designs, or send emails to each other to finish projects. Personal networks allow families to stay connected, share pictures and music, and a host of other fun activities without compromising their security.

Several people can be in the same document simultaneously to work on it. You can share events to organize political responses, social meet-ups, or a variety of other needs. Whether you want to share a grocery list or you're booking a vacation, computer networks make all of these tasks more comfortable to complete.

This technology makes it easy to share information: The average price of a broadband connection in the United States is about $50 per month for every 100 Mbps of speed you receive. Your actual price may vary based on your geographic location. When you can network with other computers online with this technology, then you have the ability to create a number of personalized benefits. Many of them we all take for granted already if we're used to their presence.

- You can stream movies and TV shows from authorized providers thanks to computer networking technologies.

- You can share files with other people almost instantly.

- You can connect multiple devices to the same internet connection at once to create personal experiences.

- You can post status updates, images, and videos to your preferred social media platforms.

Computer networks can transfer enormous file sizes in seconds: If you are old enough to remember the 1990s, then you might have used those 3.5-inch floppy disks to store information from your computer. You knew that a game was going to be complex if it came with at least 7 installation disks that you needed to manage. Older computer users might even remember the 5.25-inch floppies. With tools like Dropbox, iCloud, and similar services, you can now share files that are measured in terabytes instead of megabytes. You can even upload the file to a personal account and then share a direct access link for others to download the item.

We have opportunities to learn because of computer networks: Why is it important to share information? Because the foundation provided by computer networks gives us the opportunity to have ongoing educational opportunities every day. Online degrees are possible in a variety of fields because of this technology. We share email messages with attachments for a variety of reasons. Social media is the perfect place to share links to interesting content.

The flexibility of a network means that it can support almost any type of learning at whatever time of day is convenient for the user. Everyone can choose the sharing options that best meet their needs. It becomes an extension of who we are.

Entrepreneurs can make money because of computer networks: Fever takes advantage of computer networking technologies to deliver freelance opportunities to buyers and sellers. It was founded in 2010 and is based in Tel Aviv, Israel. Even though only 2% of the platform's sellers are above the age of 55, the gig economy gives individuals the opportunity to create a global opportunity for themselves from the comfort of their home. It is a chance for someone to earn radical income opportunities with their skills in the developing world or for busy parents to work from home to manage their schedules better.

That's one example of millions that exist in the world today. Whether you want to write a blog, sell products on Amazon, or create YouTube videos, all of those activities happen because of the presence of computer networks.

Computer networks allow us to be more productive with our time: We have instant access to almost any form of information thanks to the presence of computer networks in our lives. Instead of needing to stop to look up something in an encyclopedia, you can find the information on Google, Bing, or another search engine. We have opportunities for genuine multitasking thanks to the way web browsers can segregate data for us. Everything that we need stays in one place, even if that means it's on the device that you've stuck in your pocket.

There are numerous ways to save money with computer networks: When you can share devices on a single computer network, then there are fewer physical assets that you must purchase. You can have multiple units connected to the same printer, copy machine, or server so that the initial capital investments are minimal. Site licenses tend to be cheaper when you can deploy them along with a network as well, especially when you compare the expense to purchase several standalone licenses for people to use. You can even save money on your data backups since everything goes to a single location instead of being stored in multiple units as a partial project.

Even productivity benefits help to save money. If you are not having people key the same day multiple times, then teams can stay focused on role-based instructions instead of creating accidental duplication.

A computer network can share a single Internet connection: Instead of connecting individual units to a separate ISP account, your computer network can function as a single unit to access online information. This advantage makes the expense of purchasing cables and other equipment worthwhile because you can usually operate under a single subscription package. It is a setup that gives your digital defenses another layer of security because it funnels all traffic into a single point, whether it is coming down the stream or someone uploads something.

It provides people with an opportunity to solve problems creatively: If you have a medical emergency, then computer networks make it possible to start a crowd funding page that can cover the expense. Villages in remote locations use this technology to communicate with local providers about the basic necessities they require. Anyone can share almost anything over a blog to start building an audience of unlimited size. This advantage allows us to communicate openly, build diverse environments, and create personal and professional networks that help us to shape the world in unique ways.

Disadvantages of Computer Networking

Computer networks can lead us to a variety of distractions: The presence of a computer network can enhance productivity like arguably nothing else that has come before it. This design can also be a disadvantage if there isn't self-discipline with the personal interactions that happen with this technology. When you switch between tasks, then you can lose up to 40% of your productivity energy instantly. This issue results in a delay of up to 15 minutes before restarting your project.

Even something simple, like switching to a different tab on your preferred web browser, is enough to create this problem. You might experience more multitasking benefits, but that benefit is an experience that only 2% of the population gets to enjoy.

Computer networks require a specific setup to be useful: There must be a minimum level of electromagnetic impedance to obtain uniform coverage for a computer network. Buildings with several wireless networks often cause interference with information transfers, disrupting user access to the needed data. Individual locations with steel reinforcements make it difficult for computers to pick up the specific frequencies required for data sharing. For a computer network to operate efficiently, exceptional care must be taken during the installation process to reduce interference problems.

People can stop relying on their memory because of computer networks: Digital dependence can erode the benefits that human memory provides. When we are overly reliant on computer networks to provide us with information, then it becomes difficult to recall needed data at a moment's notice. "Many adults who could still recall their phone numbers from childhood could not remember their current work number or the numbers of family members," writes Sean Coughlan for the BBC.

A study that examined the memory habits of 6,000 adults in Europe found that over one-third of them turn to computers first to recall information. Over 50% of the participants in the UK said that they'd search online for an answer first.

National legislation has not caught up with modern computer network activities: Many of the laws that we have around the world have not yet caught up with what computer networks can provide. If someone makes a false report to the police about a dangerous incident at a person's home, then swatting activities that result in death are not counted as murder. The presence of this technology makes it easier to embezzle money when you're in a position of trust and know how to cover your digital footprint. Computers allow us to have access to information and provide more communication opportunities. It also gives us these benefits without the same security options that govern our activities outside of the digital world in some critical areas.

Computer networks change our perspective on work-life balance: Almost 50% of people take work with them when traveling on vacation. This figure includes individuals who are not self-employed. It is not unusual for professionals to bring a work computer home each night to check emails, speak with co-workers, and telecommute on projects. This disadvantage is one of the reasons why the average digital attention span for humans is about eight seconds in length. We have so many different things going on that any distraction feels like it might be an important topic that can't be missed.

Computer networks have also created a change in how we view relationships because of this issue. The average person will check their phone over 80 times per day for notifications, messages, and social media updates. When was the last time you checked-in with your spouse, partner, or significant other that many times during the day? Online communication does not provide the same benefits as a face-to-face conversation.

There are several ways to exploit the vulnerabilities of a computer network: There are infinite ways for disruptions to happen when operating a computer network. Hackers can contaminate them with malicious software, and then encrypt the information it contains for money – like they're "kidnapping" your files. You might download a file from an email that looks real without realizing it's a trap to record keystrokes to expose your credit card data.

Something as simple as a power outage can make it challenging for people to use their computers when they might require access. Viruses, information corruption, ISP outages, and DDoS assaults are all typical examples of interruptions that occur daily. A computer network is never 100% secure, even when you keep it off-line.

You can lose access to your information quickly: If you have a file server that breaks down on your computer network, then all of your information might become instantly inaccessible. When individual units become isolated, they can no longer communicate as effectively with each other. That means it takes more time and energy to get work finished each week. Trying to manage a large network is a complex process that requires training and the presence of a competent manager to maximize your opportunities for success.

One computer can create problems for the entire network: Viruses can quickly spread to other computers when an infected one is connected to a network. Even if there is no ill intent with the process, this security risk can limit productivity and increase the risk of a data breach. Security procedures, such as a firewall, cannot stop every problem that might occur when individuals use several different access points simultaneously for their collaboration efforts.

Even though other users can't see the files that someone stores locally since it remains a stand-alone machine, an experienced professional could use the network to communicate with the unit to access the data anyway.

Computer networks cause us to put all of our eggs in one basket: About $600 billion in intellectual property losses occur annually because of how we structure computer networks and use them. We can access plenty of information with this technology, but it can also be used to break the law in ways that feel anonymous. Even a common crime that happens online, like identity theft, can result in a global GDP loss of $100 billion each year.

Network Performance

Ideally, a user (or application) would expect any amount of communication to take place as fast as possible, and in a reliable manner. This is a primary requirement. One may also expect the communication to be secure. Additionally, one could expect flexibility in terms of mobility, devices, etc. That is, wherever the user is or whatever the device he or she is using, he/she may expect the same kind of seamless reliable communication across a network.

These requirements can be defined in terms of certain performance parameters of the network. Normally there are three important parameters that characterize the primary performance requirements of a network. They are (i) Throughput (Bandwidth), (ii) Delay (Latency) and (iii) Data loss. Additional parameters in terms of security and mobility may optionally be used to characterize the performance.

Throughput

Throughput or bandwidth or transfer rate is the amount of data transmitted per unit time. It is normally specified as number of bytes per second or bits per second. The common notation is to use 'Bps' for bytes per second (note the upper case B), and bps for bits per second. The transfer rates could be of the order of Kbps (kilobits per second), Mbps (mega bps), Gbps (giga bps), and so on. When we discuss bandwidth, we also differentiate between link bandwidth and end-to-end throughput. Each link involved in a communication could support different data rates (depending on the type of media and the environmental noise). When data travels across multiple links, what would matter would be the overall end-to-end throughput - i.e., the amount of data transferred per unit time from the application perspective. The throughput may not be constant - it could vary depending on the behavior of the network. You would have noticed this when downloading huge files - the data rate that is displayed will vary! Some applications (such as file download) are fine with this, but some applications may need a constant bandwidth.

Delay

Delay (Latency) is the time taken to send a message from one node to another. Here again, we talk about link delay and end-to-end delay. From an application perspective we are of course concerned with end-to-end delay. But you cannot ignore link delay, because the link delay is a component of the end-to-end delay as we will see shortly.

We view end-to-end delay as a one-way latency. However, in many situations what is more important is the round-trip time (RTT). RTT is the time it takes from the time a message is sent to the time a response is received for that message.

Let us now look at what constitutes this delay. When looking at end-to-end delay, we need to understand that there are three components to this delay: (i) propagation delay (ii) transmission delay and (iii) queuing delay. Propagation delay is the latency of the signal to travel along the entire length of the link. There is a propagation delay for every link, and is calculated as the length of the link divided by the speed of the signal. If it is an optical signal, the speed would be that of light.

Propagation delay = Distance / speed

The transmission delay is the time taken to transmit the data (a certain number of bits at a certain speed). If a transmitter has a bandwidth of rbps (that is, it is emitting data at a rate of r bps), and if the amount of data to be transmitted is x bits, then the transmission delay would be x/r secs. Greater the transmission rate, lower would be the transmission latency.

Transmission delay = Size of data / Bandwidth

Queuing delay is the delay incurred by data packets when they are waiting at the queues in the routers. When packet switching is used to send packets, packets are queued in the buffers at the routers, before they are processed and forwarded. This waiting time is the queuing delay. This is likely to vary depending on the traffic in the network. More traffic would lead to higher delays. The total latency is the sum of these three delays.

Total Latency = Propagation + Transmission + Queuing delays

Let us do a quick back-of-the-envelope calculation to understand the impact of these components.

Example: Let the length of an optical link connecting two nodes A & B be 300km. Let the size of data packet be 1 MByte. We will consider four different data rates: 1Kbps, 1Mbps, 100 Mbps, and 10Gbps. Calculate the end-to-end delay in each of the cases.

Propagation delay = 300km / $3x10^8$ m/sec = 1 msec

At 1Kbps data rate, Transmit time = 1 MB / 1kbps = approx. 8000s

At data rates of 1 Mbps, 100 Mbps, and 10Gbps, the transmit delay would reduce to 8sec, 80 ms, and 800 microseconds respectively. Hence end-to-end delay would be

8000.001secs, 8.001secs, 81ms, 1.8ms respectively. This example gives us a quick idea of the impact of data rates on the end-to-end delay. As expected, as the data rate increases, the delay decreases. What is interesting to note is that it becomes less than the propagation delay at very high data rates (at 10Gbps in this example).

It can be a little tricky to understand the importance of link bandwidth vis-à-vis link propagation delay. Which parameter is more important than the other? The answer to this question depends on the size of the data being transferred. If you were transmitting one byte of data, it really wouldn't matter if you had a 1Mbps or 100Mbps bandwidth. On the other hand, latency (propagation delay) of 1 ms or 100 ms would matter. It would be wiser to choose a path with 1 ms latency than a path with 100ms latency.

If we were transmitting a large amount of data, say 25Mbytes, a data rate of 1 Mbps or 100 Mbps will make a difference in the total data transfer latency. A 1 ms or 100ms propagation delay would be insignificant in this scenario.

Another important parameter to consider in the bandwidth-latency debate actually is a term called the delay-bandwidth product – which captures the effect of both the parameters. This product gives an idea of the amount of data that is currently in-flight or "in the pipe". The bandwidth here refers to the rate of data transmission, and the delay refers to RTT. With a data rate of 45 Mbps, and an RTT of 100ms, the delay-bandwidth product would be about 560KB, indicating that at any-time so much of data is somewhere in the network. This parameter is important in determining the amount of buffer space that needs to be used at the transmitter and receiver, or to determine the window size that should be used for high efficiency.

Packet loss

The third parameter, namely packet loss needs to be quantified, since it directly affects applications that are sensitive to loss of data. We normally classify applications as being delay tolerant or loss-tolerant (we could also use the terms loss-sensitive and delay-sensitive). Examples of delay-tolerant but loss-sensitive applications include file-transfer, e-commerce etc. Real-time video transfer or movie streaming would fall in the other category of loss-tolerant but delay- sensitive applications. It should be noted though that, even a loss-tolerant application, can only tolerate a certain number of losses. Hence we need to quantify this parameter, and also have mechanisms to handle this packet loss. Bit-error-rate (BER) is a parameter that is used to quantify errors, and percentage of packets transmitted successfully or packet delivery ratio (PDR) is used to indicate losses. When losses occur because of errors in the transmission, some error-correcting techniques could be used to recover from the error, thus preventing data loss in such cases. Or we will have to retransmit erroneous data. Alternatively, some buffering and delay tactics can be used to tolerate delays as well.

QoS Parameters

In general, these three parameters – delay, bandwidth and loss - are referred to as Quality-of Service (QoS) parameters, and are used by applications to specify the kind of service they expect from the network. The network's capability is also specified in terms of some lower/upper bounds of these parameters. Thus if an application requires some performance guarantees from the network, it can be specified in terms of these parameters or negotiated with the network.

2

Network and Internet Protocol

Network protocol refers to the set of rules that determine how data is transmitted between different devices on the same network. Hypertext transfer protocol, domain name system, transmission control protocol, etc. are some network protocols. Internet protocol is the method by which data is shared between devices on the internet. This chapter deals with network and internet protocol and their different types in an in-depth manner.

Network Protocol

Network protocols are a set of well-defined rules through which a user communicates over the internet or intranet. Both ends of the communication channel adhere to these rules for proper information exchange. Protocols are developed by industry-based people, research institutions, etc. and then once published and accepted by means of international conferences. These protocols are categorized on multiple bases like some are associated with the transport layer; some are associated with the network layer.

Understanding Networking Protocols

When we look to define the networking models, two kinds of layered models appear into the picture on which the roots of networking are laid:

- OSI Model.

- TCP/IP Model.

The OSI model is a 7 Layer model which comprises of following layers handling their tasks:

- Application Layer.

- Presentation Layer.

- Session Layer.

- Transport Layer.

- Network Layer.

- Data link layer.

- Physical Layer.

The TCP/IP model contains 4 Layers only in contrast to the OSI model and they only handle the tasks:

- Application Layer.

- Transport Layer.

- Internet.

- Network Access.

- Application layer has the user's data, handles the encoding mechanisms.

- Transport layer supports communication between the end devices.

- The Internet layer provides logical addressing.

- Network layer controls hardware devices like routers.

- Data link layer is responsible for mac addressing etc. and to communicate with the physical layer.

- The physical layer carries all stuff at the hardwired level.

Now let's understand what an IP address is and what the networking protocols in association with it are. The IP address is a decimal representation of binary numbers, unique in nature for each device such that it acts as an identity of the device connected to the network. There are two protocols put up in association with this, which are IPv4 and IPv6. In the IPv4 addressing, there are public and private IPs. The private IP is accessible inside the network while the public IP is accessible throughout the internet.

How do Networking Protocols Work?

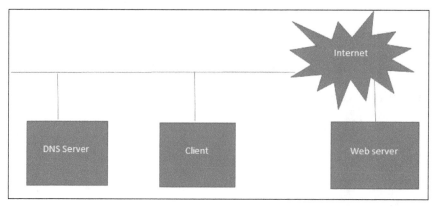

Let's understand what happens when you click at www.google.com, the client represents your system's browser here from which you submit a request at the internet, once you hit this URL, the call via channel gets transported to DNS server and it asks a query "what is the address mapped against this URL ?" Now the DNS server has cache installed, it is possible that it may have result already or in the otherwise case it will communicate with other DNS servers and return back an IP. So after the IP resolution, the request from the client reaches the web server of that host.

Types of Networking Protocols

IPv6: Refers to Internet Protocol version 6, is the future addressing format, as soon we can see the IPv4 addresses getting exhausted with a rising number of machines and the public IPs being structured up will go into version 6. It offers $3.4*10^{34}$ unique combinations in which addressing can be done and hence could represent a large number of machines connected to the internet. It's obvious that once it has to be introduced, the routing protocols and hardware may see ample changes in architecture.

TCP/IP Protocols: The TCP/IP based protocols are further classified into the following:

Web Protocols

- HTTP – It stands for Hypertext Transfer Protocol, the format of messages, their transmission and web actions associated at client and server end are managed by this protocol. Worldwide web uses it. Runs on port 80.

- HTTPS – It stands for Hyper Text Transfer Protocol Secure, so it seems to be an enhancement of HTTP only. This is used for secure communication hence whenever you are out of the local host world then go by this.

- TLS – It stands for Transport Layer Security, this is a cryptographic protocol that provides end to end communications security over networks, commonly used in transactions, the security is maintained by forgery prevention, data leak prevention, etc.

- SSL – It stands for Secure Sockets Layer, establishes encrypted link between browser and server, SSL certificate is required by the web server. A public and a private key are created cryptographically.

File Transfer Protocols

- FTP – File Transfer Protocol is used for file transfer between client and server on a computer network.

- TFTP – Trivial File Transfer Protocol is a way in which the client can get a file and put it into a remote host, the nodes which boot from LAN use it.

- SFTP – SSH File Transfer Protocol, provides a secure connection to transfer files and traverse the file system on local and remote systems.

- FTPS – It's a secure File Transfer Protocol, TLS support and SSL are added here, we are not using secure shell based protocol.

- SMB – Server Message Block, is used by windows, allows computers within the same network to share files.

- NFS – Network File system is a distributed file system, used in UNIX generally to access files among computers on the same network.

Email Protocols

- SMTP – Simple Mail Transfer Protocol is a push protocol to send an email and Post Office Protocol or Internet Message Access Protocol is used to retrieve those at the receiver side. It is implemented at the application layer.

Management Protocols

- Telnet – It is used on the internet and LAN for bilateral text communication, it uses a virtual terminal connection.

- SSH – It is a secure shell based remote login from one computer into another computer. Authentication and security can be taken care of too.

- SNMP – Simple Network Management Protocol is used for collecting and organizing information about devices in the network and modifies the information.

Media Protocols

- RTP – Real-time transport protocol is used for audio and video communication over the network.

- RTSP – Real-time streaming protocol, is a protocol for streaming, it establishes media sessions between endpoints.

Hypertext Transfer Protocol

HTTP is a protocol that is used to access web pages. So let us start with what a web page is! A web page consists of objects, which could be a HTML file, JPEG image, Java applet, audio file, video file, etc. A web page is organized as a base HTML-file which includes several referenced objects. Each object is addressable by a URL (Uniform Resource Locator). A URL consists of a host name that refers to the machine or system in the web, and a path name that gives the path on that machine where the resource is located.

Thus, retrieving a web page involves retrieving the base file and each of the objects referenced in that file. Let us look at how HTTP allows you to do that.

HTTP Overview

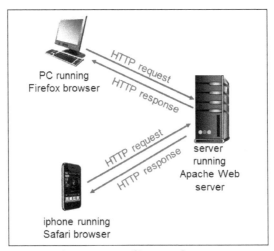

PC running
Firefox browser

HTTP request
HTTP response

HTTP request
HTTP response

server
running
Apache Web
server

iphone running
Safari browser

Figure: HTTP clients and server.

HTTP is the web's application layer protocol. It uses the client/server model. The client is the browser (IE, Firefox, Chrome, Safari etc.) that requests web objects, receives them and "displays" them. The server is the web server (implemented using Apache, IIS etc.) that sends objects in response to requests. Multiple clients can simultaneously talk to the server. There are two versions of HTTP that have been developed, version 1.0 given by RFC 1945, and HTTP 1.1 given by RFC 2068. Version 1.1 is the one that is currently prominent.

Since web access required 100% data integrity, it uses TCP. There may be some delays, but we are often willing to tolerate the delays as long as the data retrieved is not lost or corrupted. Also, HTTP can tolerate variations in bandwidth. If you access from a low bandwidth link, you anyway know that it is going to take longer. So it uses TCP.

TCP is a connection-oriented mechanism, i.e., it opens a logical connection with the other end before data transfer takes place. The HTTP server runs at the well-known port number 80. Hence, a HTTP client first initiates a TCP connection (by creating a TCP socket) to the server at port 80. This obviously means that the server would already have opened a socket at port 80, and will be waiting for requests to come from the clients. Once the server accepts the TCP connection request from the client, HTTP messages (application layer protocol messages) are exchanged between the browser (HTTP client) and the Web server (HTTP server).

It is interesting to note that HTTP is a "stateless" protocol. What this implies is that HTTP does not keep track of what messages or objects have been previously requested. Every HTTP request is treated as a fresh request, and the response is given by the server. This may appear very inefficient, (which it is to an extent), but it has a major advantage in terms of scalability. Also, there are additional features that have been added to HTTP to compensate for this inefficiency. If state were to be maintained, handling large number of clients as in the case of most web-servers would become too heavy and complex. So, to keep things simple HTTP has adopted a state-less approach, and this decision has proved itself, with the growth of the world-wide-web.

Domain Name System

Just as we humans have different identities for different purposes and for convenience, so too, the hosts and devices in the network have multiple identities. While IP addresses are used in the network for the hosts and routers to send data to each other, when human beings have to access them, they need an easy to remember alphabetic or alphanumeric name. These are referred to as domain names.

Domain Names

Domain names are alphanumeric names for IP addresses. The reason for having such names to refer to systems is obvious – it is easy for us human beings to remember names rather than large numbers (as in IP addresses). So we prefer to interact with the network nodes using names and leave it to the network to figure out the corresponding IP address. The networks answer to this challenge is the Domain Name System (DNS).

Domain Name System

The domain name system (DNS) is an Internet-wide distributed database that translates between domain names and IP addresses. This task is also referred to as name resolution. The distributed database is implemented in a hierarchy of many name servers, which have the mapping of names and addresses. It also includes an application-layer protocol – for hosts, routers, and name servers to communicate to resolve names, i.e., to do this address/name translation.

It is intriguing to note that a core Internet function is implemented as an application-layer protocol. The reason for this decision is that this is a complex task and it is easier to handle this complexity at the networks "edge" rather than at the core.

Thus any network application which needs to use the network, typically first contacts the DNS system to get the name resolved to a network (IP) address. On getting the IP address it can proceed with its work. This tells us the importance of DNS.

Another practical experience of understanding the importance of DNS is to remember the situation when the local DNS server is down. I am sure all of us would have faced this situation more than once. We would not be able to get through to the system we want to connect to:

There was a file called the HOSTS.TXT file. Before DNS (until 1985), the name-toIP address resolution was done by downloading a single file (hosts.txt) from a central server with FTP. This worked because the number of entries was limited. The hosts.txt file still works on most operating systems! It can be used to define local names. The names in the hosts.txt file are not structured.

Coming back to the current DNS system, it is a distributed set of servers that have the name-to-IP-address mapping. Now the question that comes up is – why distributed? Why not a centralized DNS server? The answer is simple – just remember the usual debate that we have between centralized and distributed systems. Centralized systems are characterized by single-point of failure. The central server fails, and all systems get stuck. Also, in this case, the amount of traffic that the centralized server has to handle is enormous, and can overwhelm the server. Maintenance of information in the server can also become complex. The distance to the centralized server can also be a cause of concern. Basically, it doesn't scale. For all these reasons, and more, the DNS has been designed to be a distributed database spread out over a vast number of servers. Let us look at how this is done.

Design Principle of DNS

The domain names are arranged in a hierarchical and logical tree structure called the domain namespace. The structure shown in Fig. shows the distribution of domain name servers starting at the root. Below the root, we have what are called as top-level domain (TLD) servers, catering to different domains. These domains are divided based on the purpose for which they are used as in edu (for education), org (for organization), com (for commerce), net (for network-related), mil (military), gov (government), or based on countries as in „in" (for India), au (for Australia), uk (for the United Kingdom), and so on.

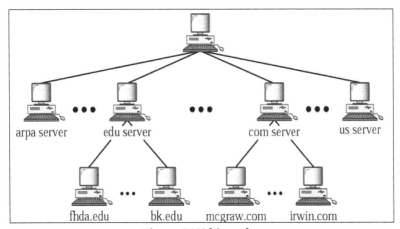

Figure: DNS hierarchy.

Under these domains, sub-categories are assigned as and how required. The names at lower layers of the hierarchy can be assigned without regard to the location on a link layer network, IP network or autonomous system. However, in practice, allocation of the domain names generally follows the allocation of IP addresses. For example, all hosts with network prefix 178.143/16 have same domain name suffix, say e-IndianUniv.edu; all hosts on network 178.143.136/24 are in the Computer Science Department of the University, and so on.

The full domain name can be traced by starting at its location in the hierarchy, and going up in the tree to the root. The servers responsible for the hosts under a particular domain are called the authoritative DNS servers. For instance, in Fig., the server shown as bk.edu would be the authoritative server for the domain bk.edu, and have the IP addresses for machines in that domain, say cs.bk.edu. In that sense, to locate an authoritative server, we just need to start at the root, and keep traversing down the tree in accordance with the domain name parsed from right to left. For example, to get the IP address for cs.bk.edu, we start at the root, then come down to the .edu server, and then to the bk.edu server which would provide the IP address for the cs.bk.edu server.

DNS Servers

As we can see from the above discussion, there are a number of distributed servers where the information required for name-address resolution – root servers, top-level domain servers, and authoritative servers. Although, theoretically speaking, there is one root server; practically there are many root servers with the same information. This is done to avoid overloading a single server, and to avoid single-point failures. There are more than 250 top-level domain servers. There are three types of top-level domains:

- Organizational: 3-character code indicates the function of the organization. This is primarily used within the USA. Examples of this category are gov, mil, edu, org, com, and net.

- Geographical: 2-character country or region code. Examples include in, va, jp, de, uk, etc.

- Reverse domains: This is a special domain used for IP address to-name mapping that gives the reverse mapping. That is, given the IP address, we can get the corresponding domain name from these servers.

Root and top-level domains are administered by an Internet central name registration authority (ICANN). Authoritative DNS servers are an organization's DNS servers, which provide authoritative hostname to IP mappings for the organization's servers (e.g., Web and mail). These can be maintained by the organization or the service provider.

In addition to these, there is a local DNS server. This is strictly not part of the hierarchy. But each ISP (residential ISP, company, university) has one server of this kind. This is also called as the "default name server". When a host makes a DNS query, the query is first sent to its local DNS server. This server acts as a proxy, and forwards the query into hierarchy. On receiving the answer (mapping) to its query, it caches the mapping, so that subsequent queries asking for the same information can be served from this server itself. It is for this reason that it gets the name "local DNS server".

Domain Name Resolution

Let us now understand the steps in domain name resolution. When an application program needs an address resolution to be carried out, it issues a request for the IP address of a hostname, to the DNS client. The DNS client contacts the local DNS server. The name server checks if it is authorized to answer the query. If yes, it responds. Otherwise, it will query other name servers, starting at the root of the tree. When the name server has the answer it sends it to the resolver (DNS client) which passes the answer to the application program. The process of the local DNS server querying the hierarchy can take place in two ways:

Recursive Querying and Iterative Querying

In a recursive query, when the local name server of a host cannot resolve a query, the server issues a query to the root server. If the root server cannot answer the query, it contacts the next server (some TLD server) in the hierarchy to resolve the query. If this server also does not have the answer, it contacts the next level server. This process continues until the authoritative server is reached. On reaching the authoritative server, it gives the answer to the upper level server which made the request. This server then passes the request up to the next server in the hierarchy. This process continues until the root server is reached. The root then passes this information to the local DNS server. An example of this is shown in Figure below.

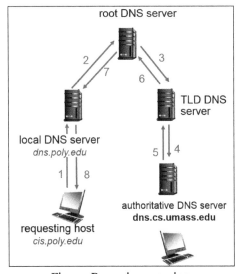

Figure: Recursive querying.

In an iterative query, when the local name server of a host cannot resolve a query, it issues a query to the root server. If the root server cannot answer the query, it sends a referral to another server that may have the answer, to the local server. The local server now contacts this server. If it has the mapping, it gives the answer; else, it gives a referral to another server (typically the next in the hierarchy). The local server contacts this server and the process continue until the authoritative server is contacted which gives the authoritative answer. An example of this is shown in Figure below.

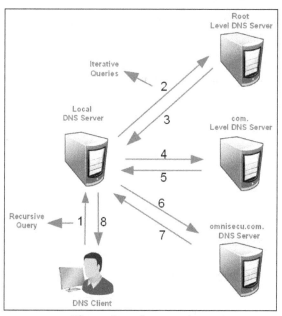

Figure: Iterative querying.

When recursive querying is used, there is a lot of load on the contacted name server. It has to keep track of the request, and forward the answer back. This could lead to high overheads, especially at the top of the hierarchy (root and TLDs). On the other hand, in iterative querying the responsibility is more on the local server. But, the local server collects more information about the hierarchy (at every step of the iterative process), which it can use to successfully answer subsequent queries. We can also use a combination of the iterative and recursive processes and use a hybrid process. This is possible because the choice of the type of query is determined by a bit in the DNS query, in the DNS message. Hence, it is possible to alternate between the two modes of querying.

DNS Caching

To reduce the DNS traffic, name servers cache information on domain name/IP address mappings. When an entry for a query is in the cache, the server does not contact other servers. If an entry is sent from a cache, the reply from the server is marked as "unauthoritative". TLD servers are typically cached in local name servers. Thus root name servers are not often visited. This reduces the load on the top of the tree.

Cache entries timeout (disappear) after some time. The time duration for which the mapping is valid is specified in a "TTL – time to live" field in the DNS record. This information is used to identify the expiry time and drop entries from the cache.

But there is a catch here. Cache entries may be out of date. If a named host changes its IP address, it would not be known until all the cache entries for that host are removed (i.e. Until the TTL expires). To take care of such situations, an update mechanism (RFC 2136) has been added to the DNS protocol using which latest updates can be conveyed to the name servers.

DNS Records

We have so far been talking about the mapping and the transactions that take place between the DNS servers at a high-level. Now let us look at the format in which the mappings are stored and then at the message formats.

All information at the servers is stored as "Resource Records (RR)" in what are called as zone files. Thus, it is a distributed database of RRs that constitute the DNS. There are many types of RRs that are used for various functions related to the management of names and addresses. We will consider 4 primary types of RRs that are essential for the functioning of the DNS. The RR is essentially a 5-tuple with the following fields:

Name, Value, Type, Class, TTL

The type field specifies the type of RR, and the name and value fields are interpreted based on the value of this type field. The class field indicates the protocol family (IN – for internet protocol). TTL is the Time-To-Live field that gives the validity of this entry when it is cached. Table gives the type and corresponding interpretation of the name and value fields, along with an example.

Table: Types of DNS Resource Records.

TYPE	NAME	VALUE
A Address Record	Hostname (www.xyz.com)	IP address (202.1.2.3)
NS Next Server record	Domain (xyz.com)	Hostname of authoritative server for this domain (dnserver.xyz.com)
CNAME Canonical Name Record	Alias name (www.xyz.com)	Canonical name for the alias (www.actualNameXYZ.com)
MX Mail Server Record	Domain name (www.xyz.com)	Mail server associated with the domain name (mail1.xyz.com)

The A type record provides the actual mapping - IPv4 address - for a given domain name. There is a AAAA (quad-A) record used for IPv6 addresses (128-bit addresses). The NS record is used to point to the next server (authoritative server for the domain) if a queried server does not have the mapping. Along with the NS record, A type record for that server is also returned in order to contact that server.

The CNAME record is used to specify aliases. For instance, you may look for cs.myuniv. edu, whereas the actual name could be computerScience.mail.edu. So when a query is sent for cs.myuniv.edu, the system automatically has to search for computerScience. mail.edu. To enable this functionality, the CNAME type allows us to specify aliases and their associated canonical (real) names.

The MX record is used to point to the mail server at a given domain name. Often, we need not know the actual name of the mail server of a given domain name. We may say, we want to send mail to aaa@xyz.com. The mail transfer agent now has to find the IP address of the mail server of xyz.com. How would it do that? It is here that the MX record is useful. The mail transfer agent would query for the MX record, get the name of the mail server, and then proceed to get the IP address of that mail server. There are many other records as well, which have been added as the DNS system continues to evolve. It would be an interesting exercise for you to check them out.

A Practical Question

What do we do if we want to register a new domain name and get an IP address assigned, say for instance "Network XYZ"?

We will have to register the name networkxyz.com at a DNS registrar (there are many registrars who provide this service). We will have to provide the names and IP addresses of authoritative name server for our domain. Actually, a primary and secondary server is to be specified. If one fails, the other acts as a backup. The registrar will then insert two RRs into the .com TLD server.

This will successfully redirect any requests for networkxyz.com to our domain's DNS server. Now at our server, we create authoritative server type A record for www.networkuptopia.com, and a type MX record for networkutopia.com for our mail server. And we are done.

DNS Message Format

There are two types of messages used by DNS: Query and reply messages. Interestingly, both messages use the same format. There is one bit in the header that identifies if a message is a query message or a reply message. The format of the message is shown in figure below.

Figure: DNS message format.

The identification field is a 16-bit number used to identify the query. The reply for a query uses the same sequence number. It is thus used to tie replies to queries. One of bits in the flags field is used to identify the message as a query or a reply. There are two bits related to use of recursion in querying - one specifying that recursion is desired, and the other specifying that recursion is available. Another flag indicates if the reply is an authoritative one (remember that replies coming from the cache are non-authoritative, and that needs to be conveyed to the requesting server).

Questions and answers respectively, refer to the information sought in the query, and the reply (RRs) given in the replies. A single query could ask a number of questions, i.e., ask for a number of domain names to be resolved. The answer would come in the form of A, CNAME, NS, etc., types of records. These records are sent under different categories to enable easy processing of information.

DNS - Benefits and Pitfalls

We can see that in addition to name resolution DNS also provides for host aliasing by supporting canonical and alias names. Similarly, it also provides mail server aliasing. In addition to these two functionalities, DNS can also be used for load distribution. Suppose we have replicated web servers to handle the huge demand of requests at our web server. We would like to have requests distributed to these servers automatically. DNS provides a cool way of accomplishing this. All we need to do is that we need to associate a set of IP addresses for one canonical name, and have DNS return addresses from this set in a round-robin fashion. Automatically, requests will be sent to different IP addresses, and the load will be distributed among the servers, without having any fancy load distribution mechanism.

As such, DNS is a very powerful tool in managing the internetworked world. But it has its downside too. Being central to the internet, it can also become a prime target for security attacks. If the DNS servers are attacked, it can bring down the entire internet! Distributed denial of service (DDoS) attacks is among the most common attacks used to bring down servers by firing too many requests to the servers. Such DDoS attacks can target root servers or the TLD servers. While it is easy to avert the attack on root servers because the root servers are bypassed by the local servers (by caching the TLD server info), it is not easy to avert the attacks on the TLD servers.

Man-in-the-middle attacks that intercept queries and pass false information are possible. DNS poisoning attacks where the attacked sends bogus replies to the DNS server which caches this information are also possible. DNS itself can be exploited, if a DNS server is compromised, and queries with spoofed source addresses are sent. To handle some of these attacks security features have been added to the DNS protocol. You should check them out if you are interested in administering a domain in a secure manner.

In this module, we have discussed the need for domain name resolution, and the challenges in designing the domain name system. We have looked at the DNS hierarchy, the different roles of DNS servers, and the DNS protocol details. We have compared iterative and recursive querying techniques. We have also seen the use of resource records to store relevant information, and the DNS messages that exchange this information.

User Datagram Protocol

The User Datagram Protocol (UDP) is a transport layer protocol defined for use with the IP network layer protocol. It is defined by RFC 768 written by John Postal. It provides a best-effort datagram service to an End System (IP host).

The service provided by UDP is an unreliable service that provides no guarantees for delivery and no protection from duplication (e.g. if this arises due to software errors within a router). The simplicity of UDP reduces the overhead from using the protocol and the services may be adequate in many cases. UDP provides a minimal, unreliable, best-effort, message-passing transport to applications and upper-layer protocols. Compared to other transport protocols.

UDP does not establish end-to-end connections between communicating end systems. UDP communication consequently does not incur connection establishment and teardown overheads and there is minimal associated end system state. Because of these characteristics, UDP can offer a very efficient communication transport to some applications, but has no inherent congestion control or reliability.

A second characteristic of UDP is that it provides no inherent On many platforms, applications can send UDP datagrams at the line rate of the link interface, which is often much greater than the available path capacity, and doing so would contribute to congestion along the path, applications therefore need to be designed responsibly.

One increasingly popular use of UDP is as a tunneling protocol, where a tunnel end-point encapsulates the packets of another protocol inside UDP datagrams and trans-mits them to another tunnel endpoint, which encapsulates the UDP datagrams and for-wards the original packets contained in the payload. Tunnels establish virtual links that appear to directly connect locations that are distant in the physical Internet topology, and can be used to create virtual (private) networks. Using UDP as a tunneling protocol is attractive when the payload protocol is not supported by middle boxes that may exist along the path, because many middle boxes support UDP transmissions.

UDP does not provide any communications security. Applications that need to protect their communications against eavesdropping, tampering, or message forgery therefore need to separately provide security services using additional protocol mechanisms.

Protocol Header

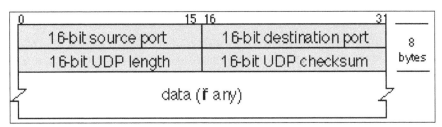

Figure: The UDP protocol header consists of 8 bytes of Protocol Control Information (PCI).

A computer may send UDP packets without first establishing a connection to the recipient. A UDP datagram is carried in a single IP packet and is hence limited to a maximum payload of 65,507 bytes for IPv4 and 65,527 bytes for IPv6. The transmis-sion of large IP packets usually requires IP fragmentation. Fragmentation decreases communication reliability and efficiency and should therefore be avoided. To trans-mit a UDP datagram, a computer completes the appropriate fields in the UDP header and forwards the data together with the header for transmission by the IP network layer.

The UDP header consists of four fields each of 2 bytes in length:

- Source Port (UDP packets from a client use this to indicate the session on the local client that originated the packet).

- Destination Port (UDP packets from a client use this to indicate the service re-quired from the remote server.

- UDP length (The number of bytes comprising the combined UDP header infor-mation and payload data).

- UDP Checksum (A checksum to verify that the end to end data has not been corrupted by routers or bridges in the network or by the processing in an end system. The algorithm to compute the checksum is the Standard Internet

Checksum algorithm. This allows the receiver to verify that it was the intended destination of the packet, because it covers the IP addresses, port numbers and protocol number, and it verifies that the packet is not truncated or padded, because it covers the size field. Therefore, this protects an application against receiving corrupted payload data in place of, or in addition to, the data that was sent. In the cases where this check is not required, the value of 0x0000 is placed in this field, in which case the data is not checked by the receiver.

Like for other transport protocols, the UDP header and data are not processed by Intermediate Systems (IS) in the network (e.g. routers), and are delivered to the final destination in the same form as originally transmitted.

At the final destination, the UDP protocol layer receives packets from the IP network layer. These are checked using the checksum (when >0, this checks correct end-to-end operation of the network service) and all invalid PDUs are discarded. UDP does not make any provision for error reporting if the packets are not delivered. Valid data are passed to the appropriate upper layer application protocol identified by the source and destination port numbers. UDP also may be used for multicast and broadcast, allowing senders to transmit to multiple receivers.

Using UDP

Application designers are generally aware that UDP does not provide any reliability, e.g., it does not retransmit any lost packets. Often, this is a main reason to consider UDP as a transport. Applications that do require reliable message delivery therefore need to implement appropriate protocol mechanisms in their applications (e.g. tftp).

UDP's best effort service does not protect against datagram duplication, i.e., an application may receive multiple copies of the same UDP datagram. Application designers therefore need to verify that their application gracefully handles datagram duplication and may need to implement mechanisms to detect duplicates.

The Internet may also significantly delay some packets with respect to others, e.g., due to routing transients, intermittent connectivity, or mobility. This can cause reordering, where UDP datagrams arrive at the receiver in an order different from the transmission order. Applications that require ordered delivery must restore datagram ordering them. The burden of needing to code all these protocol mechanism can be avoided by using TCP.

Ports

Generally, clients set the source port number to a unique number that they choose themselves - usually based on the program that started the connection.

Example Packet Calculation

A User Datagram Protocol (UDP) packet containing 1460B of broadcast UDP payload data is transmitted over a 10 Mbps Ethernet LAN. What is the size of this frame went sent over a 100BT Ethernet LAN?

This packet has the following headers:

- IFG (ignored).

- Preamble and SFD (8B).

- MAC Header (14B).

- IP Packet header (20B - assuming no options).

- UDP Header (8B).

- UDP Payload (1460B).

- CRC-32 (4B).

    Total =8+12+20+8+1460+4 =1514B.

The main purpose of the UDP Checksum is to detect problems that may arise within Intermediate Systems (where there is no CRC on the data). While the packet is being processed by the router the packet data is protected by the CRC. Router processing errors may otherwise pass undetected.

Transmission Control Protocol

The transmission Control Protocol (TCP) is one of the most important protocols of Internet Protocols suite. It is most widely used protocol for data transmission in communication network such as internet.

Features

- TCP is reliable protocol. That is, the receiver always sends either positive or negative acknowledgement about the data packet to the sender, so that the sender always has bright clue about whether the data packet is reached the destination or it needs to resend it.

- TCP ensures that the data reaches intended destination in the same order it was sent.

- TCP is connection oriented. TCP requires that connection between two remote points be established before sending actual data.

- TCP provides error-checking and recovery mechanism.

- TCP provides end-to-end communication.

- TCP provides flow control and quality of service.

- TCP operates in Client/Server point-to-point mode.

- TCP provides full duplex server, i.e. it can perform roles of both receiver and sender.

Header

The length of TCP header is minimum 20 bytes long and maximum 60 bytes.

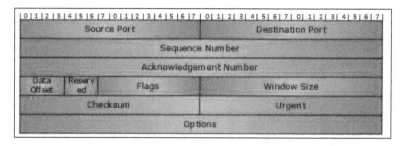

- Source Port (16-bits) - It identifies source port of the application process on the sending device.

- Destination Port (16-bits) - It identifies destination port of the application process on the receiving device.

- Sequence Number (32-bits) - Sequence number of data bytes of a segment in a session.

- Acknowledgement Number (32-bits) - When ACK flag is set, this number contains the next sequence number of the data byte expected and works as acknowledgement of the previous data received.

- Data Offset (4-bits) - This field implies both, the size of TCP header (32-bit words) and the offset of data in current packet in the whole TCP segment.

- Reserved (3-bits) - Reserved for future use and all are set zero by default.

- Flags (1-bit each):

  ○ NS - Nonce Sum bit is used by Explicit Congestion Notification signaling process.

  ○ CWR - When a host receives packet with ECE bit set, it sets Congestion Windows Reduced to acknowledge that ECE received.

- ○ ECE -It has two meanings:

  - ▪ If SYN bit is clear to 0, then ECE means that the IP packet has its CE (congestion experience) bit set.

  - ▪ If SYN bit is set to 1, ECE means that the device is ECT capable.

- ○ URG - It indicates that Urgent Pointer field has significant data and should be processed.

- ○ ACK - It indicates that Acknowledgement field has significance. If ACK is cleared to 0, it indicates that packet does not contain any acknowledgement.

- ○ PSH - When set, it is a request to the receiving station to PUSH data (as soon as it comes) to the receiving application without buffering it.

- ○ RST - Reset flag has the following features:

  - ▪ It is used to refuse an incoming connection.

  - ▪ It is used to reject a segment.

  - ▪ It is used to restart a connection.

- ○ SYN - This flag is used to set up a connection between hosts.

- ○ FIN - This flag is used to release a connection and no more data is exchanged thereafter. Because packets with SYN and FIN flags have sequence numbers, they are processed in correct order.

- Windows Size - This field is used for flow control between two stations and indicates the amount of buffer (in bytes) the receiver has allocated for a segment, i.e. how much data is the receiver expecting.

- Checksum - This field contains the checksum of Header, Data and Pseudo Headers.

- Urgent Pointer - It points to the urgent data byte if URG flag is set to 1.

- Options - It facilitates additional options which are not covered by the regular header. Option field is always described in 32-bit words. If this field contains data less than 32-bit, padding is used to cover the remaining bits to reach 32-bit boundary.

Addressing

TCP communication between two remote hosts is done by means of port numbers (TSAPs). Ports numbers can range from 0 – 65535 which are divided as:

- System Ports (0 – 1023).

- User Ports (1024 – 49151).

- Private/Dynamic Ports (49152 – 65535).

Connection Management

TCP communication works in Server/Client model. The client initiates the connection and the server either accepts or rejects it. Three-way handshaking is used for connection management.

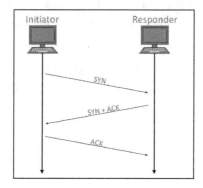

Establishment

Client initiates the connection and sends the segment with a Sequence number. Server acknowledges it back with its own Sequence number and ACK of client's segment which is one more than client's Sequence number. Client after receiving ACK of its segment sends an acknowledgement of Server's response.

Release

Either of server and client can send TCP segment with FIN flag set to 1. When the receiving end responds it back by Acknowledging FIN, that direction of TCP communication is closed and connection is released.

Bandwidth Management

TCP uses the concept of window size to accommodate the need of Bandwidth management. Window size tells the sender at the remote end, the number of data byte segments the receiver at this end can receive. TCP uses slow start phase by using window size 1 and increases the window size exponentially after each successful communication.

For example, the client uses windows size 2 and sends 2 bytes of data. When the acknowledgement of this segment received the windows size is doubled to 4 and next sent the segment sent will be 4 data bytes long. When the acknowledgement of 4-byte data segment is received, the client sets windows size to 8 and so on. If an acknowledgement is missed, i.e. data lost in transit network or it received NACK, then the window size is reduced to half and slow start phase starts again.

Error Control and Flow Control

TCP uses port numbers to know what application process it needs to handover the data segment. Along with that, it uses sequence numbers to synchronize itself with the remote host. All data segments are sent and received with sequence numbers. The Sender knows which last data segment was received by the Receiver when it gets ACK. The Receiver knows about the last segment sent by the Sender by referring to the sequence number of recently received packet.

If the sequence number of a segment recently received does not match with the sequence number the receiver was expecting, then it is discarded and NACK is sent back. If two segments arrive with the same sequence number, the TCP timestamp value is compared to make a decision.

Multiplexing

The technique to combine two or more data streams in one session is called Multiplexing. When a TCP client initializes a connection with Server, it always refers to a well-defined port number which indicates the application process. The client itself uses a randomly generated port number from private port number pools.

Using TCP Multiplexing, a client can communicate with a number of different application processes in a single session. For example, a client requests a web page which in turn contains different types of data (HTTP, SMTP, FTP etc.) the TCP session timeout is increased and the session is kept open for longer time so that the three-way handshake overhead can be avoided. This enables the client system to receive multiple connections over single virtual connection. These virtual connections are not good for Servers if the timeout is too long.

Congestion Control

When large amount of data is fed to system which is not capable of handling it, congestion occurs. TCP controls congestion by means of Window mechanism. TCP sets a window size telling the other end how much data segment to send. TCP may use three algorithms for congestion control:

- Additive increase, Multiplicative Decrease.
- Slow Start.
- Timeout React.

Timer Management: TCP uses different types of timer to control and management various tasks.

Keep-Alive Timer

- This timer is used to check the integrity and validity of a connection.

- When keep-alive time expires, the host sends a probe to check if the connection still exists.

Retransmission Timer

- This timer maintains stateful session of data sent.

- If the acknowledgement of sent data does not receive within the Retransmission time, the data segment is sent again.

Persist Timer

- TCP session can be paused by either host by sending Window Size 0.

- To resume the session a host needs to send Window Size with some larger value.

- If this segment never reaches the other end, both ends may wait for each other for infinite time.

- When the Persist timer expires, the host re-sends its window size to let the other end know.

- Persist Timer helps avoid deadlocks in communication.

Timed-Wait

- After releasing a connection, either of the hosts waits for a Timed-Wait time to terminate the connection completely.

- This is in order to make sure that the other end has received the acknowledgement of its connection termination request.

- Timed-out can be a maximum of 240 seconds (4 minutes).

Crash Recovery

TCP is very reliable protocol. It provides sequence number to each of byte sent in segment. It provides the feedback mechanism i.e. when a host receives a packet; it is bound to ACK that packet having the next sequence number expected (if it is not the last segment).

When a TCP Server crashes mid-way communication and re-starts its process it sends TPDU broadcast to all its hosts. The hosts can then send the last data segment which was never unacknowledged and carry onwards.

Internet Protocol

In order to send somebody information over the internet, you need the correct address – just like sending a regular letter through the mail. In this case however, it is the IP address. Just as a letter receives a stamp to ensure it arrives to the correct recipient, data packets get an IP address. The difference between an IP address and a postal address is that they do not correlate with a specific location per se: instead, they are automatically or manually assigned to networked devices during the connection set up. "Internet Protocol" plays an important role in this process.

The Internet Protocol (IP for short) is the primary protocol in the internet protocol family, and is therefore of fundamental importance when it comes to exchanging messages in computer networks. The connectionless protocol published in 1974 by the Institute of Electrical and Electronics Engineers (IEEE) and specified as standard in RFC 791, is primarily intended to ensure a successful packet dispatch from sender to addressee. To do this, the Internet Protocol specifies a format that defines what kind of description these data packets have.

Internet Protocol (IP) is a connection free protocol that is an integral part of the Internet protocol suite (a collection of around 500 network protocols) and is responsible for the addressing and fragmentation of data packets in digital networks. Together with the transport layer TCP (Transmission Control Protocol), IP makes up the basis of the internet. To be able to send a packet from sender to addressee, the Internet Protocol creates a packet structure which summarizes the sent information. So, the protocol determines how information about the source and destination of the data is described and separates this information from the informative data in the IP header. This kind of packet format is also known as an IP-Datagram.

In 1974 the Institute of Electrical and Electronics Engineers (IEEE) published a research paper by the American computer scientists Robert Kahn and Vint Cerf, who described a protocol model for a mutual packet network connection based on the internet predecessor ARPANET. In addition to the TCP transmission control protocol, the primary component of this model was the IP protocol which (aside from a special abstraction layer) allowed for communication across different physical networks. After this, more and more research networks were consolidated on the basis of "TCP/IP" protocol combination, which in 1981 was definitively specified as a standard in the RFC 971.

IPv4 and IPv6: What is behind the Different Version Numbers?

Today, those who are concerned with the characteristics of a particular IP address e.g., one that would make computers addressable in a local network, will no doubt encounter the two variants IPv4 and IPv6. However, despite undergoing extensive changes in the past, in no way is this the fourth or sixth generation of IP protocol. IPv4 actually is the first official version of the Internet Protocol, whilst the version number relates to the fact that the fourth version of the TCP protocol is used. IPv6 is the direct successor of IPv4 – the development of IPv5 was suspended prematurely for economic reasons.

Even though there have been no further releases since IPv4 and IPv6, the Internet Protocol has been revised since its first mention in 1974 (before this it was just a part of TCP and did not exist independently). The focus was essentially on optimizing connection set-up and addressing. For example, the bit length of host addresses were increased from 16 to 32 bits, therefore extending the address space to approximately four billion possible proxies. The visionary IPv6 has 128-bit address fields and allows for about 340 sextillion (a number with 37 zeroes) different addresses, thus meeting the long term need for Internet addresses.

How is the IP Header of a Datagram Constructed?

The Internet Protocol ensures that each data packet is preceded by the important structural features in the header and is assigned to the appropriate transport protocol (usually TCP). The header data area has been fundamentally revised for version 6, which is why it is necessary to specify between the IPv4 and IPv6 headers.

Construction of IPv4 Headers

Every IP header always begins with a 4 Bit long specification of the Internet protocol version number – either IPv4 or IPv6. Then there are a further 4 Bits, which contain information about the length of the IP header (IP header length), as this does not always remain constant. The total length of the header is always calculated from this value, multiplied by 32 bits. Thus, the smallest possible header length is 160 bytes (equivalent to 20 bytes) when no options are added. The maximum value is 15 to 480 bit (equivalent to 60 bytes). Bits 8 to 15 (type of service) include instructions for handling and prioritizing the datagram. Here the host can specify the importance of points such as reliability, throughput and delay in data transmission, for example:

Bits	0–3	4–7	8–11	12–15	16–18	19–23	24–27	28–31
0	Version	Head Length	Type of Service		Total length (Packet)			
32	Identification				Flags	Fragment Spacing		
64	Lifespan (TTL)		Protocol		Header checksum			
96	Source Address							
128	Destination Address							
160	Options							

Figure: Construction of IPv4 headers.

The total length specifies the total size of the data packet- in other words; it adds the size of the useful data to the header length. Since the field has a length of 16 bits, the maximum limit is 65,635 bytes. It is stipulated in RFC 791 that each host has to be able to process at least 576 bytes. An IP datagram can be fragmented on its way from the host to routers or other devices if desired, but the fragments should not be smaller than the 576 bytes mentioned. The other fields on the IPv4 header have the following meanings:

- Identification: All fragments of a datagram have the same identification number that they receive from the sender. By matching this 16 bit field, the target host can assign individual fragments to a particular datagram.

- Flags: Every IP header contains 3 flag bits, which contain information and guidelines for fragmentation. The first bit is reserved and always has the value 0. The second bit, called "Don't Fragment", informs whether or not the packet may be fragmented (0) or not (1). The last "More Fragments" bit indicates whether further fragments follow (1) or whether the packet is complete or will be completed with the current fragment (0).

- Fragment alignment: This field informs the target host about where a single fragment belongs, so that the entire datagram can be complied again easily. The 13 bit length means that the datagram can be split into 8192 fragments.

- Lifespan (Time to Live, TTL): To ensure that a packet on the network cannot migrate from node to node indefinitely, it is sent with a maximum lifespan (Time to Live). The RFC standard provides the unit of seconds for this 8 bit field, while the maximum lifetime is 255 seconds. The TTL is reduced by at least 1 for each network node that has passed. If the value 0 is reached, the data packet is automatically discarded.

- Protocol: The protocol field (8 bit) assigns the respective transport protocol to the data packet, for example the value 6 for TCP or the value 17 for the UDP protocol. The official list of all possible protocols has been managed and maintained by IANA (Internet Assigned Numbers Authority) since 2002.

- Header/Checksum: The 16 bit "Checksum" field contains the checksum for the header. This has to be recalculated at every network node, due to the dwindling TTL per interim. The accuracy of the user information remains unverified for efficiency reasons.

- Source address and destination address: Every 32 bits (4 bytes) are reserved for the assigned IP address of the originating and target hosts. These IP addresses are usually written in the form of 4 decimal numbers separated by dots. The lowest address is 0.0.0.0., and the highest is 255.255.255.255.

- Options: The options field expands the IP protocol with additional information which is not provided in the standard design. Since these are just optional additions, the field has a variable length, which is limited by the maximum header length. Examples of possible options include: "Security" (indicates how secret a datagram is), "Record Route" (indicates all network nodes that have passed, their IP address to follow the packet route), and "Time Stamp" (adds the time at which a particular node was passed).

Construction of IPv6 Headers

Bits	0–3	4–7	8–11	12–15	16–18	19–23	24–27	28–31
0	Version	Traffic Class		Flow Label				
32	User-data size				Next Header		Hop-Limit	
64	Source address							
128								
192	Data address							
256								

Figure: Construction of IPv6 Headers.

Unlike its predecessor's header, the IPv6 protocol has a fixed size of 320 bits (40 bytes). Less frequently required information can be attached separately between the standard header and the user data. These extension headers can be compared to the option field of the IPv4 protocol and can be adapted at any time without having to change the actual header. Amongst other things, you can determine packet routes, specify fragmentation information, or initiate encrypted communication via IPsec. To optimize performance, a header checksum does not exist.

Like IPv4, the actual IP header begins with the 4-bit version number of the Internet Protocol. The following field called "Traffic Class" is equivalent to the "Type of Service" entry in the older protocol variant. The same rules apply to these 8 bits as in the previous version: they inform the target host about the qualitative processing of the datagram. A new feature of IPv6 is the Flow Label (20 bit), which makes it possible to identify data streams from continuous data packets. This allows for the reservation of bandwidth and the optimization of routing.

The following list explains the additional header information for the improved IP protocol:

- Size of user data: IPv6 transmits a value for the size of the transported user data, including the extension headers (total 16 bits). In the previous version, this value had to be calculated separately from the total length minus the header line length.

- Next Header: The 8-bit "Next Header" field is the counterpart of the protocol specification in IPv4 and therefore has also assumed its function – the assignment of the desired transport protocol.

- Hop-Limit: The Hop limit (8 bit) defines the maximum number of intermediate stations that a packet can pass through before it is discarded. Just like the TTL in IPv4, the value is reduced by at least 1 with each node.

- Source and destination address: Most of the IPv6 headers contain the addresses of sender and addressee. As previously mentioned, these have a length of 128 bits (quadruple of IPv4 addresses). There are also significant differences in the standard notation. The newer version of the Internet Protocol uses hexadecimal numbers and divides them into 8 blocks of 16 bits each. Double points are used instead of simple dots to separate them. For example, a full IPv6 address looks something like this: 2001:0db8:85a3:08d3:1319:8a2e:0370:7344.

How does Internet Protocol Addressing Work?

In order for the datagrams in their header to make the basic specification of the initial and destination addresses, they must first be assigned to the network subscribers. They are usually assigned between internal and external, or public IP addresses. Three address ranges are reserved for the former, which are used for communication in local networks:

- 10.0.0.0 bis 10.255.255.255.

- 172.16.0.0 bis 172.31.255.255.

- 192.168.0.0 bis 192.168.255.255.

The prefix "fc00: /7" is provided for IPv6 networks. Addresses in these networks are not routed in the internet and can therefore be freely selected and used in private or company networks. Addresses are successfully assigned either by manual input or automatically as soon as the device connects to the network, as long as the automatic address assignment is activated and a DHCP server is in use. With the help of a subnet mask, this type of local network can also be selectively segmented into other areas.

External IP addresses are routed automatically by the respective internet provider when they connect to the internet. All devices on the internet via a common router access the same external IP. Typically, the providers assign a new internet address every 24 hours from an address range, which was assigned to them by the IANA. This also applies to the almost inexhaustible arsenal of IPv6 addresses, which are only partly released for normal use. Furthermore, it is not just divided into private and public addresses, but it can be distinguished by much more versatile classification possibilities in so-called "address scopes":

- Host Scope: The loopback address 0:0:0:0:0:0:0: can use a host to send IPv6 datagrams to it.

- Link Local Scope: For IPv6 connectivity is it essential that each host has its own address, even if it is only valid on a local network. This link local address is identified by the prefix"fe80: /10"and is used for example, for communication with the standard gateway (router) in order to generate a public IP address.

- Unique Local Scope: This is the aforementioned address range "fc00: /7", which is exclusively reserved for the configuration of local networks.

- Site Local Scope: The site local scope is an now outdated prefix "fec0: /10", which was also defined for local networks. However, as soon as different networks were connected or VPN connections were made between networks that were numbered with site-local addresses, the standard was considered overtaken.

- Global Scope: Any host that wants to connect to the internet at least needs its own public address. This is obtained by auto-configuration, either by accessing the SLAAC (stateless address configuration) or DHCPv6 (state-oriented address configuration).

- Multicast Scope: Network nodes, routers, servers and other network services can be grouped into multicast groups using IPv6. Each of these groups has its own address, which allows a single packet to reach all the hosts involved. The prefix "ff00: /8"indicates that a multicast address follows.

How IP Protocol Regulates Fragmentation?

Whenever a data packet needs to be sending via TCP/IP, the overall size is automatically checked. If the size is above the maximum transmission unit of the respective network interface, the information becomes fragmented i.e., deconstructed into smaller data blocks. The sending host (IPv6) or an intermediate router (IPv4) takes over this task. By default, the packet is composed by the recipient, who accesses the fragmentation information stored in the IP header or in the extension header. In exceptional cases, the reassembling can also be taken over by a firewall, as long as it can be configured accordingly.

Since IPv6 generally no longer provides fragmentation and no longer allows router fragmentation, the IP packet must already have a suitable size before sending. If a router reaches IPv6 datagrams that are higher than the maximum transmission unit, the router will discard them and inform the sender of an ICMPv6 type 2 "Packet Too Big" message. The data sending application can now either create smaller, non-fragmented packets, or initiate fragmentation. Subsequently, the appropriate extension header is added to the IP packet, so that the target host can also reassemble the individual fragments after reception.

Real-Time Transport Protocol

The Real-time Transport Protocol is a network protocol used to deliver streaming audio and video media over the internet, thereby enabling the Voice over Internet Protocol (VoIP).

RTP Design Goals & Philosophy

RTP has been designed with certain design goals. They are:

- It should be a flexible protocol. It should provide mechanisms, but should not dictate algorithms that should be used. It should support various coding standards - H261, MPEG1/2/. etc.

- It should be protocol neutral. That is, underlying protocol can be anything - UDP/IP, private ATM networks, or any other network protocol.

- It should be scalable. It should work for unicast, as well as multicast, from small groups to very large groups.

- It should separate control and the data concerns. Some functions may be taken over by a conference control protocol (e.g. RTSP) too.

- It should meet the requirements of:

  ◦ Interactive multimedia applications which have strict real-time constraints; as well as,

  ◦ Streaming applications, whose constraints are not so strict.

- It should allow similar applications to talk to each other. Allow them to negotiate on coding schemes.

- It should help recipients determine timing relationships among the data. It should provide for time-stamping and synchronization of multiple-media.

- It is enough to provide an indication of packet loss. Handling it can be left to the application.

- It should provide an indication of "frame-boundary". The frame boundary will differ with respect to the application. In case of audio, it could be a talk spurt; and in case of video, it could be I/P/B frames.

- It should provide a generic identity for senders - independent of IP address.

- And all of the above without too much header overhead.

Two Key Ideas

Keeping the above requirements in mind, there are two key ideas that are used in the design of RTP. They are (i) Application-level framing and (ii) End-to-end principle:

- Application-level framing: An application knows what it needs best. Hence framing and other such issues such as formats are left to the applications. We can have different profiles (formats) for different applications. The major advantage is that we get app-specific flexibility.

- End-to-end principle: In tune with the Internet principle that the network can be simple or dumb, the end systems take the responsibility of providing service irrespective of n/w capabilities. That is, the intelligence is in the applications.

Let us look at the features of RTP (RFC 3550) to understand how these ideas are implemented.

RTP Features

RTP runs in end systems, and RTP packets are encapsulated in UDP segments. It manages delivery of real time data, by specifying packet structure for packets carrying audio, and/or video data. It is designed with interoperability in mind. If two VoIP applications run RTP, they can work together.

RTP packet provides:

- Payload type identification.
- Source Identifier.
- Sequence numbering for loss detection.
- Time stamping for timing recovery.
- Marker for significant events in the data stream.

Thus it caters to most of the goals. It supports content labeling and timing information with respect to the data. Content labeling helps in source identification, loss detection, and resequencing. Timing helps in intra-media synchronization, to remove jitter with play out buffers; and inter-media synchronization, for example, lip synchronization between audio-video. RTP runs on top of UDP. Thus UDP+RTP together is to be viewed as the transport layer. Thus RTP libraries provide transport-layer interface that extends UDP to provide:

- Port numbers, IP addresses.
- Payload type identification.
- Packet sequence numbering.
- Time-stamping.

There is no fixed UDP port for RTP; it is negotiated out of band. The UDP port for RTCP is always set to UDP port for RTP + 1. Usually, one media is transported per RTP session (i.e. port pair).

RTP Packet Format

The RTP packet format is given in Fig. Each row is of 32 bits length. The first three rows are mandatory in the RTP header. The fourth row and the extension header are optional – used only when needed. This is followed by the payload. The payload will carry a payload-specific header. Thus, we can see that RTP tries to minimize the header overhead. Let us look at the purpose of each of the fields in the header.

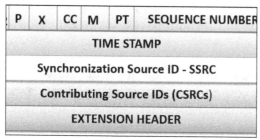

Figure: RTP Packet Format.

The first row has 7 fields:

- A 2-bit version number (V).

- A padding bit (P) which is set if the RTP payload is padded.

- An extension bit (X) that is set if the extension header is present.

- A 4-bit count field (CC) that gives a count of the number of contributing sources; (we will come to what we mean by contributing source).

- A marker bit (M) to indicate frame boundaries.

- A 7-bit payload type (PT) field.

- A 16-bit sequence number to detect missing or mis-ordered packets.

Use of the M-bit and the PT bits are defined by the application profile. Payload type indicates the type of encoding currently being used. If sender changes encoding during call, sender informs the receiver via the payload type field. For instance:

- Payload type 0: PCM mu-law, 64 kbps.

- Payload type 3: GSM, 13 kbps.

- Payload type 7: LPC, 2.4 kbps.

- Payload type 26: Motion JPEG.

- Payload type 31: H.261.

- Payload type 33: MPEG2 video.

The sequence number is incremented by one for each RTP packet sent. The Timestamp field (32 bits long) is a counter of ticks. The granularity of ticks is appspecific. It gives the sampling instant of the first byte in that RTP data packet. For audio, timestamp clock increments by one for each sampling period (e.g., each 125 usecs for 8 KHz sampling clock). If application generates chunks of 160 encoded samples (20msec), timestamp increases by 160 for each RTP packet when source is active (sequence number increases by one). Timestamp clock continues to increase at constant rate when source is inactive. The difference in timestamps is used for synchronization.

The SSRC field (32 bits long) identifies the source of the RTP stream. Each stream in an RTP session (say video conference) has a distinct SSRC. It is also possible that more than one RTP stream is combined and carried in a single packet. In that case, each of them become a contributing source, and the device which is combining them becomes the synchronizing source. Their ids are given in the CSRCs and SSRC respectively.

Thus, up to SSRC is the mandatory part of the RTP header – i.e., 12 bytes. Rest of the header is used only when necessary. From the packet format, we can see that all the goals set out for RTP have been met. Any application specific detail required is part of the payload – application level framing.

Thus, the control and data concerns are separated. All the other general requirements in terms of timing, synchronization, loss identification, marking etc., are taken into account.

RTP Example

As an example consider sending of 64 kbps PCM-encoded voice over RTP. The application collects encoded data in chunks, e.g., every 20 msec; 160 bytes in a chunk. The audio chunk + RTP header form the RTP packet, which is encapsulated in an UDP segment. The RTP header indicates type of audio encoding in each packet. The RTP header also contains sequence numbers, and timestamps. If the sequence number is x, and the timestamp is y, in a given packet, the values in the next subsequent packet will be x+1 and y+160, if part of the same talk spurt (since each chunk has 160 samples). The sender can change the encoding during the conference.

Consider another example – that of VoIP using RTP. Two different offices on public telephone networks could be connected using a VoIP gateway on either side, as shown in figure.

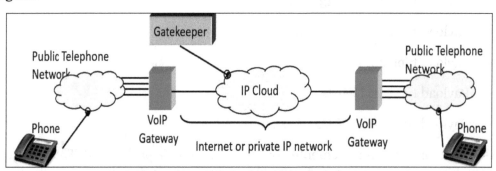

Figure: VoIP using RTP: Multiplexing using SSRC.

Only one RTP session needs to be established between the VoIP gateways. Many phone calls can be carried on this session by multiplexing using different SSRC IDs within the RTP session.

RTP Mixers/Translators

RTP supports the notion of using devices/entities known as mixers and translators to combine the streams from different sources, or change encoding schemes etc. There are many types of translators and mixers used for different purposes, such as adding or re-moving encryptions, changing the underlying encoding scheme, replicating between a multicasting address and one or more unicast address etc. The main difference between a translator and a mixer is that, the translator passes data from the different sources separately. It does not change their source id, whereas a mixer combines them to form a new stream. This new stream will have a different SSRC – the mixer becomes the SSRC, and the combined streams become the CSRCs.

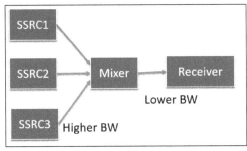

Figure: RTP mixer.

One simple scenario to understand the use of a mixer is as follows. Consider the case of an audio conference, where one of the participants has a low bandwidth link. Instead of all the participants dropping to a low-quality transmission, a mixer could be used near the low-bandwidth receiver, to receive the transmissions from the other sources, combine them (synchronize, add new time stamp etc.,) and send them at a lower rate on the low bandwidth link.

Real-Time Streaming Protocol

The Real-Time Streaming Protocol (RTSP) is a tried-and-true technology used to con-trol audio/video transmission between two endpoints and facilitate the transportation of low-latency streaming content across the internet.

Along with the Real-Time Messaging Protocol (RTMP), RTSP once dominated the video streaming landscape. Although that's no longer the case today, RTSP remains standard in many surveillance and closed-circuit television (CCTV) architectures. The reason for this is simple: it's still the protocol of choice for IP cameras.

RTSP is an application-layer protocol used for commanding streaming media servers via pauses and play capabilities. It thereby facilitates real-time control of the streaming media by communicating with the server — without actually transmitting the data itself. Rather, RTSP servers often leverage the Real-Time Transport Protocol (RTP) in conjunction with the Real-Time Control Protocol (RTCP) to move the actual streaming data.

The official definition from a 1998 proposal of the standard states:

> "The Real-Time Streaming Protocol (RTSP) establishes and controls either a single or several time-synchronized streams of continuous media such as audio and video. It does not typically deliver the continuous streams itself, although interleaving of the continuous media stream with the control stream is possible. In other words, RTSP acts as a "network remote control" for multimedia servers."

So, when a user initiates a video stream from an IP camera using RTSP, the device sends an RTSP request to the streaming server that jumpstarts the setup process. The video and audio data can then be transmitted using RTP. You can thus think of RTSP in terms of a television remote control for media streaming, with RTP acting as the broadcast itself.

RTSP: A Snapshot

- Audio Codecs: AAC, AAC-LC, HE-AAC+ v1 & v2, MP3, Speex, Opus, Vorbis.

- Video Codecs: H.265 (preview), H.264, VP9, VP8.

- Playback Compatibility: Not widely supported and rarely used for playback (Quicktime Player and other RTSP/RTP-compliant players, VideoLAN VLC media player, 3Gpp-compatible mobile devices).

- Benefits: Low-latency and ubiquitous in IP cameras.

- Drawbacks: Not optimized for quality of experience and scalability.

- Latency: 2 seconds.

- Variant Formats: The entire stack of RTP, RTCP (Real-Time Control Protocol), and RTSP is often referred to as RTSP.

RTSP Requests

RTSP uses the following commands, typically sent from the client to the server, when negotiating and controlling media transmissions:

- Options: This request determines what other types of requests the media server will accept.

- Describe: A describe request identifies the URL and type of data.

- Announce: The announce method describes the presentation when sent from the client to the server and updates the description when sent from server to client.

- Setup: Setup requests specify how a media stream must be transported before a play request is sent.

- Play: A play request starts the media transmission by telling the server to start sending the data.

- Pause: Pause requests temporarily halt the stream delivery.

- Record: A record request initiates a media recording.

- Teardown: This request terminates the session entirely and stops all media streams.

- Redirect: Redirect requests inform the client that it must connect to another server by providing a new URL for the client to issue requests to.

Other types of RTSP requests include 'get parameter,' 'set parameter,' and 'embedded (interleaved) binary data.

RTSP and IP Cameras

Most IP cameras use the RTSP protocol to pull data to the media server. From surveillance to conferencing, IP cameras work great when you want to live-stream from one location without getting too fancy. These user-friendly streaming devices don't require a separate encoder, and RTSP works great when pairing IP cameras with a stateful server. What's more, broadcasters can then aggregate the content for delivery to any device with a live transcoding solution.

Typical RTSP Workflow

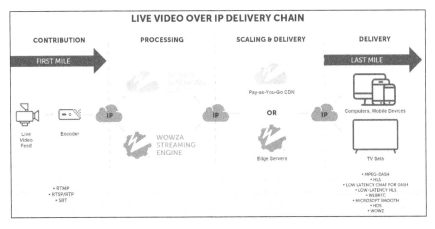

RTSP is a stateful protocol used more often for video contribution (ingest) than for last-mile delivery and playback (egress). Android and iOS devices don't have RTSP compatible players out of the box, which is the primary reason why RTSP is rarely used for streaming from end to end. Instead, most broadcasters leverage a streaming software or service to repackage the RTSP stream into a more user-friendly format like HLS.

Real-Time Control Protocol

Real-Time Control Protocol (RTCP) is the companion control protocol for RTP. It does not guarantee anything either. It only provides feedback about the packets sent through RTP. RTCP is designed to work in conjunction with RTP, where all participants – senders and receivers -send control and feedback information about the RTP session to the others. The main objective of RTCP is to report End-to-End Delay, Delay Jitter, and Loss Rate. The purpose of this report is to control performance. It allows the sender to adjust its transmission based on this feedback, say by switching to a lower-bitrate codec.

Each RTCP packet contains sender and/or receiver reports that report statistics useful to the application: # packets sent, # packets lost, and inter-arrival jitter. RTCP packets are transmitted periodically. There are several functions that RTCP serves by providing feedback on the quality of data distribution. It lets everybody evaluate the number of participants. It provides a persistent transport-level canonical name for a source, CNAME. For example, user@host, which will not change, even if the SSRC does? It helps to provide binding across multiple media tools for a single user (eg., for audio-video synchronization).

RTCP packets are distributed in the same manner as data packets (n®m multicast). Multiple RTCP packets can be concatenated by translators/mixers to form a compound RTCP packet. RTCP packets being control packets, we would also like to limit their number – we do not want RTCP claiming too much of bandwidth. Given that, each sender and receiver will send RTCP packets, we have to be careful when the number of participants is large. Hence, RTCP has an in-built mechanism to support scalability with session size. It imposes a requirement that RTCP traffic should not exceed 5% of total session bandwidth. This requires an evaluation of the number of participants, and requires each participant to adjust its reporting rate accordingly.

RTCP Packet Format

The RTCP packet format is shown in figure below. In keeping with the philosophy of Low overhead, the header is kept simple with five fields occupying only 32 bits. It has a 2-bit version field, 2-bit priority field, 4-bit item count, 8-bit type, and a 16-bit length field.

V	P	Item Count	Type	Length
Data				

Table: RTCP packet format.

The item-count describes the number of items carried in the packet, with the item itself defined based on the type of the packet. The type would be one of the following:

- 193 – NACK.

- 200 – SR: Sender Report (Tx statistics).

- 201 – RR: Receiver Report (Rx statistics).

- 202 – SDES packet (Source description items – CNAME).

- 203 – BYE packet (end of participation).

- 204 – APP packet (application specific functions).

Sender reports (SRs) carry the SSRC of the RTP stream, current time, number of packets sent, and number of bytes sent etc. Receiver reports (RRs) give information about the fraction of packets lost, last sequence number, average interarrival jitter, etc.

Source description packets (SDES) give the description of the sender - e-mail address of sender, sender's name, SSRC of associated RTP stream, and provide mapping between the SSRC and the user/host name. Let us look at the formats of each of these packets.

SR RTCP Packets

The format of the SR packet is given in figure.

V	P	RC	PT=200	Length
SSRC of the sender				
NTP timestamp (MSB)				
NTP timestamp (LSB)				
RTP timestamp				
Sender's packet count				
Sender's octet count				
First reception report block (SSRC_1)				
...				
Last reception report block (SSRC_n)				

Figure: SR packet format.

It includes:

- SSRC of sender (to identify source of data).

- NTP timestamp (gives time at which report was sent).

- RTP timestamp (the corresponding RTP time).

- Packet count (total number of packets sent).

- Octet count (total number of octets sent).

This is followed by zero or more receiver reports. We will look at the RR format in the Next section. For example, if source 1 reports, and there are 2 other sources, the SR report would be as follows:

RR Packet Format

V	P	RC	PT=201	Length
SSRC of the sender					
SSRC of the first source					
Fract. lost	Cum. no of packets lost				
Ext. highest sequence number received					
Interarrival jitter estimate					
Last sender report timestamp (LSR)					
Delay since last sender report (DLSR)					
...					
Last reception report block					

Figure: RR packet format.

Each receiver report block includes:

- SSRC of source (to identify the source to which this RR block pertains).
- Fraction lost (Fraction of packets lost since the time the previous RR (SR) sent.
- (Frlost= int(256*lost/expected)).
- Cumulative # of packets lost (gives an indication of the long term loss).
- Highest seq # received (Useful to compare losses).
- interarrival jitter (smoothed interpacket distortion).
- LSR (time of last SR rcvd).
- DLSR (delay since receiving last SR).

We will look at how this timing information is used in the next few sections.

SDES Packet

The format of the SDES packet is given in figure.

V	P	SC	PT=202	Length
SSRC/CSRC of the sender					
Type	length	text			
text continued					
...					
Last chunk					

Figure: SDES packet format.

Information about the sender/source is conveyed in this packet, in the form of <type,length,value> fields. CNAME (Canonical name), NAME, EMAIL, PHONE,

LOCATION, etc., are the types of information conveyed in this packet. The SDES information should be sent periodically by a source, so that any new participant will become aware of the senders in a short time.

BYE Packet

The format of the BYE packet is shown in figure. It is sent when a participant is leaving the session. It includes information about why it is leaving the session (low bandwidth/poor quality, etc).

V	P	SC	PT=203	Length
SSRC/CSRC of the sender				
length			reason for leaving	
...				
Last chunk				

Figure: BYE packet.

APP Packet

The format of the APP packet is shown in figure.

V	P	Sub	PT=204	Length
SSRC/CSRC of the sender				
name (ASCII)				
application-dependent data				

Figure: APP packet.

This packet consists of APP-dependent data and is defined by the application.

Timing Calculations

We will now look at how the information in the RR reports help in calculating values of RTT and jitter.

RTT Calculation

RTT is calculated from the SR and RR fields – NTP in SR, LSR and DLSR in RR.

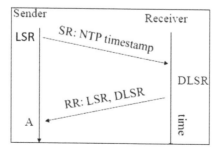

Note that the time at which an SR is sent is available in the NTP timestamp. That is copied in the LSR field of the RR packet. RR packet also has the delay since receiving the last SR. Thus the RTT can be calculated if the time of arrival (A) of the RR packet is noted as:

$$RTT = A - LSR - DLSR$$

Jitter Calculation

Jitter is the variation in delay, and is calculated as the weighted average of the deviation of the current packets delay, and the previous average. If Si is the RTP timestamp from packet i, Ri is the time of arrival in RTP timestamp units for packet i, then for two packets i and j, deviation in delay D (I,j) is given by:

$$D (i,j) = (Rj - Ri) - (Sj - Si) = (Rj - Sj) - (Ri - Si)$$

The jitter after arrival of packet is then calculated as:

$$J(i) = J(i-1) + (|D(i-1,i)| - J(i-1))/16$$

RTCP: Stream Synchronization

Using the timing info, the RTCP can synchronize different media streams within an RTP session. For example, in a videoconferencing application, each sender generates one RTP stream for video, and one for audio. Timestamps in RTP packets are tied to the video, audio sampling clocks, not to the wall-clock time. Hence they need to be synchronized. This is done with the help of the time stamps – NTP, and RTP – in the SR packet. Remember that each SR packet contains (for the most recently generated packet in the associated RTP stream), timestamp of RTP packet, and wall-clock time for when packet was created. Receivers use this association to synchronize play out of audio, and video.

RTCP Traffic Bandwidth

While RTCP packets give plenty of information, they consume bandwidth. Especially, when there are multiple senders in a multicast video session, the RTCP traffic can become too high, and clog the available session bandwidth. To avoid this, RTCP restricts the amount of packets sent by regulating the timing of the packets. This regulation is done by considering the number of senders and receivers. RTCP is normally restricted to 5% of the session (data) bandwidth. Hence,

Total BW required = Session BW + 5% of Session BW.

Of this, ¼ of RTCP bandwidth is for senders (this can be modified based on profile) – i.e., 1.25% of session bandwidth is for the senders, and 3.75% for the receivers. We can also have different bandwidths allocated for active and non-active participants. We also have bounds on time-interval between RTCP packets. If it is too small, it leads to bursts of traffic. If it is too large, it leads to not receiving feedback for a long time. Hence a minimum time-interval is decided based on the number of participants. The minimum time-interval for a new participant is about 5 secs, so that the others in the group get to know about the new entrant within a reasonable amount of time.

The time interval is thus a function of (members, senders, avg-rtcp-pkt-size, and rtcp-bw). Let us understand this RTCP bandwidth scaling with some numbers. Consider one sender sending video at 2 Mbps. That is, session bandwidth = 2Mbps. RTCP attempts to limit RTCP traffic to 5% of this value, i.e., 100 Kbps. RTCP gives 75% of this rate to receivers, and remaining 25% to sender. 75 kbps is equally shared among receivers. With R receivers, each receiver gets to send RTCP traffic at 75/R kbps. The number of senders and receivers are determined by the number of distinct SRs and RRs received. Sender gets to send RTCP traffic at 25 kbps. Participant determines RTCP packet transmission period by calculating the average RTCP packet size (across entire session) and dividing by the allocated rate.

Compound RTCP

This is another feature provided by RTCP. Multiple RTCP packets from one participant may be combined and sent as 1 compound RTCP packet. It consists of a fixed part, and a number of structured elements of RTCP types (SR/RR/SDES etc). An SR/RR should be sent in each compound packet. SDES is to be included (for new receivers to receive C name of sender asap). This feature is useful when Mixers/Translators are used. They become responsible for combining multiple RTCP packets into compound packets.

Session Initiation Protocol

The SIP protocol described in RFC 3261 has been designed with a long-term vision that:

All telephone calls and video conference calls take place over the Internet. People will be identified by names or e-mail addresses, rather than by phone numbers. One can reach the callee (if callee so desires), no matter where callee roams, no matter what IP device the c allee is currently using. Accordingly, the capabilities provided by SIP can be grouped into five categories:

- User location: Determining the correct device with which to communicate to reach a particular user.

- User availability: Determining if the user is willing or able to take part in a particular communication session.

- User capabilities: Determining such items as the choice of media and coding scheme to use.

- Session setup: Establishing session parameters such as port numbers to be used by the communicating parties.

- Session management: A range of functions including transferring sessions (e.g. to implement "call forwarding") and modifying session parameters.

SIP Characteristics

SIP is designed to be a simple client-server based protocol with HTTP-like characteristics. It is a text-based protocol – with message syntax and header fields identical to HTTP/1.1. It provides the basic services to initiate the session, and leaves the details of description of the session, and its announcement to the supplementary SDP/SAP protocols. SIP provides mechanisms: for call setup, i.e., for the caller to let the callee know that she wants to establish a call; for the caller, and callee to agree on media type, and encoding; for ending the call. It provides support for call management: we can add new media streams during call; change encoding during call; invite others, transfer, hold calls etc. Identification of callee is done via the current IP address, but it maps a mnemonic identifier to current IP address. The elements in a SIP environment are depicted in figure.

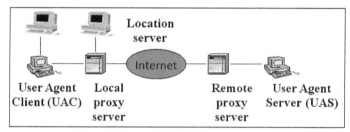

Figure: Elements in a SIP Environment.

The client and server are referred to as User Agent Client (UAC) and User Agent Server (UAS). There are proxy servers that the user agents connect to. There is a location server that the proxy servers are aware of, whose services they use to determine the callee.

Messages in SIP

A message-response mechanism similar to HTTP is used to manage the call. The messages used in SIP are given in Table 34.1, and the response codes in table.

Table: SIP messages.

Operators	Description
INVITE	Invite a user to a call
ACK	Confirmation for the final response
BYE	Terminate a call between endpoints

CANCEL	Terminate the search for a user or request for a call
OPTIONS	Features supported for a call
REGISTER	Register current location of the client with location server
INFO	Use for mid-session signaling

Table: Reply Codes in SIP.

Reply Code	Description
1xx (Informational)	Trying, ringing and queued
2xx (Successful)	The request was successful
3xx (Redirection)	Give information about the receiver's new location
4xx (Request Failures)	Failure responses from a particular server
5xx (Server Failures)	Failure responses given when a server itself has erred
6xx (Global Failures)	Busy, decline, requests not acceptable

We can see that the messages are self-explanatory, and the status codes are similar to the ones used in HTTP. Let us now look at the steps involved in a typical call-setup:

- UAC sends an INVITE message to UAS with the SIP URL.

- If the destination IP address is known, it sends the request directly to the destination. If it is unknown, the message is redirected to the local proxy server (with location server).

- In redirection mode, the callee's new location is sent back.

- In proxy mode, it forwards the request to the destination.

- The UAS answers with a 200 (OK) status.

- Then the UAC sends an ACK message.

The session is established. This message flow for a basic SIP session is shown in Fig.34.3. It shows a UAC at cisco.com calling a UAS at princeton.edu. There are two proxy servers involved at the two ends. While the proxies forward the INVITE message, then send back a "trying" and "ringing" status to the caller. When the callee accepts the call, an OK status is sent. The transfer of media then takes place, and a BYE message is sent to terminate the session.

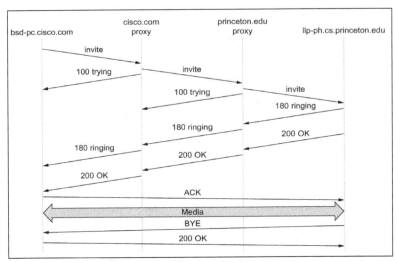

Figure: Message flow in a basic SIP session.

Figure illustrates the scenario of Alice setting up a call to Bob whose IP address is known, with details of the messages sent. Alice's SIP invite message indicates her port number, IP address, encoding she prefers to receive (say PCM mu-law). Bob's 200 OK messages indicate his port number, IP address, and preferred encoding (say GSM). SIP messages can be sent over TCP or UDP. Here they are sent over RTP/UDP. The default SIP port number is 5060. Note that the audio can be transferred in two different formats on either side. It is also possible that the preferred codec is not available at the other end. In such cases, a negotiation is carried out.

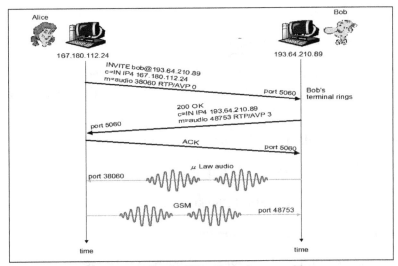

Figure: Example of a SIP call to a known address.

Suppose Bob doesn't have PCM mu-law encoder, Bob will reply with 606 Not Acceptable statuses, and listing his encoders. Alice can then send a new INVITE message choosing a different encoder. Bob can also reject calls with replies such as "busy," "gone," "payment required," "forbidden", etc. If Alice does not know Bob's IP address, but knows the intermediate server through which she can reach Bob, then the invite message she sends would be as given below:

- INVITE sip:bob@domain.com SIP/2.0

- Via: SIP/2.0/UDP 167.180.112.24

- From: sip:alice@hereway.com

- To: sip:bob@domain.com

- Call-ID: a2e3a@pigeon.hereway.com

- Content-Type: application/sdp

- Content-Length: 885

- c=IN IP4 167.180.112.24

- m=audio 38060 RTP/AVP 0

Here Alice does not know Bob's IP address, but knows the intermediate server address. Hence, intermediate SIP servers are needed, whose address is specified in the "via" line. Alice specifies in the header that the SIP client will send & receive SIP messages over UDP.

Name Translation and Locating User

We will next look at what is done when the caller has only the callee's name or e-mail address. In this case, we need some mechanism by which the name can be translated to an IP address, and the callee can be located. The callee could move around, and so may have different IP addresses at different points of time. Also, he could use different devices, such as laptop, PC, smart phone etc. In all these cases, we need to locate the user and connect to him/her.

Also, the user may have certain preferences. The response from the callee could be based on time of day (work, home), or based on who the caller is (don't want boss to call you at home), or the status of callee (calls sent to voicemail when callee is already talking to someone). To manage all these situations, the SIP server performs two important functions: that of Registrar, and that of proxy.

SIP Registrar

When Bob starts the SIP client, client sends SIP REGISTER message to Bob's registrar server. The register message would have the following format:

- REGISTER sip:domain.com SIP/2.0

- Via: SIP/2.0/UDP 193.64.210.89

- From: sip:bob@domain.com

- To: sip:bob@domain.com

- Expires: 3600

This message informs the server of its identity and location. The registrar can then use this information to locate the server and forward the invite message to it.

SIP Proxy

As a proxy server, the server is responsible for routing SIP messages to the callee, possibly through multiple proxies. Referring back to the same example, when Alice sends invite message to her proxy server, the invite contains the address sip:bob@domain.com. It is the proxy's responsibility to locate the callee, possibly though multiple proxies. The callee, Bob, then sends the response back through the same set of SIP proxies. The proxy then returns Bob's SIP response message to Alice. SIP proxy is analogous to a local DNS server plus TCP setup.

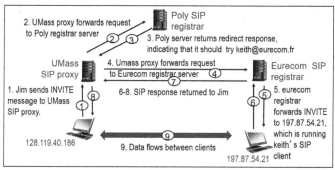

Figure: A final SIP example.

An example showing all these functions is given in Fig. The messages exchanged between the entities, in sequence, is also shown. Here jim@umass.edu calls keith@poly.edu. But keith has moved to eurecom.fr, but has informed its registrar. Hence the SIP registrar is aware of that, and performs a redirect to the other registrar. Once the call is set up, all communication between the client and the server takes place directly, not along this path.

3

Routing and its Protocol

Routing is the process in which data packets are transferred from the source to the destination through the optimal path from one network to the other. Routing protocol is the formula used by routers to determine the optimal network transfer and the appropriate path between the networks. This chapter sheds light on routing and its related topics for a thorough understanding of the subject.

Routing

Routing and forwarding are two terms that are commonly used together in the context of network layer. It is useful to reiterate the difference between the two. Forwarding refers to the selection of an output port based on destination address and routing table, while routing refers to the process by which the routing table is built. Forwarding actually uses a forwarding table that is derived from the routing table. The forwarding table is used when a packet is being forwarded and hence must contain enough information to accomplish the forwarding function. A row in the forwarding table contains the mapping from a network number to an outgoing interface and some MAC information, such as Ethernet Address of the next hop. A routing table, on the other hand, is built by the routing algorithm as a precursor to build the forwarding table, and generally contains a mapping from network numbers to next hops. An example row in a forwarding table and a routing table is shown in Table.

Table: Example rows from (a) routing and (b) forwarding tables.

(a) Routing table		
Prefix Length	Next Hop	
	171.69.243.12	
(b) Forwarding table		
Prefix Length	Interface	MAC Address
18/8	If 0	8:0:2b:e3:1b:1:4

Routing Algorithms

The task of routing is to select a path from the source to the destination in a network that consists of multiple routers interconnected by many links. The challenge in arriving at a method to do so is that, the method should be efficient, scalable, stable, robust, and fair. It should be able to achieve its goal with low delay. It should scale to any number of devices, networks, routers and links. It should be stable in that it should provide a route that is stable. It should be robust – against failure of certain links, routers etc. It should be fair – providing all networks/devices equal service (at least for the same cost).

Most routing algorithms arrive at this method by modeling the network as a graph, with the routers represented by nodes, and the links represented by the edges. A cost could be associated with the edges. The basic problem of routing then boils down to finding the lowest-cost path between any two nodes. (Nodes are the routers connected to different networks – thus router to router path gives us network to network path). The cost of a path equals the sum of the costs of all the edges that make up the path.

Graph Abstraction

The graph model of a network can be formally stated as follows (shown for the example network given in figure):

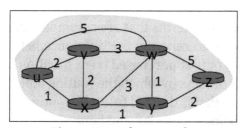

Figure: Network as a graph.

Graph: $G = (N,E)$

   N = set of routers = {u, v, w, x, y, z}

   E = set of links ={ (u,v), (u,x), (v,x), (v,w), (x,w), (x,y), (w,y), (w,z), (y,z) }

   Let $c(x, x') = $ cost of link (x, x')

   e.g., $c(w,z) = 5$

The cost could always be 1, or inversely proportional to the bandwidth of the link, or inversely proportional to the congestion level on the link. Then, the path cost through nodes x1... xp, is calculated as:

$$\text{Cost of path } (x_1, x_2, x_3, x_p) = c(x_1, x_2) + c(x_2, x_3) + \ldots + c(xp_{-1}, xp)$$

The routing problem can then be stated in terms of this abstraction as finding the least cost path between any two nodes. For example, to find the least cost path between nodes u and w, we need to identify the paths and their costs, and then pick the one with the least cost. We often replace cost with distance; hence the two terms are used interchangeably. There are different ways in which this can be done, giving rise to different classes of routing algorithms.

Routing Algorithm Classification

One of the questions that can be asked is, "Is the network graph information global or decentralized?" In other words, do all the routers have the complete topology, and costs of all links (global), or do they have only local information, as in who are their neighbors, and the link cost to the neighbors only (local or decentralized).

In the networking world, we have two predominant routing algorithms – one of each type. We have the link state algorithm which is a global information based algorithm, and we have the distance vector routing algorithm which is based on local information.

The second question that comes up is "Is the algorithm static or dynamic?" Does it react quickly to changes in the network or not? Static algorithms are fine if the routes hardly change, but in an internet kind of scenario, we need dynamic algorithms which react to route changes quickly. This implies that routers must exchange information periodically, or whenever a change occurs. In the IP network, we need dynamic algorithms. Both algorithms mentioned above are dynamic in nature. We will delve into link state algorithm in the next module.

Distance Vector Algorithm

The basis of the distance vector algorithm is the Bellman-Ford equation (that is used in dynamic programming). The Bellman-Ford equation is given as follows:

Let,

$$d_x(y) := \text{cost of least-cost path from x to y}$$

Then,

$$d_x(y) = \min_v \{c(x,v) + d_v(y)\}, \text{ where v is the set of all neighbours of x.}$$

That is, cost of least-cost path from x to y, is the minimum of the sum of the cost to neighbour v, and the cost from v to y (taken over all neighbours v). This equation gives us a recursive relation to calculate the minimum cost between any two nodes.

For example, considering the same network given in Figure., the distance from u to z, is calculated as follows:

We know that, $d_v(z) = 5$, $d_x(z) = 3$, $d_w(z) = 3$. Then as per Bellman-Ford's equation,

$$d_u(z) = \min \{c(u,v) + d_v(z), c(u,x) + d_x(z), c(u,w) + d_w(z)\}$$

$$= \min \{2 + 5, 1 + 3, 5 + 3\} = 4$$

The node achieving the minimum cost – x in this example, becomes the next hop in the shortest path, and is used in the forwarding table. Let us now look at how this idea is implemented in the network. Every node x maintains an estimate of its least cost to every other node y, $D_x(y)$, where y ∈ N - the set of all nodes in the network. It then exchanges this vector with its neighbors. To start with, each node x, knows its cost to each neighbor v: c(x,v). So for each neighbor v, x maintains D_v = [$D_v(y)$: y ∈ N]. Unknown values are initialized to infinity or a very large value.

It then exchanges this distance vector estimate with its neighbours. When a node x, receives new DV estimate from neighbor, it updates its own DV using B-F equation:

$$D_x(y) \leftarrow \min_v\{c(x,v) + D_v(y)\} \text{ for each node } y \in N.$$

Over a period of time (a few exchanges), under normal circumstances, the distance vector converges to the least cost values. This algorithm is iterative, and asynchronous. Each local iteration is caused by a local link cost change or a DV update message from a neighbor. Each node notifies its neighbors whenever its DV changes. And these nodes notify their neighbors if necessary (i.e., if a change occurs in their DV). Also, there are periodic updates that take place as well. Even if there is no change, these updates indicate that all is well.

Distance Vector – An Example

Consider the simple network shown in Figure with 3 nodes x, y and z.

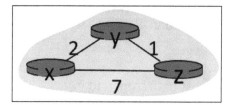

Figure: Example network – 1.

The initial distance vectors at each node are shown in the second column in Table 18.2. Initial vectors at x, y and z show the direct costs to the neighbors. The vectors from the neighbors are initially set to ∞ After the first exchange, at x, the vectors from y and z are received. Hence it recomputes its distances as shown in the distance calculation column, and chooses the minimum distance as 2 to y, and 3 to z. similar calculations take place at nodes y and z. No changes are seen in y, whereas z changes its distance to x as 3.

Node x table	Initial values Cost to x y z	After 1st exchange Cost to x y z	Distance calculation
From x	0 2 7	0 2 3	Dx(y) = min{c(x,y) + Dy(y), c(x,z) + Dz(y)}
From y	∞∞∞	2 0 1	[= min{2+0 , 7+1} = 2 Dx(z) = min{c(x,y)
From z	∞∞∞	7 1 0	+ Dy(z), c(x,z) + Dz(z)}
			= min{2+1 , 7+0} = 3

Node y table	Initial values Cost to x y z		
From x	∞∞∞	0 2 7	
From y	2 0 1	2 0 1	
From z	∞∞∞	7 1 0	
Node z table	Initial values Cost to x y z	After 1 exchange – cost to x y z	
From x	∞∞∞	0 2 7	Distance to z updated
From y	∞∞∞	2 0 1	
From z	7 1 0	3 1 0	

This set of new vectors at x and z are then exchanged in the next round. But that causes no change in the distance values. Hence, no other updates are triggered. The node y does not send any vector, as no information at y has changed.

Distance Vector – Another Example

Consider another example – a network shown in Figure, where the cost of every link is 1.

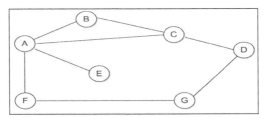

Figure: Example network – 2.

The initial vector at each of the nodes will have the values shown in each row of Table. The directly connected links have a distance/cost of 1, and the distance to all other nodes is set to infinity. These vectors are exchanged with the neighbors, and at the end of 4 exchanges the distances will stabilize to the values shown in Table.

Table: Initial distance vectors at each node for network.

Information Stored at Node	Distance to Reach Node						
	A	B	C	D	E	F	G
A	0	1	1	∞	1	1	∞
B	1	0	1	∞	∞	∞	∞
C	1	1	0	1	∞	∞	∞
D	∞	∞	1	0	∞	∞	∞
E	1	∞	∞	∞	0	∞	∞

F	1	∞	∞	∞	∞	0	1
G	∞	∞	∞	1	∞	1	0

Table: Final distance vectors at each node for network.

Information Stored at Node	Distance to Reach Node						
	A	B	C	D	E	F	G
A	0	1	1	2	1	1	2
B	1	0	1	2	2	2	3
C	1	1	0	1	2	2	2
D	2	2	1	0	3	2	1
E	1	2	2	3	0	2	3
F	1	2	2	2	2	0	1
G	2	3	2	1	3	1	0

Handling Link Failure

Let us look at how the algorithm can dynamically handle link failures. Considering the same example given above, when a node detects a link failure, it sets its distance to the node connected by that link to infinity, and passes the updated information to its other neighbors.

Let us say, F detects that link to G has failed, then, F sets distance to G to infinity and sends update to A. A sets distance to G to infinity since it uses F to reach G. A receives periodic update from C with 2-hop path to G. A sets distance to G to 3 and sends update to F. F decides it can reach G in 4 hops via A. That is, in a few hops, all nodes get identical information.

However, it may not be as simple in some cases. Slightly different circumstances can prevent the network from stabilizing. Suppose the link from A to E goes down. In the next round of updates, A advertises a distance of infinity to E, but B and C advertise a distance of 2 to E. Depending on the exact timing of events, the following might happen:

- Node B, upon hearing that E can be reached in 2 hops from C, concludes that it can reach E in 3 hops and advertises this to A.

- Node A concludes that it can reach E in 4 hops and advertises this to C.

- Node C concludes that it can reach E in 5 hops; and so on.

This cycle stops only when the distances reach some number that is large enough to be considered as infinity. This is called the "Count-to-infinity problem" faced by the distance vector algorithm.

Count-to-infinity Problem and Solutions

The count-to-infinity problem occurs because; the nodes just trust the information coming from their neighbors, as they do not have a global view (topology) of the network. As can be seen in the example described above, A does not realize that there is no other path from B to E, and trusts the local information at B.

How do we solve this problem? One simple solution is to use some relatively small number as an approximation of infinity. Then, in that many number of exchanges, everybody will get the distance to the unreachable node as the equivalent of infinity.

For example, if the maximum number of hops to get across a certain network may never be more than 16, this value could be set as the approximation for infinity.

Another technique to improve the time to stabilize routing is called the split horizon technique. With this approach, when a node sends a routing update to its neighbors, it does not send those routes it learned from each neighbor back to that neighbor itself. For example, if B has the route (E, 2, A) in its table, then it knows it must have learned this route from A, and so whenever B sends a routing update to A, it does not include the route (E, 2) in that update. This way we try to avoid giving incorrect information from B.

In a stronger version of split horizon, called split horizon with poison reverse, B actually sends that back route to A, but it puts negative information in the route to ensure that A will not eventually use B to get to E. For example, B sends the route (E, ∞) to A.

Router

The router is a physical or virtual internetworking device that is designed to receive, analyze, and forward data packets between computer networks. A router examines a destination IP address of a given data packet, and it uses the headers and forwarding tables to decide the best way to transfer the packets. There are some popular companies that develop routers; such are Cisco, 3Com, HP, Juniper, D-Link, Nortel, etc. Some important points of routers are given below:

- A router is used in LAN (Local Area Network) and WAN (Wide Area Network) environments. For example, it is used in offices for connectivity, and you can also establish the connection between distant networks such as from Bhopal.

- It shares information with other routers in networking.

- It uses the routing protocol to transfer the data across a network.

- Furthermore, it is more expensive than other networking devices like switches and hubs.

A router works on the third layer of the OSI model, and it is based on the IP address of a computer. It uses protocols such as ICMP to communicate between two or more networks. It is also known as an intelligent device as it can calculate the best route to pass the network packets from source to the destination automatically.

A virtual router is a software function or software-based framework that performs the same functions as a physical router. It may be used to increase the reliability of the network by virtual router redundancy protocol, which is done by configuring a virtual router as a default gateway. A virtual router runs on commodity servers, and it is packaged with alone or other network functions, like load balancing, firewall packet filtering, and wide area network optimization capabilities.

Why Routers?

A router is more capable as compared to other network devices, such as a hub, switch, etc., as these devices are only able to execute the basic functions of the network. For example, a hub is a basic networking device that is mainly used to forward the data between connected devices, but it cannot analyze or change anything with the transferring data. On the other hand, the router has the capability to analyze and modify the data while transferring it over a network and it can send it to another network. For example, generally, routers allow sharing a single network connection between multiple devices.

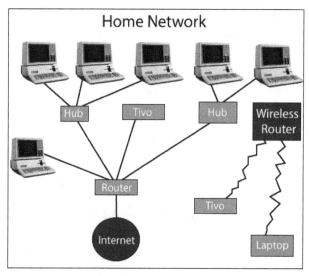

How does Router work?

A router analyzes a destination IP address of a given packet header and compares it with the routing table to decide the packet's next path. The list of routing tables provides directions to transfer the data to a particular network destination. They have a set of rules that compute the best path to forward the data to the given IP address.

Routers use a modem such as a cable, fiber, or DSL modem to allow communication between other devices and the internet. Most of the routers have several ports to connect different devices to the internet at the same time. It uses the routing tables to determine where to send data and from where the traffic is coming.

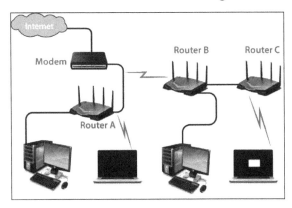

A routing table mainly defines the default path used by the router. So, it may fail to find the best way to forward the data for a given packet. For example, the office router along a single default path instructs all networks to its internet services provider.

There are two types of tables in the router that are static and dynamic. The static routing tables are configured manually, and the dynamic routing tables are updated automatically by dynamic routers based on network activity.

Features of Router

- A router works on the 3rd layer (Network Layer) of the OSI model, and it is able to communicate with its adjacent devices with the help of IP addresses and subnet.

- A router provides high-speed internet connectivity with the different types of ports like gigabit, fast-Ethernet, and STM link port.

- It allows the users to configure the port as per their requirements in the network.

- Routers' main components are central processing unit (CPU), flash memory, RAM, Non-Volatile RAM, console, network, and interface card.

- Routers are capable of routing the traffic in a large networking system by considering the sub-network as an intact network.

- Routers filter out the unwanted interference, as well as carry out the data encapsulation and decapsulation process.

- Routers provide the redundancy as it always works in master and slave mode.

- It allows the users to connect several LAN and WAN.

- Furthermore, a router creates various paths to forward the data.

Applications of Routers

There are various areas where a router is used:

- Routers are used to connect hardware equipment with remote location networks like BSC, MGW, IN, SGSN, and other servers.

- It provides support for a fast rate of data transmission because it uses high STM links for connectivity; that's why it is used in both wired and wireless communication.

- Internet service providers widely use routers to send the data from source to destination in the form of e-mail, a web page, image, voice, or a video file. Furthermore, it can send data all over the world with the help of an IP address of the destination.

- Routers offer access restrictions. It can be configured in a way that allows for few users to access the overall data and allows others to access the few data only, which is defined for them.

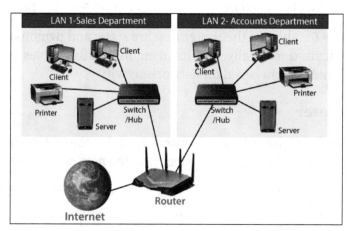

- Routers are also used by software testers for WAN communications. For example, the software manager of an organization is located in Agra, and its executive is located at a different place like Pune or Bangalore. Then the router provides the executive the method to share his software tools and other applications with the manager with the help of routers by connecting their PCs to the router using WAN architecture.

- In wireless networks, by configuring VPN in routers, it can be used in the client-server model, which allows sharing the internet, video, data, voice, and hardware resources.

- In modern times, routers have the facility of inbuilt USB ports within the hardware. They have enough internal storage capacity. External storage devices can be used with routers to store and share data.

- Routers are used to set up the operation and maintenance center of an organization, which is known as the NOC center. All equipment at a distant location is connected by routers on optical cable at a central location, which also offer redundancy through the main link and protection link topology.

Types of Routers

There are various types of routers in networking; such are given below:

- Wireless Router: Wireless routers are used to offer Wi-Fi connectivity to laptops, smartphones, and other devices with Wi-Fi network capabilities, and it can also provide standard ethernet routing for a small number of wired network systems. Wireless routers are capable of generating a wireless signal in your home or office, and it allows the computers to connect with routers within a range, and use the internet. If the connection is indoors, the range of the wireless router is about 150 feet, and when the connection is outdoors, and then its range is up to 300 feet.

  Furthermore, you can make more secure wireless routers with a password or get your IP address. Thereafter, you can log in to your router by using a user ID and password that will come with your router.

- Brouter: A brouter is a combination of the bridge and a router. It allows transferring the data between networks like a bridge. And like a router, it can also route the data within a network to the individual systems. Thus, it combines these two functions of bridge and router by routing some incoming data to the correct systems while transferring the other data to another network.

- Core router: A core router is a type of router that can route the data within a network, but it is not able to route the data between the networks. It is a computer communication system device and the backbone of networks, as it helps to link all network devices. It is used by internet service providers (ISPs), and it also provides various types of fast and powerful data communication interfaces.

- Edge router: An edge router is a lower-capacity device that is placed at the boundary of a network. It allows an internal network to connect with the external networks. It is also called as an access router. It uses an External BGP

(Border Gateway Protocol) to provide connectivity with remote networks over the internet. There are two types of edge routers in networking:

- ○ Subscriber edge router.

- ○ Label edge router.

The subscriber edge router belongs to an end-user organization, and it works in a situation where it acts on a border device. The label edge router is used in the boundary of Multiprotocol Label Switching (MPLS) networks. It acts as a gateway between the LAN, WAN, or the internet.

- Broadband routers: Broadband routers are mainly used to provide high-speed internet access to computers. It is needed when you connect to the internet through phone and use voice over IP technology (VOIP).

All broadband routers have the option of three or four Ethernet ports for connecting the laptop and desktop systems. A broadband router is configured and provided by the internet service provider (ISP). It is also known as a broadband modem, asymmetric digital subscriber line (ADSL), or digital subscriber line (DSL) modem.

Benefits of Router

There are so many benefits of a router, which are given below:

- Security: Router provides the security, as LANs work in broadcast mode. The information is transmitted over the network and traverses the entire cable system. Although the data is available to each station, but the station which is specifically addressed reads the data.

- Performance enhancement: It enhances the performance within the individual network. For example, if a network has 14 workstations, and all generate approximately the same volume of traffic. The traffic of 14 workstations runs through the same cable in a single network. But if the network is divided into two sub-networks each with 7 workstations, then a load of traffic is reduced to half. As each of the networks has its own servers and hard disk, so fewer PCs will need the network cabling system.

- Reliability: Routers provide reliability. If one network gets down when the server has stopped, or there is a defect in the cable, then the router services and other networks will not be affected. The routers separate the affected network, whereas the unaffected networks remain connected, without interrupting the work and any data loss.

- Networking Range: In networking, a cable is used to connect the devices, but its length cannot exceed 1000 meters. A router can overcome this limitation by performing the function of a repeater (Regenerating the signals). The physical range can be as per the requirement of a particular installation, as long as a router is installed before the maximum cable range exceeds.

Routing Protocols

Routing protocols specify a way for the router to identify other routers on the network and make dynamic decisions to send all network messages. There are several protocols, which are given below:

- Open Shortest Path First (OSPF): It is used to calculate the best route for the given packets to reach the destination, as they move via a set of connected networks. It is identified by the Internet Engineering Task Force (IETF) as Interior Gateway Protocol.

- Border Gateway Protocol (BGP): It helps manage how packets are routed on the internet via exchange of information between edge routers. It provides network stability for routers if one internet connection goes down while forwarding the packets, it can adapt another network connection quickly to send the packets.

- Interior Gateway Routing Protocol (IGRP): It specifies how routing information will be exchanged between gateways within an independent network. Then, the other network protocols can use the routing information to determine how transmissions should be routed.

- Enhanced Interior Gateway Routing Protocol (EIGRP): In this protocol, if a router is unable to find a path to a destination from the tables, it asks route to its neighbors, and they pass the query to their neighbors until a router has found the path. When the entry of routing table changes in one of the routers, it informs its neighbors only about the changes, but do not send the entire table.

- Exterior Gateway Protocol (EGP): It decides how routing information can be exchanged between two neighbor gateway hosts, each of which has its own router. Additionally, it is commonly used to exchange routing table information between hosts on the internet.

- Routing Information Protocol (RIP): It determines how routers can share information while transferring traffic among connected group of local area networks. The maximum number of hops that can be allowed for RIP is 15, which restricts the size of networks that RIP can support.

Difference between Bridge and Router

Bridge	Router
A bridge is a networking device that is used to connect two local area networks (LANs) by using media access control addresses and transmit the data between them.	A router is also a networking device that sends the data from one network to another network with the help of their IP addresses.

A bridge is able to connect only two different LAN segments.	A router is capable of connecting the LAN and WAN.
A bridge transfers the data in the form of frames.	A router transfers the data in the form of packets.
It sends data based on the MAC address of a device.	It sends data based on the IP address of a device.
The bridge has only one port to connect the device.	The router has several ports to connect the devices.
The bridge does not use any table to forward the data.	The router uses a routing table to send the data.

Difference between Hub, Switch and Router

There are three primarily networking devices that connect the computers from one to another. These devices are hub, switch, and router. These all have the ability to connect one computer to another, but there is some difference between them. The difference between a hub, switch, and router are given below:

Hub: A hub is a basic networking device that is used to connect computers or other networking devices together. A hub does not use any routing table to send the data to the destination. Although it can identify basic errors of networks like collisions, it can be a security risk to broadcast all information to the multiple ports. As the hub is a dumb device, it does not need an IP address. Furthermore, Hubs are cheaper than a switch or router.

Switch: A switch is a hardware device that also connects computers to each other. A switch is different as compared to a hub in that way; it handles packets of data. Whenever a switch receives a packet, it decides the device to which the packet can be sent, and sends it to that device only. A hub broadcasts the packet to all computers, but the switch does not circulate the packet to all devices, which means bandwidth is not shared with the network, and thus it increases the efficiency of the network. That's why switches are more preferred as compared to a hub.

Router: A router is more different from a switch or hub. It is mainly used to route the data packets to another network instead of transmitting the data to the local networks only. A router is commonly found in homes and offices as it allows your network to communicate with other networks through the internet. Basically, a router provides more features to your networks like firewall, VPN, QoS, traffic monitoring, etc.

What is Routing Table in Router?

A routing table determines the path for a given packet with the help of an IP address of a device and necessary information from the table and sends the packet to the destination network. The routers have the internal memory that is known as Random Access Memory (RAM). All the information of the routing table is stored in RAM of routers.

For Example

Destination (Network ID)	Subnet mask	Interface
200.1.2.0	255.255.255.0	Eth0
200.1.2.64	255.255.255.128	Eth1
200.1.2.128	255.255.255.255	Eth2
Default		Eth3

A routing Table Contains the Following Entities

- It contains an IP address of all routers which are required to decide the way to reach the destination network.

- It includes extrovert interface information.

- Furthermore, it is also contained IP addresses and subnet mask of the destination host.

Network Element in Router

There are two types of a network element in the router which are as follows:

Control plane: A router supports a routing table that determines which path and physical interface connection should be used to send the packet. It is done by using internal pre-configured directives, which are called static routes, or by learning routes with the help of routing protocol. A routing table stores the static and dynamic routes. Then the control-plane logic eliminates the unnecessary directives from the table and constructs a forwarding information base that is used by the forwarding plane.

Forwarding plane: A router sends data packets between incoming and outgoing interface connections. It uses information stored in the packet header and matches it to entries in the FIB, which is supplied by the control plane; accordingly, it forwards the data packet to the correct network type. It is also called the user plane or data plane.

How to buy a Router?

There are many points to keep in mind while buying a router:

- Type of Connection: Which kind of router should you buy depends on the type of connection you have. For example, if you want to use the internet connection from your telephone services providers like BSNL or MTNL, you will need an ADSL router. In this router, you have to use the hardware that is provided to you with your connection. Although this router may have limited functionalities on some fronts. Alternatively, you can purchase an advanced router that allows you sharing storage, including printer over a wireless connection.

If you use the connection provided by the local cable operator, you will need a non-ADSL router.

- Standard: The routers support standards like 802.11ac, 802.11n, etc. The routers that support 802.11ac standard, enhances the speed to transfer the data more than three times the speed of 802.11n standard routers. It uses the 5GHz frequency band, which is less crowded as compared to the regular 2.4GHz band. Furthermore, it also provides better network performance for file transfers and streaming media content. The routers that support 802.11ac standard are beneficial as they are compatible with 'n' standard, by which your older devices can also work without any problem.Alternatively; you can save some money and full fill your requirements by purchasing 'n' standard routers.

- Dual-band: Most of 'n' standard routers operate in the 2.4GHz frequency, but a dual-band router is better as it supports the 5GHz band. Furthermore, it can also connect with smartphones and laptops on 5GHz, while other routers can operate over 2.4GHz only.

- USB port: Routers with USB ports allow you to plug flash drives, including printers, to share these resources over the network. These functions are suitable for a small area as they can be used within the wireless network without using the internet. Some routers provide backup internet by 3G data dongles when your main connection goes down. But these routers work with specific brands only. So, before purchasing a router, check if it supports the dongle you are using.

- Multiple antennas: External antennas are strong enough to increase the overall range of your router as well as are suitable for environments where you need signals across multiple walls or doors.

OSPF Routing

The OSPF protocol which implements the LS algorithm is an open, publicly available protocol with 3 versions - OSPF v2: RFC 2328, and OSPF v3: RFC 2740. It is an intradomain routing protocol. It has mechanisms for LSP dissemination throughout the network, topology construction at each node, and route computation using Dijkstra's algorithm. LSPs are flooded through OSPF advertisements to the entire domain. They are carried in OSPF messages directly over IP (rather than TCP or UDP).

A look at the OSPF message format is enough to understand how the LS algorithm is implemented. There are different types of OSPF messages – for sending the Hello messages, and to send LS advertisements. The header of the OSPF message is given in figure.

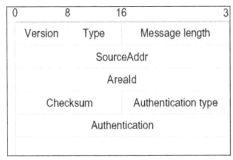

Figure: OSPF message header.

The SourceAddr is the address of the router sending the message, areaId is the ID of the area to which the router belongs – (the domain or autonomous system (AS) is divided into areas for easy manageability). Checksum is the usual IP-like checksum. Authentication type and authentication information are used to provide some level of security in sending the OSPF messages. The format of the LSA message is shown in figure.

LS Age		Options	Type = 1
Link-state ID			
Advertising router			
LS sequence number			
LS checksum		Length	
0	Flags	0	Number of links
Link ID			
Link data			
Link type	Num_TOS		Metric
Optional TOS information			
More links			

Figure: OSPF LSA message format.

The fields in the LSA message are pretty much self-explanatory. LSAge is the TTL information for the LSA packet. Link-state ID and Advertising router give the address of the router sending the LSP. LS sequence number is the SEQNO in the LS algorithm.Every LSA, can carry information about more than one link. The number of links for which the information is carried is specified in the field of the same name. The LinkID and Link data fields identify the individual links. The metric and Num_TOS give the type of metric being used to specify the cost (bandwidth, congestion etc.,), and the numeric value of that metric. The link specific fields are repeated for each link at the advertising router.

OSPF – Additional Features

It is interesting to note that OSPF provides support for many interesting features associated with routing. Some of these are mentioned below:

- Support for equal-cost multipath routing: If there exist more than one path to a destination with the same cost, it supports sending of packets along the multiple paths. Support for TOS-based routing – It supports different parameters to be specified – for providing different IP Type-of-Service. Multiple routes for multiple ToS are supported. A separate shortest path tree will be constructed for each ToS.

- Support for variable subnet length: Each route distributed has a destination and mask to support advertising routing info for groups of subnets.

- Integrated unicast and multicast support: Multicast OSPF (MOSPF) uses the same topology database as OSPF.

- Support for two levels of hierarchy: An area is a group of contiguous networks and hosts. OSPF allows for the entire AS to be split into multiple "areas", to provide scalability – We can route to an area - inter-area routing, and then route within the area – intra-area routing. Dividing into areas helps in reducing the number of networks that each router will have to handle for an entire AS. The topology of an area is invisible from the outside. With this support for areas a typical OSPF hierarchy-based network would be as shown in figure.

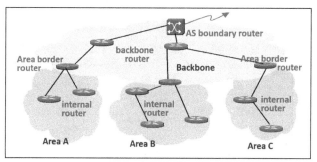

Figure: A hierarchical AS.

The entire AS is divided into areas, which connect to a backbone network inside the AS, which in turn connects to the AS boundary router which connects to other ASes. Area border routers "summarize" distances to networks of that area, and advertise that information to other Area Border routers. Area internal routers only participate in intraarea routing, and LSA's are sent only within the area. They receive external routes broadcasted by area border router, and integrate that information. The backbone routers run OSPF routing limited to backbone. The AS Boundary routers connect to other AS's.

OSPF vs RIP

Many of these features of OSPF are not present in RIP making OSPF a more sophisticated protocol:

Security: all OSPF messages are authenticated to prevent malicious intrusion. There is no such support in RIP. Multiple same-cost paths are allowed, whereas only one path in RIP.

For each link, multiple cost metrics for different TOS (e.g., satellite link cost set "low" for best effort ToS; high for real time ToS), which is not supported in RIP.

Integrated uni- and multicast support, which again is not supported by RIP. Hierarchical OSPF in large domains helps scalability, which does not feature in RIP. RIP is mostly used in small networks.

RIP Routing

RIP is an interior gateway protocol (IGP) that uses a distance-vector algorithm to determine the best route to a destination, using the hop count as the metric.

In a RIP network, each router's forwarding table is distributed among the nodes through the flooding of routing table information. Because topology changes are flooded throughout the network, every node maintains the same list of destinations. Packets are then routed to these destinations based on path-cost calculations done at each node in the network.

Distance-Vector Routing Protocols

Distance-vector routing protocols transmit routing information that includes a distance vector, typically expressed as the number of hops to the destination. This information is flooded out all protocol-enabled interfaces at regular intervals (every 30 seconds in the case of RIP) to create a network map that is stored in each node's local topology database. Figure shows how distance-vector routing works.

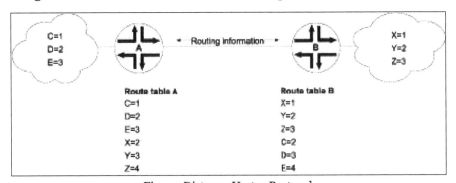

Figure: Distance-Vector Protocol.

In Figure, Routers A and B have RIP enabled on adjacent interfaces. Router A has known RIP neighbors Routers C, D, and E, which are 1, 2, and 3 hops away, respectively. Router B has known RIP neighbors Routers X, Y, and Z, which are 1, 2, and 3 hops away, respectively. Every 30 seconds, each router floods its entire routing table information out all RIP-enabled interfaces. In this case, flooding exchanges routing table information across the RIP link.

When Router A receives routing information from Router B, it adds 1 to the hop count to determine the new hop count. For example, Router X has a hop count of 1, but when

Router A imports the route to X, the new hop count is 2. The imported route also includes information about where the route was learned, so that the original route is imported as a route to Router X through Router B with a hop count of 2.

When multiple routes to the same host are received, RIP uses the distance-vector algorithm to determine which path to import into the forwarding table. The route with the smallest hop count is imported. If there are multiple routes with the same hop count, all are imported into the forwarding table, and traffic is sent along the paths in round-robin fashion.

The RIP IGP uses the Bellman-Ford, or distance-vector, algorithm to determine the best route to a destination. RIP uses the hop count as the metric. RIP enables hosts and routers to exchange information for computing routes through an IP-based network. RIP is intended to be used as an IGP in reasonably homogeneous networks of moderate size.

RIP version 1 packets contain the minimal information necessary to route packets through a network. However, this version of RIP does not support authentication or subnetting. RIP uses User Datagram Protocol (UDP) port 520.

RIP has the following architectural limitations:

- The longest network path cannot exceed 15 hops (assuming that each network, or hop, has a cost of 1).

- RIP depends on counting to infinity to resolve certain unusual situations—when the network consists of several hundred routers, and when a routing loop has formed, the amount of time and network bandwidth required to resolve a next hop might be great.

- RIP uses only a fixed metric to select a route. Other IGPs use additional parameters, such as measured delay, reliability, and load.

RIP Packets

RIP packets contain the following fields:

- Command: Indicates whether the packet is a request or response message. Request messages seek information for the router's routing table. Response messages are sent periodically and also when a request message is received. Periodic response messages are called update messages. Update messages contain the command and version fields and 25 destinations (by default), each of which includes the destination IP address and the metric to reach that destination.

- Version number: Version of RIP that the originating router is running.

- Address family identifier: Address family used by the originating router. The family is always IP.

- Address: IP address included in the packet.

- Metric: Value of the metric advertised for the address.

- Mask: Mask associated with the IP address (RIP version 2 only).

- Next hop: IP address of the next-hop router (RIP version 2 only).

Routing information is exchanged in a RIP network by RIP request and RIP response packets. A router that has just booted can broadcast a RIP request on all RIP-enabled interfaces. Any routers running RIP on those links receive the request and respond by sending a RIP response packet immediately to the router. The response packet contains the routing table information required to build the local copy of the network topology map.

In the absence of RIP request packets, all RIP routers broadcast a RIP response packet every 30 seconds on all RIP-enabled interfaces. The RIP broadcast is the primary way in which topology information is flooded throughout the network.

Once a router learns about a particular destination through RIP, it starts a timer. Every time it receives a new response packet with information about the destination, the router resets the timer to zero. However, if the router receives no updates about a particular destination for 180 seconds, it removes the destination from its RIP routing table.

In addition to the regular transmission of RIP packets every 30 seconds, if a router detects a new neighbor or detects that an interface is unavailable, it generates a triggered update. The new routing information is immediately broadcast out all RIP-enabled interfaces, and the change is reflected in all subsequent RIP response packets.

Maximizing Hop Count

The successful routing of traffic across a RIP network requires that every node in the network maintain the same view of the topology. Topology information is broadcast between RIP neighbors every 30 seconds. If Router A is many hops away from a new host, Router B, the route to B might take significant time to propagate through the network and be imported into Router A's routing table. If the two routers are 5 hops away from each other, Router A cannot import the route to Router B until 2.5 minutes after Router B is online (30 seconds per hop). For large numbers of hops, the delay becomes prohibitive. To help prevent this delay from growing arbitrarily large, RIP enforces a maximum hop count of 15 hops. Any prefix that is more than 15 hops away is treated as unreachable and assigned a hop count equal to infinity. This maximum hop count is called the network diameter.

Split Horizon and Poison Reverse Efficiency Techniques

Because RIP functions by periodically flooding the entire routing table out to the network, it generates a lot of traffic. The split horizon and poison reverse techniques can help reduce the amount of network traffic originated by RIP hosts and make the transmission of routing information more efficient.

If a router receives a set of route advertisements on a particular interface, RIP determines that those advertisements do not need to be retransmitted out the same interface. This technique, known as split horizon, helps limit the amount of RIP routing traffic by eliminating information that other neighbors on that interface have already learned. Figure shows an example of the split horizon technique.

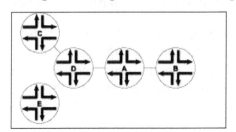

Figure: Split Horizon Example.

In Figure, Router A advertises routes to Routers C, D, and E to Router B. In this example, Router A can reach Router C in 2 hops. When Router A advertises the route to Router B, Router B imports it as a route to Router C through Router A in 3 hops. If Router B then re-advertised this route to Router A, Router A would import it as a route to Router C through Router B in 4 hops. However, the advertisement from Router B to Router A is unnecessary, because Router A can already reach the route in 2 hops. The split horizon technique helps reduce extra traffic by eliminating this type of route advertisement.

Similarly, the poison reverse technique helps to optimize the transmission of routing information and improve the time to reach network convergence. If Router A learns about unreachable routes through one of its interfaces, it advertises those routes as unreachable (hop count of 16) out the same interface. Figure shows an example of the poison reverse technique.

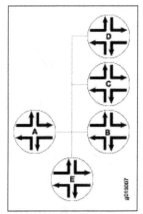

Figure: Poison Reverse Example.

In figure, Router A learns through one of its interfaces that routes to Routers C, D, and E are unreachable. Router A re-advertises those routes out the same interface as unreachable. The advertisement informs Router B that Routers C, D, and E are definitely not reachable through Router A.

Limitations of Unidirectional Connectivity

Because RIP processes routing information based solely on the receipt of routing table updates, it cannot ensure bidirectional connectivity. As figure shows, RIP networks are limited by their unidirectional connectivity.

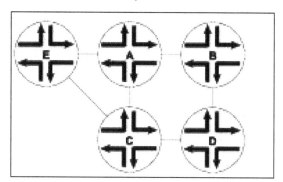

Figure: Limitations of Unidirectional Connectivity.

In figure, Routers A and D flood their routing table information to Router B. Because the path to Router E has the fewest hops when routed through Router A, that route is imported into Router B's forwarding table. However, suppose that Router A can transmit traffic but is not receiving traffic from Router B because of an unavailable link or invalid routing policy. If the only route to Router E is through Router A, any traffic destined for Router A is lost, because bidirectional connectivity was never established. OSPF establishes bidirectional connectivity with a three-way handshake.

RIPng Overview

The Routing Information Protocol next generation (RIPng) is an interior gateway protocol (IGP) that uses a distance-vector algorithm to determine the best route to a destination, using hop count as the metric. RIPng exchanges routing information used to compute routes and is intended for IP version 6 (IPv6)-based networks. RIPng is disabled by default. On devices in secure context, IPv6 is disabled. You must enable IPv6 to use RIPng.

RIPng Protocol

The RIPng IGP uses the Bellman-Ford distance-vector algorithm to determine the best route to a destination, using hop count as the metric. RIPng allows hosts and routers to exchange information for computing routes through an IP-based network. RIPng is intended to act as an IGP for moderately-sized autonomous systems. RIPng is a distinct routing protocol from RIPv2. RIPng is a UDP-based protocol and uses UDP port 521. RIPng has the following architectural limitations:

- The longest network path cannot exceed 15 hops (assuming that each network, or hop, has a cost of 1).

- RIPng is prone to routing loops when the routing tables are reconstructed. Especially when RIPng is implemented in large networks that consist of several hundred routers, RIPng might take an extremely long time to resolve routing loops.

- RIPng uses only a fixed metric to select a route. Other IGPs use additional parameters, such as measured delay, reliability, and load.

RIPng Standards

RIPng is defined in the following documents:

- RFC 2080, RIPng for IPv6.

- RFC 2081, RIPng Protocol Applicability Statement.

RIPng Packets

A RIPng packet header contains the following fields:

- Command: Indicates whether the packet is a request or response message. Request messages seek information for the router's routing table. Response messages are sent periodically or when a request message is received. Periodic response messages are called update messages. Update messages contain the command and version fields and a set of destinations and metrics.

- Version number: Specifies the version of RIPng that the originating router is running. This is currently set to Version 1.

The rest of the RIPng packet contains a list of routing table entries consisting of the following fields:

- Destination prefix: 128-bit IPv6 address prefix for the destination.

- Prefix length: Number of significant bits in the prefix.

- Metric: Value of the metric advertised for the address.

- Route tag: A route attribute that must be advertised and redistributed with the route. Primarily, the route tag distinguishes external RIPng routes from internal RIPng routes when routes must be redistributed across an exterior gateway protocol (EGP).

Inter-Domain Routing

Inter-Domain routing, as the name suggests, is the protocol in which Routing algorithm works within and between domains. In case of Inter-Domain the interaction is between different domains so information of components of other domains is also required. In Inter-Domain Routing Interior-gateway protocols such as RIP (resource information protocol) and OSPF (open shortest path first) are being used. For Inter-Domain Routing internet within the domain and in domain with which the interaction is going on should be connected and available. Inter-Domain Routing is more complex and more dependent as compared to that of Intra-Domain Routing.

Classless Inter-Domain Routing

Classless Inter-Domain Routing (CIDR) allows far more flexible network sizes than those allowed by classful addresses. CIDR allows for many network sizes beyond the arbitrary classful network sizes.

The Class A network 10.0.0.0 contains IP addresses that begins with 10: 10.1.2.3.4, 10.187.24.8, 10.3.96.223, etc. In other words, 10.* is a Class A address. The first 8 bits of the dotted-quad IPv4 address is the network (10); the remaining 24 bits are the host address: 3.96.223 in the last previous example. The CIDR notation for a Class A network is /8 for this reason: 10.0.0.0/8. The "/8" is the netmask, which means the network portion is 8 bits long, leaving 24 bits for the host.

Similarly, the class C network of 192.0.2.0 contains any IP address that begins with 192.0.2: 192.0.2.177, 192.0.2.253, etc. That class C network is 192.0.2.0/24 in CIDR format: the first 24 bits (192.0.2) describe the network; the remaining 8 bits (177 or 253 in the previous example) describe the host.

Once networks are described in CIDR notation, additional routable network sizes are possible. Need 128 IP addresses? Chop a Class C (/24) in half, resulting in two /25 networks. Need 64 IP addresses? Chop a /24 network into quarters, resulting in four /26 networks with 64 IP addresses each.

Hierarchical Inter-Domain Routing Architecture (HIDRA)

The Hierarchical Inter-Domain Routing Architecture (HIDRA) is a proposal with two concerns, the first one is to reduce the size of routing tables at core networks and the second is related with deployment concerns. HIDRA is a hierarchical network architecture that uses mapping and encapsulation, and also employs IPv4 addresses for location and identification purposes, to maximize the compatibility with existent approaches. HIDRA uses BGP as a proactive mapping system (with the overhead of transmitting routes that may not be necessary), nevertheless the mapping devices are placed at the edges, near end-nodes. In an optimized HIDRA mode, end-nodes can perform encapsulation before transmission. In a reactive mapping mode, HIDRA adds more information to the mapping (e.g., priority) enabling traffic engineering. As one of the concerns in HIDRA is deployment, detailed steps are provided to enable migration from existing architectures to HIDRA. For instance, a default route must be installed to send all traffic to an encapsulation point. An implementation in a Linux testbed is used to test HIDRA. Nevertheless, reactive mapping optimizations are not specified.

Hybrid proposals rely on the locator-identifier split paradigm; nonetheless, some organize the network in an hierarchical way to facilitate deployment and management. The Node ID Internetworking Architecture (NIIA) organizes the network as a tree, and employs default routes to parent nodes to enable inter-domain routing. In addition, NIIA supports multiple registrations of nodes in the tree (useful when there are multiple interfaces). Notwithstanding, no implementations are available, as summarized in Table 8. Less-Is-More Architecture (LIMA) uses a hierarchical structure to enable efficient inter-domain routing and relies on transport protocols such as SCTP and MPTCP to enable multiaddressing configurations. iMark includes support for simultaneous connections between heterogeneous networks. Nonetheless, details to enable its implementation are missing, such as the mechanism to generate identifiers. HiiMap organizes the network according to a region prefix, allowing trust relationships with authorities. MILSA has the advantage of not introducing changes on DNS, or even relying on this service to support mobility.

Table: Comparison of hierarchical multihoming proposals.

Protocol	Approach	Multihoming Goals				Strengths	Weak Aspects	Implementation	
		R	U	L	F			Simulators	OS
LIMA	Loc/ID split	✓	✓	✓	✓	Includes protocols supporting multihoming	Requires changes to DHCP and DNS	–	–
iMark	Loc/ID split	✓	✓	✓	✓	Support concurrent connections	Specification not complete	–	–
HiiMap	Loc/ID split	✓	✓	X	X	Support security	No public implementation available	–	–
HRA	Loc/ID split	✓	✓	X	X	Scalable and supports mobility	Does not support flow distribution	–	–
SILMS	Loc/ID split	✓	X	X	✓	Supports flow distribution	Only for IPv6	–	–
MILSA	Loc/ID split	✓	✓	✓	✓	Supports flow distribution	No public implementation	–	–
TurfNet	Loc/ID split	✓	✓	X	X	Supports mobility	No public implementation	–	–
NIIA	Loc/ID split	✓	✓	X	X	Includes security	No public implementation	–	–
PoMo	Loc/ID split	✓	✓	✓	✓	Includes security	Extra-information on packets	–	–
HAIR	Routing architecture	✓	✓	✓	✓	Hierarchical network organization	Missing details on implementation	–	In Linux [181]
HIDRA	Routing architecture	✓	✓	✓	✓	Includes deployment concerns	Optimize mode not specified (e.g., reactive)	–	In Linux [145]

Hierarchical Architecture for Internet Routing (HAIR) is a hierarchical proposal that aims to enable traffic engineering and puts emphasis on the role of end-hosts by moving core functionalities to end-hosts. Nonetheless, it lacks details regarding identifiers. Hierarchical Inter-Domain Routing Architecture (HIDRA) is also a proposal that aims to foster deployment. For instance, it relies on existing routing protocols such as BGP to allow a proactive mapping system. Proposals, like Hierarchical Routing Architecture (HRA) support mobility by extending HIP and BGP protocols. SILMS has the limitation of only supporting IPv6.

Instead of aiming compatibility, other proposals pursue a security-oriented paradigm. PoMo and Node ID Internetworking Architecture (NIIA) include native security mechanisms, aiming to protect the identity of nodes.

Border Gateway Protocol

The network is actually organized in a hierarchical manner. The challenges and concerns at different levels of the hierarchy are different. The network is very heterogeneous. There are many owners of the different pieces of the network, with different goals for the network. There are many service providers in the internet. Thus a simple "one size fits all" kind of solution may not work.

A look at the organization of a simple multi-provider inter-network would help to understand this concern.

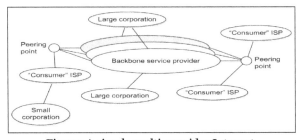

Figure: A simple multi-provider Internet.

There are many backbone service providers who provide the infrastructure to connect many large networks as required by large corporations, and other smaller "consumer" service providers. There are peering points through which these service providers connect to each other. The smaller ISPs may provide network service to smaller corporations and consumers. It is also possible that there could be further levels in the hierarchy with one consumer provider supporting many other smaller service providers and so on. And the numbers are large.

There are millions of networks that we have to deal with in the Internet. It will not be possible to store all the destination addresses in routing tables. Imagine exchanging routing table information or link state information of so many networks across routers. Just the exchange of this information will clog the network – leaving hardly any bandwidth for actual data exchange.

Further given that there are so many independent (autonomous) service providers, each provider may want to control routing in his/her own network in their own manner, depending on geographic, economic or political reasons.

Hence, the routing problem from anywhere to anywhere-else has to handle this hetero-geneity and scale. For this reason, the Internet is treated as an interconnection of au-tonomous systems, with a certain hierarchy. And the routing problem is broken down into manageable pieces within this hierarchy.

Internet Organization - Autonomous Systems and Hierarchical Routing

An autonomous system (AS) is under the control of a single administrative entity, such as a University, company, internet service provider (ISP), etc. A corporation's internal network might be a single AS. The network of a single ISP might be an AS. Thus an AS corresponds to an administrative domain. Routing inside this domain in under the control of that administration. For routing across domains we need a common mech-anism. The ASes are therefore referred to as routing domains as well. We will use the term domain and AS interchangeably in this context.

We now divide the routing problem hierarchically - into two parts – routing within a single AS, and routing between AS. In other words, routing is now viewed as intrado-main routing, and inter-domain routing. Each AS is free to choose its own intradomain routing protocol (RIP or OSPF). The inter-domain routing protocol is an internetwide standard. This organization helps to handle scale by aggregating routing information and also provides autonomy.

Routers inside an AS run the same (intra-AS or intra-domain) routing protocol. This obviously means that routers in different AS can run different intra-AS routing proto-col. The "Gateway routers" which are at the "edge" of their own AS, have links to gate-way routers in other ASes, and run the inter-domain routing protocol.

The forwarding tables at the routers are configured by both intra-domain and interdo-main routing algorithms:

- Intra-AS routing sets entries for internal destinations.

- Both inter-AS & intra-AS routing set entries for external destinations.

Let us understand how this can be done with an example, and then we will look at the actual protocol used for this purpose. Consider the scenario given in figure.

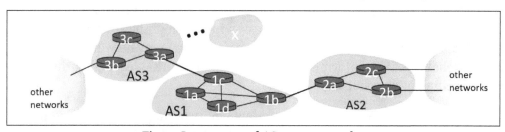

Figure: Interconnected ASes – an example.

Suppose a router in AS1 receives a datagram destined outside of AS1. The router should forward the packet to a gateway router. The question is which one? To answer that the AS1 must learn which destinations are reachable through AS2, and which through AS3, and propagate this reachability information to all routers in AS1. This is the job of inter-AS routing! For example, let us look at how the forwarding table in router 1d would be set.

Suppose AS1 learns (via inter-AS protocol) that subnet x is reachable via AS3 (gateway 1c), but not via AS2. The inter-AS protocol propagates this reachability information to all internal routers. Router 1d determines from the intra-AS routing information that its interface 'I' is on the least cost path to 1c. Then, it installs a forwarding table entry (x,I), indicating that network x can be reached through interface 'I'.

This is a simple case where there is just one path to reach x. Suppose x is reachable through both AS2 and AS3. AS1 learns this from the inter-AS protocol. To configureure the forwarding table, router 1d must determine which gateway it should forward packets towards for destination x. This is the job of the intra-AS routing protocol! This may be achieved through what is called as hot potato routing, which essentially means sending the packet towards closest of two routers. The routing information from intra-AS protocol is used to determine the costs of least-cost paths to each of the gateways. Then the gateway that has the smallest least cost is chosen, and the interface 'l' through which this gateway can be reached is entered in the forwarding table as (x,l).

Thus an interplay of intra-AS and inter-AS protocols is at work to determine the actual entries in the forwarding table. Having looked at what we expect the inter-AS protocol to do, we will now delve in to the details of the de facto inter-domain routing protocol – BGP.

Border Gateway Protocol (BGP)

BGP can be viewed as the "glue that holds the Internet together". BGP provides each AS a means to:

- Obtain subnet reachability information from neighboring AS-es : eBGP (external).

- Propagate reachability information to all AS-internal routers : iBGP (internal BGP).

- Determine "good" routes to other networks based on reachability information and policy.

Basically it allows each subnet to advertise its existence to the rest of Internet: "I am here!" Let us look at some BGP terminology first. BGP uses certain terms to identify the traffic, and the type of AS.

Local traffic: Is traffic that originates at or terminates on nodes within an AS and Transit traffic is traffic that passes through an AS.

There are three types of AS defined by BGP – stub AS, multihomed AS, and transit AS.

- Stub AS: Is an AS that has only a single connection to one other AS. Such an AS will only carry local traffic; typically small corporations fall under this category.

- Multihomed AS: Is an AS that has connections to more than one other AS, but refuses to carry transit traffic; typically large corporations.

- Transit AS: Is an AS that has connections to more than one other AS, and is designed to carry both transit and local traffic (e.g. backbone providers).

BGP Philosophy

The goal of BGP is to find any path to the intended destination that is loop free. We are concerned more with reachability here rather than optimality. Note the difference from intra-AS protocols – where we are concerned with shortest distance or least cost paths. In the inter-AS scenario, finding a path anywhere close to optimal is considered to be a great achievement. Why is this so? The answer again goes back to scalability, and autonomy.

- Scalability: An Internet backbone router must be able to forward any packet destined anywhere in the Internet. It should have a routing table that will provide a match for any valid IP address.

- Autonomy: Given the diverse concerns of ASes, it is impossible to calculate meaningful path costs for a path that crosses multiple ASes. For instance, a cost of 1000 across one provider might imply a great path, but it might mean an unacceptably bad one from another provider.

Further we have an additional issue of trust. A provider A might be unwilling to believe certain advertisements from provider B. Or a provider A may choose not to go through a provider B for many reasons – which could be political, competition etc. This essentially means that we go for "policy-based" routing in BGP! That is, entire path (or path vector) to reach a network is advertised by the routers and each AS is free to choose whichever path based on its own set of policies.

BGP Protocol

Each AS has one BGP speaker that advertises local networks, and other reachable networks (if it is a transit AS), and gives path information. In addition to the BGP speakers, the AS has one or more border "gateways" which need not be the same as the speakers. The border gateways are the routers through which packets enter and leave the AS.

BGP protocol works by exchanging BGP messages between two BGP gateways ("peers") over BGP sessions. A BGP session can be viewed as a semi-permanent TCP connection. The messages advertise paths to different destination network prefixes, giving it the name of a "path vector" protocol. When an AS advertises a prefix to another AS, it promises that it will forward datagrams towards that prefix. An AS can aggregate prefixes in its advertisement thereby reducing the amount of information exchanged. BGP advertises complete paths as an enumerated list of ASs to reach a particular network.

This again is easy to understand with an example. Let us consider the same example given in Figure. above. When AS3 wants to advertise reachability to a network present in AS3 to AS1, say, 212.34.56/22, it uses a eBGP session between its BGP peers, say 3a and 1c, and AS3 sends prefix reachability info to AS1. 1c can then use iBGP to distribute this new prefix info to all routers in AS1. 1b can then re-advertise new reachability info to AS2 over a 1b-to-2a eBGP session, specifying that the said network prefix 212.34.56/22 can be reached through AS1 and AS3. In addition it would also advertise reachability info for the networks in AS1 itself to AS2. In this manner, path information to reach different networks is passed on. When a router learns of a new prefix, it creates an entry for the prefix in its forwarding table.

The advertised information consists of prefix and attributes (prefix + attributes = "route"). It essentially gives the list of subnets that can be reached by an AS_PATH. AS_PATH is an attribute that contains AS IDs through which prefix advertisement has passed: e.g., AS3, AS1. A loop is easily found, if current AS is already in the AS_PATH. Another important attribute is NEXT-HOP, which indicates the specific internal-AS router to the next-hop AS. There may be multiple links from current AS to next-hop-AS.

The gateway router receiving the route advertisement uses its import policy (policy-based routing) to accept or decline the path. For example, if it has a policy which says "never route through AS x", it would reject that path. When a router learns about more than one route to a destination AS, it selects route based on the following criteria:

- Local preference value attribute: Policy decision.

- Shortest AS-PATH.

- Closest NEXT-HOP router: Hot potato routing.

- Additional criteria.

To illustrate with an example, let us assume that a network prefix, say 138.16.64/22, is reachable through two ASes say, AS2 and AS3 to router 1c in AS1. Assume that AS2 and AS3 advertise the following paths:

- AS-PATH: AS2 AS17 to 138.16.64/22; NEXT-HOP: 111.99.86.55.

- AS-PATH AS3 AS131 AS201 to 138.16.64/22; NEXT-HOP: 134.45.23.66.

NEXT-HOP attribute is the IP address of the router interface that begins the AS PATH – i.e., the address to reach AS2 in the first path, and to reach AS3 in the second path.

Let us assume that the policy is to choose the shortest AS-PATH. As per this policy, it will select the path via AS2 (2-hop path as opposed to the 3-hop path via AS3). Then it looks at the corresponding NEXT-HOP info and identifies the AS2's entry point as 111.99.86.55. Next, it uses OSPF or RIP to find the shortest path from 1c to 111.99.86.55. It then identifies the port, say port 4, along the OSPF shortest path. It then adds the following prefix-port entry to its forwarding table: (138.16.64/22, port 4).

BGP Routing Policy

The policy could be based on multiple criteria. One simple criterion could be based on whether it is a provider network or a customer network. A provider network would advertise routes for its customers, whereas a customer would not propagate that information to other customers. Peers may propagate information to each other. Consider the example given in figure.

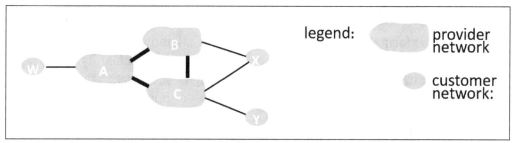

Figure: BGP policy – example.

Let A, B, C be provider networks. X, W, Y is customers (of the corresponding provider networks). X is dual-homed: attached to two networks. Obviously, X does not want to route from B via itself to C. So X will not advertise to B a route to C. For example, A advertises path AW to B. B advertises path BAW to X. Should B advertise a path BAW to C? No way! B gets no "revenue" for routing CBAW since neither W nor C are B's customers. B wants to force C to route to w via A, so it will not advertise a path to W. B will want to route only to/from its customers. Accordingly the import policies will be set.

BGP Messages

Some of the important BGP messages used are:

- Open: To open a TCP connection to a peer and authenticate the sender.

- Update: To advertise a new path (or withdraw old path).

- Keepalive: To keep the connection alive in absence of UPDATES; also ACKs OPEN request.

- Notification: To reports errors in previous message, and to close connection.

Thus BGP helps to disseminate network prefix information across the internet.

Combining Intra-Domain and Inter-Domain Routing

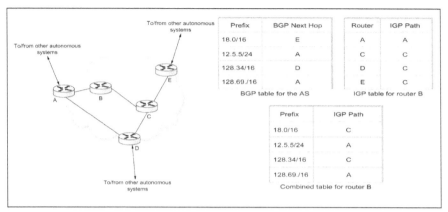

Figure: Integrating Inter and intra domain routing.

One last piece that we need to look at before we conclude on inter-domain routing is integration of information coming from intra-domain and inter-domain protocols. We have already mentioned this earlier, but we will try to understand it better with an example. Consider the AS shown in figure. Let us focus on an internal router, say B.

Assume that the based on information advertised by BGP, the BGP table is shown in the top-left table of the figure. Four different prefixes are reachable through E, A, D, and A respectively. Now the intra-domain routing protocol will give the next-hop information to reach these routers from B. That is shown as the IGP table for router B. These two pieces of information are combined as shown in the combined table. For example, prefix 18.0/16 is reachable through router E, which can be reached through C from B. Hence the combined table at B shows an entry of <18.0/16, C>. That entire router B has to do is send packets for 18.0/16 on the link to C. Similar entries at C will forward the packet towards its destination.

4

Network Topology: Basics

Network topology refers to the manner in which the links and nodes of a network are arranged physically or logically in relation to one another. It defines the way different nodes are placed and interconnected with each other. Network topology and its different types like ring network, bus network, star network and mesh network are discussed in detail in this chapter.

Network Topology

Network topology is the arrangement of the various elements (links, nodes, etc.) of a computer network. Essentially, it is the topological structure of a network and may be depicted physically or logically. *Physical topology* is the placement of the various components of a network, including device location and cable installation, while *logical topology* illustrates how data flows within a network, regardless of its physical design. Distances between nodes, physical interconnections, transmission rates, or signal types may differ between two networks, yet their topologies may be identical.

An example is a local area network (LAN). Any given node in the LAN has one or more physical links to other devices in the network; graphically mapping these links results in a geometric shape that can be used to describe the physical topology of the network. Conversely, mapping the data flow between the components determines the logical topology of the network.

Topology

Two basic categories of network topologies exist, physical topologies and logical topologies.

The cabling layout used to link devices is the physical topology of the network. This refers to the layout of cabling, the locations of nodes, and the interconnections between the nodes and the cabling. The physical topology of a network is determined by the capabilities of the network access devices and media, the level of control or fault tolerance desired, and the cost associated with cabling or telecommunications circuits.

In contrast, logical topology is the way that the signals act on the network media, or the way that the data passes through the network from one device to the next without regard to the physical interconnection of the devices. A network's logical topology is not necessarily the same as its physical topology. For example, the original twisted pair Ethernet using repeater hubs was a logical bus topology carried on a physical star topology. Token ring is a logical ring topology, but is wired as a physical star from the media access unit. Logical topologies are often closely associated with media access control methods and protocols. Some networks are able to dynamically change their logical topology through configuration changes to their routers and switches.

Classification

The study of network topology recognizes eight basic topologies: point-to-point, bus, star, ring or circular, mesh, tree, hybrid, or daisy chain.

Point-to-point

The simplest topology with a dedicated link between two endpoints. Easiest to understand, of the variations of point-to-point topology, is a point-to-point communications channel that appears, to the user, to be permanently associated with the two endpoints. A child's tin can telephone is one example of a *physical dedicated* channel.

Using circuit-switching or packet-switching technologies, a point-to-point circuit can be set up dynamically and dropped when no longer needed. Switched point-to-point topologies are the basic model of conventional telephony.

The value of a permanent point-to-point network is unimpeded communications between the two endpoints. The value of an on-demand point-to-point connection is proportional to the number of potential pairs of subscribers and has been expressed as Metcalfe's Law.

Bus

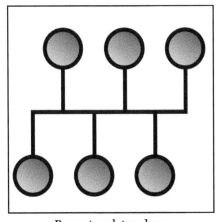

Bus network topology.

In local area networks where bus topology is used, each node is connected to a single cable, by the help of interface connectors. This central cable is the backbone of the network and is known as the bus (thus the name). A signal from the source travels in both directions to all machines connected on the bus cable until it finds the intended recipient. If the machine address does not match the intended address for the data, the machine ignores the data. Alternatively, if the data matches the machine address, the data is accepted. Because the bus topology consists of only one wire, it is rather inexpensive to implement when compared to other topologies. However, the low cost of implementing the technology is offset by the high cost of managing the network. Additionally, because only one cable is utilized, it can be the single point of failure.

Linear Bus

The type of network topology in which all of the nodes of the network are connected to a common transmission medium which has exactly two endpoints (this is the 'bus', which is also commonly referred to as the backbone, or trunk) – all data that is transmitted between nodes in the network is transmitted over this common transmission medium and is able to be received by all nodes in the network simultaneously.

Note: When the electrical signal reaches the end of the bus, the signal is reflected back down the line, causing unwanted interference. As a solution, the two endpoints of the bus are normally terminated with a device called a terminator that prevents this reflection.

Distributed Bus

The type of network topology in which all of the nodes of the network are connected to a common transmission medium which has more than two endpoints that are created by adding branches to the main section of the transmission medium – the physical distributed bus topology functions in exactly the same fashion as the physical linear bus topology (i.e., all nodes share a common transmission medium).

Star

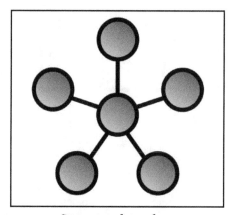

Star network topology.

In local area networks with a star topology, each network host is connected to a central hub with a point-to-point connection. So it can be said that every computer is indirectly connected to every other node with the help of the hub. In Star topology, every node (computer workstation or any other peripheral) is connected to a central node called hub, router or switch. The switch is the server and the peripherals are the clients. The network does not necessarily have to resemble a star to be classified as a star network, but all of the nodes on the network must be connected to one central device. All traffic that traverses the network passes through the central hub. The hub acts as a signal repeater. The star topology is considered the easiest topology to design and implement. An advantage of the star topology is the simplicity of adding additional nodes. The primary disadvantage of the star topology is that the hub represents a single point of failure.

Extended Star

A type of network topology in which a network that is based upon the physical star topology has one or more repeaters between the central node and the peripheral or 'spoke' nodes, the repeaters being used to extend the maximum transmission distance of the point-to-point links between the central node and the peripheral nodes beyond that which is supported by the transmitter power of the central node or beyond that which is supported by the standard upon which the physical layer of the physical star network is based.

If the repeaters in a network that is based upon the physical extended star topology are replaced with hubs or switches, then a hybrid network topology is created that is referred to as a physical hierarchical star topology, although some texts make no distinction between the two topologies.

Distributed Star

A type of network topology that is composed of individual networks that are based upon the physical star topology connected in a linear fashion – i.e., 'daisy-chained' – with no central or top level connection point (e.g., two or more 'stacked' hubs, along with their associated star connected nodes or 'spokes').

Ring

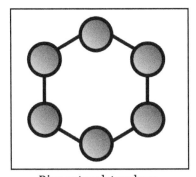

Ring network topology.

A ring topology is a bus topology in a closed loop. Data travels around the ring in one direction. When one node sends data to another, the data passes through each intermediate node on the ring until it reaches its destination. The intermediate nodes repeat (retransmit) the data to keep the signal strong. Every node is a peer; there is no hierarchical relationship of clients and servers. If one node is unable to retransmit data, it severs communication between the nodes before and after it in the bus.

Mesh

The value of fully meshed networks is proportional to the exponent of the number of subscribers, assuming that communicating groups of any two endpoints, up to and including all the endpoints, is approximated by Reed's Law.

Fully Connected Network

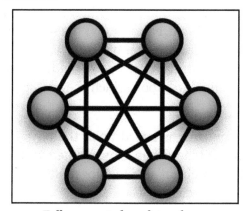

Fully connected mesh topology.

In a *fully connected network*, all nodes are interconnected. (In graph theory this is called a complete graph.) The simplest fully connected network is a two-node network. A fully connected network doesn't need to use packet switching or broadcasting. However, since the number of connections grows quadratically with the number of nodes:

$$c = \frac{n(n-1)}{2}.$$

This makes it impractical for large networks.

Partially Connected Network

In a partially connected network, certain nodes are connected to exactly one other node; but some nodes are connected to two or more other nodes with a point-to-point link. This makes it possible to make use of some of the redundancy of mesh topology that is physically fully connected, without the expense and complexity required for a connection between every node in the network.

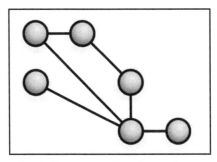

Partially connected mesh topology.

Hybrid

Hybrid networks combine two or more topologies in such a way that the resulting network does not exhibit one of the standard topologies (e.g., bus, star, ring, etc.). For example, a tree network (or *star-bus network*) is a hybrid topology in which star networks are interconnected via bus networks. However, a tree network connected to another tree network is still topologically a tree network, not a distinct network type. A hybrid topology is always produced when two different basic network topologies are connected.

A *star-ring* network consists of two or more ring networks connected using a multistation access unit (MAU) as a centralized hub.

Snowflake topology is a star network of star networks.

Two other hybrid network types are *hybrid mesh* and *hierarchical star*.

Daisy Chain

Except for star-based networks, the easiest way to add more computers into a network is by daisy-chaining, or connecting each computer in series to the next. If a message is intended for a computer partway down the line, each system bounces it along in sequence until it reaches the destination. A daisy-chained network can take two basic forms: linear and ring.

- A linear topology puts a two-way link between one computer and the next. However, this was expensive in the early days of computing, since each computer (except for the ones at each end) required two receivers and two transmitters.

- By connecting the computers at each end, a ring topology can be formed. An advantage of the ring is that the number of transmitters and receivers can be cut in half, since a message will eventually loop all of the way around. When a node sends a message, the message is processed by each computer in the ring. If the ring breaks at a particular link then the transmission can be sent via the reverse path thereby ensuring that all nodes are always connected in the case of a single failure.

Centralization

The star topology reduces the probability of a network failure by connecting all of the peripheral nodes (computers, etc.) to a central node. When the physical star topology is applied to a logical bus network such as Ethernet, this central node (traditionally a hub) rebroadcasts all transmissions received from any peripheral node to all peripheral nodes on the network, sometimes including the originating node. All peripheral nodes may thus communicate with all others by transmitting to, and receiving from, the central node only. The failure of a transmission line linking any peripheral node to the central node will result in the isolation of that peripheral node from all others, but the remaining peripheral nodes will be unaffected. However, the disadvantage is that the failure of the central node will cause the failure of all of the peripheral nodes.

If the central node is *passive*, the originating node must be able to tolerate the reception of an echo of its own transmission, delayed by the two-way round trip transmission time (i.e. to and from the central node) plus any delay generated in the central node. An *active* star network has an active central node that usually has the means to prevent echo-related problems.

A tree topology (a.k.a. hierarchical topology) can be viewed as a collection of star networks arranged in a hierarchy. This tree has individual peripheral nodes (e.g. leaves) which are required to transmit to and receive from one other node only and are not required to act as repeaters or regenerators. Unlike the star network, the functionality of the central node may be distributed.

As in the conventional star network, individual nodes may thus still be isolated from the network by a single-point failure of a transmission path to the node. If a link connecting a leaf fails, that leaf is isolated; if a connection to a non-leaf node fails, an entire section of the network becomes isolated from the rest.

To alleviate the amount of network traffic that comes from broadcasting all signals to all nodes, more advanced central nodes were developed that are able to keep track of the identities of the nodes that are connected to the network. These network switches will "learn" the layout of the network by "listening" on each port during normal data transmission, examining the data packets and recording the address/identifier of each connected node and which port it is connected to in a lookup table held in memory. This lookup table then allows future transmissions to be forwarded to the intended destination only.

Decentralization

In a partially connected mesh topology, there are at least two nodes with two or more paths between them to provide redundant paths in case the link providing one of the paths fails. Decentralization is often used to compensate for the single-point-failure disadvantage that is present when using a single device as a central node (e.g., in star and tree networks). A special kind of mesh, limiting the number of hops between two nodes, is a hypercube. The number of arbitrary forks in mesh networks makes them more difficult to design and implement, but their decentralized nature makes them very useful. In 2012 the IEEE published the Shortest Path Bridging protocol to ease configuration tasks and allows all paths to be active which increases bandwidth and redundancy between all devices.

This is similar in some ways to a grid network, where a linear or ring topology is used to connect systems in multiple directions. A multidimensional ring has a toroidal topology, for instance.

A *fully connected network*, *complete topology*, or *full mesh topology* is a network topology in which there is a direct link between all pairs of nodes. In a fully connected network with n nodes, there are n(n-1)/2 direct links. Networks designed with this topology are usually very expensive to set up, but provide a high degree of reliability due to the multiple paths for data that are provided by the large number of redundant links between nodes. This topology is mostly seen in military applications.

Ring Network

A ring network is a network topology in which each node connects to exactly two other nodes, forming a single continuous pathway for signals through each node - a ring. Data travels from node to node, with each node along the way handling every packet.

Rings can be unidirectional, with all traffic travelling either clockwise or anticlockwise around the ring, or bidirectional (as in SONET/SDH). Because a unidirectional ring topology provides only one pathway between any two nodes, unidirectional ring networks may be disrupted by the failure of a single link. A node failure or cable break might isolate every node attached to the ring. In response, some ring networks add a "counter-rotating ring" (C-Ring) to form a redundant topology: in the event of a break, data are wrapped back onto the complementary ring before reaching the end of the cable, maintaining a path to every node along the resulting C-Ring. Such "dual ring" networks include Spatial Reuse Protocol, Fiber Distributed Data Interface (FDDI), and Resilient Packet Ring. 802.5 networks - also known as IBM token ring networks - avoid the weakness of a ring topology altogether: they actually use a *star* topology at the *physical* layer and a media access unit (MAU) to *imitate* a ring at the *datalink* layer.

Some SONET/SDH rings have two sets of bidirectional links between nodes. This allows maintenance or failures at multiple points of the ring usually without loss of the primary traffic on the outer ring by switching the traffic onto the inner ring past the failure points.

Advantages

- Very orderly network where every device has access to the token and the opportunity to transmit.

- Performs better than a bus topology under heavy network load.

- Does not require a central node to manage the connectivity between the computers.

- Due to the point to point line configuration of devices with a device on either side (each device is connected to its immediate neighbor), it is quite easy to install and reconfigure since adding or removing a device requires moving just two connections.

- Point to point line configuration makes it easy to identify and isolate faults.

- Reconfiguration for line faults of bidirectional rings can be very fast, as switching happens at a high level, and thus the traffic does not require individual re-routing.

Disadvantages

- One malfunctioning workstation can create problems for the entire network. This can be solved by using a dual ring or a switch that closes off the break.

- Moving, adding and changing the devices can affect the network.

- Communication delay is directly proportional to number of nodes in the network.

- Bandwidth is shared on all links between devices.

- More difficult to configure than a Star: node adjunction = Ring shutdown and reconfiguration.

Misconceptions

- "Token Ring is an example of a ring topology." 802.5 (Token Ring) networks do not use a ring topology at layer 1. As explained above, IBM Token Ring (802.5) networks *imitate* a ring at layer 2 but use a physical star at layer 1.

- "Rings prevent collisions." The term "ring" only refers to the layout of the cables. It is true that there are no collisions on an IBM Token Ring, but this is because of the layer 2 Media Access Control method, not the physical topology (which again is a star, not a ring.) Token passing, not rings, prevent collisions.

- "Token passing happens on rings." Token passing is a way of managing access to the cable, implemented at the MAC sublayer of layer 2. Ring topology is the cable layout at layer one. It is possible to do token passing on a bus (802.4) a star (802.5) or a ring (FDDI). Token passing is not restricted to rings.

Bus Network

A bus network is a network topology in which nodes are directly connected to a common linear (or branched) half-duplex link called a bus.

Function

A host on a bus network is called a *Station* or *workstation*. In a bus network, every station receives all network traffic, and the traffic generated by each station has equal transmission priority. A bus network forms a single network segment and collision domain. In order for nodes to transmit on the same bus simultaneously, they use a media access control technology such as carrier sense multiple access (CSMA) or a bus master.

If any link or segment of the bus is severed, all network transmission ceases due to signal bounce caused by the lack of a terminating resistor.

Advantages and Disadvantages

Advantages

- Easy to connect a computer or peripheral to a linear bus.
- Requires less cable length than a star topology resulting in lower costs.
- It works well for small networks.

Disadvantages

- Entire network shuts down if there is a break in the main cable or one of the T connectors break.
- Large amount of packet collisions on the network, which results in high amounts of packet loss.

Star Network

Star networks are one of the most common computer network topologies. In its simplest form, a star network consists of one central node, typically a switch or hub, which acts as a conduit to transmit messages. In star topology, every node (computer work-station or any other peripheral) is connected to a central node. The switch is the server and the peripherals are the clients.

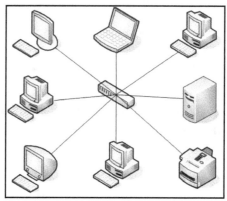

Star topology.

A star network is an implementation of a Spoke–hub distribution paradigm in comput-er networks. Thus, the hub and leaf nodes, and the transmission lines between them, form a graph with the topology of a star. Data on a star network passes through the hub, switch, or concentrator before continuing to its destination. The hub, switch, or con-centrator manages and controls all functions of the network. It also acts as a repeater for the data flow. This configuration is common with twisted pair cable and optical fibre cable. However, it can also be used with coaxial cable.

The star topology reduces the damage caused by line failure by connecting all of the sys-tems to a central node. When applied to a bus-based network, this central hub rebroadcasts all transmissions received from any peripheral node to all peripheral nodes on the network, sometimes including the originating node. All peripheral nodes may thus communicate with all others by transmitting to, and receiving from, the central node only. The failure of a transmission line linking any peripheral node to the central node will result in the isolation of that peripheral node from all others, but the rest of the systems will be unaffected.

Advantages and Disadvantages

Advantages:

- If one computer or its connection breaks it doesn't affect the other computers and their connections.

- Devices can be added or removed without disturbing the network.

Disadvantages:

- An expensive network layout to install because of the amount of cables needed.

- The central hub is a single point of failure for the network.

Passive Vs. Active

If the central node is *passive*, the originating node must be able to tolerate the reception of an echo of its own transmission, delayed by the two-way transmission time (i.e. to and from the central node) plus any delay generated in the central node. An *active* star network has an active central node that usually has the means to prevent echo-related problems.

Mesh Networking

A mesh network is a network topology in which each node relays data for the network. All mesh nodes cooperate in the distribution of data in the network.

Mesh networks can relay messages using either a *flooding* technique or a *routing* technique. With routing, the message is propagated along a path by *hopping* from node to node until it reaches its destination. To ensure all its paths' availability, the network must allow for continuous connections and must reconfigure itself around broken paths, using *self-healing* algorithms such as Shortest Path Bridging. Self-healing allows a routing-based network to operate when a node breaks down or when a connection becomes unreliable. As a result, the network is typically quite reliable, as there is often more than one path between a source and a destination in the network. Although mostly used in wireless situations, this concept can also apply to wired networks and to software interaction.

A mesh network whose nodes are all connected to each other is a fully connected network. Fully connected wired networks have the advantages of security and reliability: problems in a cable affect only the two nodes attached to it. However, in such networks, the number of cables, and therefore the cost, goes up rapidly as the number of nodes increases.

Mesh networks can be considered a type of an *ad-hoc* network. Thus, mesh networks are closely related to mobile ad hoc networks (MANETs), although MANETs also must deal with problems introduced by the mobility of the nodes.

Wired

Shortest path bridging allows Ethernet switches to be connected in a mesh topology and for all paths to be active.

Wireless

Wireless mesh networks were originally developed for military applications. Mesh networks are typically wireless. Over the past decade, the size, cost, and power requirements of radios has declined, enabling multiple radios to be contained within a single mesh node, thus allowing for greater modularity; each can handle multiple frequency bands and support a variety of functions as needed—such as client access, backhaul service, and scanning (required for high-speed handoff in mobile applications)—even customized sets of them.

Work in this field has been aided by the use of game theory methods to analyze strategies for the allocation of resources and routing of packets.

Early wireless mesh networks all use nodes that have a single half-duplex radio that, at any one instant, can either transmit or receive, but not both at the same time. This requires a shared mesh configuration.

Some later wireless mesh networks use nodes with more complex radio hardware that can receive packets from an upstream node and transmit packets to a downstream node simultaneously (on a different frequency or a different CDMA channel), which is a prerequisite for a switched mesh configuration.

Examples

- The first widely deployed mesh network was created for the military market. DoD JTRS radios are mesh networks (SRW). Harris ANW2 (2007), running on AN/PRC-117, AN/PRC-152A are mesh networks.

- In rural Catalonia, Guifi.net was developed in 2004 as a response to the lack of broadband internet, where commercial internet providers weren't providing a connection or a very poor one. Nowadays with more than 30,000 nodes it is only halfway a fully connected network, but following a peer to peer agreement it remained an open, free and neutral network with extensive redundancy.

- ZigBee digital radios are incorporated into some consumer appliances, including battery-powered appliances. ZigBee radios spontaneously organize a mesh network, using AODV routing; transmission and reception are synchronized. This means the radios can be off much of the time, and thus conserve power.

- Thread is a consumer wireless networking protocol built on open standards and IPv6/6LoWPAN protocols. Thread's features include a secure and reliable mesh network with no single point of failure, simple connectivity and low power. Thread networks are easy to set up and secure to use with banking-class encryption to close security holes that exist in other wireless protocols. In 2014 Google Inc's Nest Labs announced a working group with the companies Samsung, ARM Holdings, Freescale, Silicon Labs, Big Ass Fans and the lock company Yale to promote Thread.

Building a Rural Wireless Mesh Network: A DIY Guide.

- In early 2007, the US-based firm Meraki launched a mini wireless mesh router. This is an example of a wireless mesh network (on a claimed speed of up to 50 megabits per second). The 802.11 radio within the Meraki Mini has been optimized for long-distance communication, providing coverage over 250 metres.

  This is an example of a single-radio mesh network being used within a community as opposed to multi-radio long range mesh networks like BelAir or MeshDynamics that provide multifunctional infrastructure, typically using tree based topologies and their advantages in O(n) routing.

- The Naval Postgraduate School, Monterey CA, demonstrated such wireless mesh networks for border security. In a pilot system, aerial cameras kept aloft by balloons relayed real time high resolution video to ground personnel via a mesh network.

- SPAWAR, a division of the US Navy, is prototyping and testing a scalable, secure Disruption Tolerant Mesh Network to protect strategic military assets, both stationary and mobile. Machine control applications, running on the mesh nodes, "take over", when internet connectivity is lost. Use cases include Internet of Things e.g. smart drone swarms.

- An MIT Media Lab project has developed the XO-1 laptop or "OLPC"(One Laptop per Child) which is intended for disadvantaged schools in developing nations and uses mesh networking (based on the IEEE 802.11s standard) to create a robust and inexpensive infrastructure. The instantaneous connections made by the laptops are claimed by the project to reduce the need for an external infrastructure such as the Internet to reach all areas, because a connected node could share the connection with nodes nearby. A similar concept has also been implemented by Greenpacket with its application called SONbuddy.

- In Cambridge, UK, on 3 June 2006, mesh networking was used at the "Strawberry Fair" to run mobile live television, radio and Internet services to an estimated 80,000 people.

- Broadband-Hamnet, a mesh networking project used in amateur radio, is a "a high-speed, self-discovering, self-configuring, fault-tolerant, wireless computer network" with very low power consumption and a focus on emergency communication.

- The Champaign-Urbana Community Wireless Network (CUWiN) project is developing mesh networking software based on open source implementations of the Hazy-Sighted Link State Routing Protocol and Expected Transmission Count metric. Additionally, the Wireless Networking Group in the University of Illinois at Urbana-Champaign are developing a multichannel, multi-radio wireless mesh testbed, called Net-X as a proof of concept implementation of some of the multichannel protocols being developed in that group. The implementations are based on an architecture that allows some of the radios to switch channels to maintain network connectivity, and includes protocols for channel allocation and routing.

- FabFi is an open-source, city-scale, wireless mesh networking system originally developed in 2009 in Jalalabad, Afghanistan to provide high-speed internet to parts of the city and designed for high performance across multiple hops. It is an inexpensive framework for sharing wireless internet from a central provider across a town or city. A second larger implementation followed a year later near Nairobi, Kenya with a freemium pay model to support network growth. Both projects were undertaken by the Fablab users of the respective cities.

- SMesh is an 802.11 multi-hop wireless mesh network developed by the Distributed System and Networks Lab at Johns Hopkins University. A fast handoff scheme allows mobile clients to roam in the network without interruption in connectivity, a feature suitable for real-time applications, such as VoIP.

- Many mesh networks operate across multiple radio bands. For example, Firetide and Wave Relay mesh networks have the option to communicate node to node on 5.2 GHz or 5.8 GHz, but communicate node to client on 2.4 GHz (802.11). This is accomplished using software-defined radio (SDR).

- The SolarMESH project examined the potential of powering 802.11-based mesh networks using solar power and rechargeable batteries. Legacy 802.11 access points were found to be inadequate due to the requirement that they be continuously powered. The IEEE 802.11s standardization efforts are considering power save options, but solar-powered applications might involve single radio nodes where relay-link power saving will be inapplicable.

- The WING project (sponsored by the Italian Ministry of University and Research and led by CREATE-NET and Technion) developed a set of novel algorithms and protocols for enabling wireless mesh networks as the standard access architecture for next generation Internet. Particular focus has been given to interference and traffic aware channel assignment, multi-radio/multi-interface support, and opportunistic scheduling and traffic aggregation in highly volatile environments.

- WiBACK Wireless Backhaul Technology has been developed by the Fraunhofer Institute for Open Communication Systems (FOKUS) in Berlin. Powered by solar cells and designed to support all existing wireless technologies, networks are due to be rolled out to several countries in sub-Saharan Africa in summer 2012.

- Recent standards for wired communications have also incorporated concepts from Mesh Networking. An example is ITU-T G.hn, a standard that specifies a high-speed (up to 1 Gbit/s) local area network using existing home wiring (power lines, phone lines and coaxial cables). In noisy environments such as power lines (where signals can be heavily attenuated and corrupted by noise) it's common that mutual visibility between devices in a network is not complete. In those situations, one of the nodes has to act as a relay and forward messages between those nodes that cannot communicate directly, effectively creating a mesh network. In G.hn, relaying is performed at the Data Link Layer.

References

- Jim Duffy (11 May 2012). "Largest Illinois healthcare system uproots Cisco to build $40M private cloud". PC Advisor. Retrieved 11 May 2012

- "IEEE Approves New IEEE 802.1aq Shortest Path Bridging Standard". Tech Power Up. 7 May 2012. Retrieved 11 May 2012

- D. Fedyk, Ed.,; P. Ashwood-Smith, Ed.,; D. Allan, A. Bragg,; P. Unbehagen (April 2012). "IS-IS Extensions Supporting IEEE 802.1aq". IETF. Retrieved 12 May 2012

- Peter Ashwood-Smith (24 February 2011). "Shortest Path Bridging IEEE 802.1aq Overview" (PDF). Huawei. Retrieved 11 May 2012

- Jim Duffy (11 May 2012). "Largest Illinois healthcare system uproots Cisco to build $40M private cloud". PC Advisor. Retrieved 11 May 2012

- "IEEE Approves New IEEE 802.1aq Shortest Path Bridging Standard". Tech Power Up. 7 May 2012. Retrieved 11 May 2012

- D. Fedyk, Ed.,; P. Ashwood-Smith, Ed.,; D. Allan, A. Bragg,; P. Unbehagen (April 2012). "IS-IS Extensions Supporting IEEE 802.1aq". IETF. Retrieved 12 May 2012

- Peter Ashwood-Smith (24 February 2011). "Shortest Path Bridging IEEE 802.1aq Overview" (PDF). Huawei. Retrieved 11 May 2012

- Bicsi, B. (2002). Network Design Basics for Cabling Professionals. McGraw-Hill Professional. ISBN 9780071782968

- Sosinsky, Barrie A. (2009). "Network Basics". Networking Bible. Indianapolis: Wiley Publishing. p. 16. ISBN 978-0-470-43131-3. OCLC 359673774. Retrieved 2016-03-26

- Bradley, Ray. Understanding Computer Science (for Advanced Level): The Study Guide. Cheltenham: Nelson Thornes. p. 244. ISBN 978-0-7487-6147-0. OCLC 47869750. Retrieved 2016-03-26

- "Teach-ICT OCR GCSE Computing - computer network topologies, bus network, ring network, star network". teach-ict.com. Retrieved 2015-10-15

- "Broadband-Hamnet wins International Association of Emergency Managers Awards". ARRL. Retrieved 2015-05-02

- "What is star network? - Definition from WhatIs.com". Searchnetworking.techtarget.com. Retrieved 2014-06-24

5

Transmission of Data and Link Control

Data transmission is the process of sending data over a communication medium to one or more digital devices. A data link control is a service that ensures reliable data transfer by managing error detection and flow control. This chapter closely examines the process of data transmission and link control in computer networks to provide an easy understanding of the topic.

Data Transmission

Data transmission, digital transmission or digital communications is the transfer of data (a digital bit stream or a digitized analog signal) over a point-to-point or point-to-multipoint communication channel. Examples of such channels are copper wires, optical fibers, wireless communication channels, storage media and computer buses. The data are represented as an electromagnetic signal, such as an electrical voltage, radiowave, microwave, or infrared signal.

Analog or analogue transmission is a transmission method of conveying voice, data, image, signal or video information using a continuous signal which varies in amplitude, phase, or some other property in proportion to that of a variable. The messages are either represented by a sequence of pulses by means of a line code (*baseband transmission*), or by a limited set of continuously varying wave forms (*passband transmission*), using a digital modulation method. The passband modulation and corresponding demodulation (also known as detection) is carried out by modem equipment. According to the most common definition of digital signal, both baseband and passband signals representing bit-streams are considered as digital transmission, while an alternative definition only considers the baseband signal as digital, and passband transmission of digital data as a form of digital-to-analog conversion.

Data transmitted may be digital messages originating from a data source, for example a computer or a keyboard. It may also be an analog signal such as a phone call or a video signal, digitized into a bit-stream for example using pulse-code modulation (PCM) or more advanced source coding (analog-to-digital conversion and data compression) schemes. This source coding and decoding is carried out by codec equipment.

Distinction between Related Subjects

Courses and textbooks in the field of *data transmission* as well as *digital transmission* and *digital communications* have similar content.

Digital transmission or data transmission traditionally belongs to telecommunications and electrical engineering. Basic principles of data transmission may also be covered within the computer science/computer engineering topic of data communications, which also includes computer networking or computer communication applications and networking protocols, for example routing, switching and inter-process communication. Although the Transmission control protocol (TCP) involves the term "transmission", TCP and other transport layer protocols are typically *not* discussed in a textbook or course about data transmission, but in computer networking.

The term tele transmission involves the analog as well as digital communication. In most textbooks, the term analog transmission only refers to the transmission of an analog message signal (without digitization) by means of an analog signal, either as a non-modulated baseband signal, or as a passband signal using an analog modulation method such as AM or FM. It may also include analog-over-analog pulse modulatated baseband signals such as pulse-width modulation. In a few books within the computer networking tradition, "analog transmission" also refers to passband transmission of bit-streams using digital modulation methods such as FSK, PSK and ASK. Note that these methods are covered in textbooks named digital transmission or data transmission, for example.

The theoretical aspects of data transmission are covered by information theory and coding theory.

Protocol Layers and Sub-topics

Courses and textbooks in the field of data transmission typically deal with the following OSI model protocol layers and topics:

- Layer 1, the physical layer:
  - Channel coding including:
    - Digital modulation schemes.
    - Line coding schemes.
    - Forward error correction (FEC) codes.
  - Bit synchronization.
  - Multiplexing.
  - Equalization.
  - Channel models.

- Layer 2, the data link layer:

  o Channel access schemes, media access control (MAC).

  o Packet mode communication and Frame synchronization.

  o Error detection and automatic repeat request (ARQ).

  o Flow control.

- Layer 6, the presentation layer:

  o Source coding (digitization and data compression), and information theory.

  o Cryptography (may occur at any layer).

Applications and History

Data (mainly but not exclusively informational) has been sent via non-electronic (e.g. optical, acoustic, mechanical) means since the advent of communication. Analog signal data has been sent electronically since the advent of the telephone. However, the first data electromagnetic transmission applications in modern time were telegraphy (1809) and teletypewriters (1906), which are both digital signals. The fundamental theoretical work in data transmission and information theory by Harry Nyquist, Ralph Hartley, Claude Shannon and others during the early 20th century, was done with these applications in mind.

Data transmission is utilized in computers in computer buses and for communication with peripheral equipment via parallel ports and serial ports such as RS-232 (1969), Firewire (1995) and USB (1996). The principles of data transmission are also utilized in storage media for Error detection and correction since 1951.

Data transmission is utilized in computer networking equipment such as modems (1940), local area networks (LAN) adapters (1964), repeaters, hubs, microwave links, wireless network access points (1997), etc.

In telephone networks, digital communication is utilized for transferring many phone calls over the same copper cable or fiber cable by means of Pulse code modulation (PCM), i.e. sampling and digitization, in combination with Time division multiplexing (TDM) (1962). Telephone exchanges have become digital and software controlled, facilitating many value added services. For example, the first AXE telephone exchange was presented in 1976. Since the late 1980s, digital communication to the end user has been possible using Integrated Services Digital Network (ISDN) services. Since the end of the 1990s, broadband access techniques such as ADSL, Cable modems, fiber-to-the-building (FTTB) and fiber-to-the-home (FTTH) have become widespread to small offices and homes. The current tendency is to replace traditional telecommunication services by packet mode communication such as IP telephony and IPTV.

Transmitting analog signals digitally allows for greater signal processing capability.

The ability to process a communications signal means that errors caused by random processes can be detected and corrected. Digital signals can also be sampled instead of continuously monitored. The multiplexing of multiple digital signals is much simpler to the multiplexing of analog signals.

Because of all these advantages, and because recent advances in wideband communication channels and solid-state electronics have allowed scientists to fully realize these advantages, digital communications has grown quickly. Digital communications is quickly edging out analog communication because of the vast demand to transmit computer data and the ability of digital communications to do so.

The digital revolution has also resulted in many digital telecommunication applications where the principles of data transmission are applied. Examples are second-generation (1991) and later cellular telephony, video conferencing, digital TV (1998), digital radio (1999), telemetry, etc.

Data transmission, digital transmission or digital communications is the physical transfer of data (a digital bit stream or a digitized analog signal) over a point-to-point or point-to-multipoint communication channel. Examples of such channels are copper wires, optical fibers, wireless communication channels, storage media and computer buses. The data are represented as an electromagnetic signal, such as an electrical voltage, radiowave, microwave, or infrared signal.

While analog transmission is the transfer of a continuously varying analog signal over an analog channel, digital communications is the transfer of discrete messages over a digital or an analog channel. The messages are either represented by a sequence of pulses by means of a line code (baseband transmission), or by a limited set of continuously varying wave forms (passband transmission), using a digital modulation method. The passband modulation and corresponding demodulation (also known as detection) is carried out by modem equipment. According to the most common definition of digital signal, both baseband and passband signals representing bit-streams are considered as digital transmission, while an alternative definition only considers the baseband signal as digital, and passband transmission of digital data as a form of digital-to-analog conversion.

Data transmitted may be digital messages originating from a data source, for example a computer or a keyboard. It may also be an analog signal such as a phone call or a video signal, digitized into a bit-stream for example using pulse-code modulation (PCM) or more advanced source coding (analog-to-digital conversion and data compression) schemes. This source coding and decoding is carried out by codec equipment.

Serial and Parallel Transmission

In telecommunications, serial transmission is the sequential transmission of signal elements of a group representing a character or other entity of data. Digital serial transmissions are bits sent over a single wire, frequency or optical path sequentially. Because it requires less signal processing and less chances for error than parallel transmission, the transfer rate of each individual path may be faster. This can be used over longer distances as a check digit or parity bit can be sent along it easily.

In telecommunications, parallel transmission is the simultaneous transmission of the signal elements of a character or other entity of data. In digital communications, parallel transmission is the simultaneous transmission of related signal elements over two or more separate paths. Multiple electrical wires are used which can transmit multiple bits simultaneously, which allows for higher data transfer rates than can be achieved with serial transmission. This method is used internally within the computer, for example the internal buses, and sometimes externally for such things as printers, The major issue with this is "skewing" because the wires in parallel data transmission have slightly different properties (not intentionally) so some bits may arrive before others, which may corrupt the message. A parity bit can help to reduce this. However, electrical wire parallel data transmission is therefore less reliable for long distances because corrupt transmissions are far more likely.

Types of Communication Channels

Some communications channel types include:

- Data transmission circuit.
- Full-duplex.
- Half-duplex.
- Multi-drop:
  o Bus network.
  o Mesh network.
  o Ring network.
  o Star network.
  o Wireless network.
- Point-to-point.
- Simplex.

Asynchronous and Synchronous Data Transmission

Asynchronous start-stop transmission uses start and stop bits to signify the beginning bit ASCII character would actually be transmitted using 10 bits. For example, "0100 0001" would become "1 0100 0001 0". The extra one (or zero, depending on parity bit) at the start and end of the transmission tells the receiver first that a character is coming and secondly that the character has ended. This method of transmission is used when data are sent intermittently as opposed to in a solid stream. In the previous example the start and stop bits are in bold. The start and stop bits must be of opposite polarity. This allows the receiver to recognize when the second packet of information is being sent.

Synchronous transmission uses no start and stop bits, but instead synchronizes transmission speeds at both the receiving and sending end of the transmission using clock signal(s) built into each component. A continual stream of data is then sent between the two nodes. Due to there being no start and stop bits the data transfer rate is quicker although more errors will occur, as the clocks will eventually get out of sync, and the receiving device would have the wrong time that had been agreed in the protocol for sending/receiving data, so some bytes could become corrupted (by losing bits). Ways to get around this problem include re-synchronization of the clocks and use of check digits to ensure the byte is correctly interpreted and received.

Framing and Synchronization

Normally, units of data transfer are larger than a single analog or digital encoding symbol. It is necessary to recover clock information for both the signal (so we can recover the right number of symbols and recover each symbol as accurately as possible), and obtain synchronization for larger units of data (such as data words and frames). It is necessary to recover the data in words or blocks because this is the only way the receiver process will be able to interpret the data received; for a given bit stream. Depending on the byte boundaries, there will be seven or eight ways to interpret the bit stream as ASCII characters, and these are likely to be very different. So, it is necessary to add other bits to the block that convey control information used in the data link control procedures. The data along with preamble, postamble, and control information forms a frame. This framing is necessary for the purpose of synchronization and other data control functions.

Synchronization

Data sent by a sender in bit-serial form through a medium must be correctly interpreted at the receiving end. This requires that the beginning, the end and logic level and duration of each bit as sent at the transmitting end must be recognized at the receiving end. There are three synchronization levels: *Bit, Character and Frame*. Moreover, to achieve synchronization, two approaches known as *asynchronous* and *synchronous* transmissions are used.

Frame synchronization is the process by which incoming frame alignment signals (i.e., distinctive bit sequences) are identified, i.e. distinguished from data bits, permitting the data bits within the frame to be extracted for decoding or retransmission. The usual practice is to insert, in a dedicated time slot within the frame, a non-information bit that is used for the actual synchronization of the incoming data with the receiver.

In order to receive bits in the first place, the receiver must be able to determine how fast bits are being sent and when it has received a signal symbol. Further, the receiver needs to be able to determine what the relationship of the bits in the received stream have to one another, that is, what the logical units of transfer are, and where each received bit fits into the logical units. We call these logical units *frames*. This means that in addition to bit (or transmission symbol) synchronization, the receiver needs word and frame synchronization.

Synchronous Communication (bit-oriented)

Timing is recovered from the signal itself (by the carrier if the signal is analog, or by regular transitions in the data signal or by a separate clock line if the signal is digital). Scrambling is often used to ensure frequent transitions needed. The data transmitted may be of any bit length, but is often constrained by the frame transfer protocol (data link or MAC protocol).

Bit-oriented framing only assumes that bit synchronization has been achieved by the underlying hardware, and the incoming bit stream is scanned at all possible bit positions for special patterns generated by the sender. The sender uses a special pattern (a flag pattern) to delimit frames (one flag at each end), and has to provide for data transparency by use of bit stuffing. A commonly used flag pattern is HDLC's 01111110 flag as shown in figure. The bit sequence 01111110 is used for both preamble and postamble for the purpose of synchronization. A frame format for bit-oriented synchronous frame is shown in figure. Apart from the flag bits there are control fields. This field contains the commands, responses and sequences numbers used to maintain the data flow accountability of the link, defines the functions of the frame and initiates the logic to control the movement of traffic between sending and receiving stations.

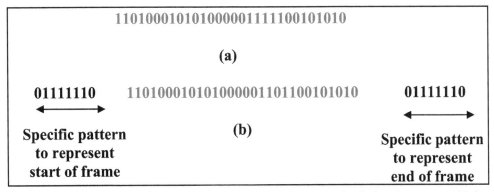

Bit oriented framing (a) Data to be sent to the peer, (b) Data after being character stuffed.

8-bit flag	Control fields	Data field	Control fields	8-bit flag

Synchronous frame format

Frame format for synchronous communication.

Summary of the approach:

- Initially 1 or 2 synchronization characters are sent.

- Data characters are then continuously sent without any extra bits.

- At the end, some error detection data is sent.

Advantages:

- Much less overhead.

- No overhead is incurred except for synchronization characters.

Disadvantages:

- No tolerance in clock frequency is allowed.

- The clock frequency should be same at both the sending and receiving ends.

Bit stuffing: If the flag pattern appears anywhere in the header or data of a frame, then the receiver may prematurely detect the start or end of the received frame. To overcome this problem, the sender makes sure that the frame body it sends has no flags in it at any position (note that since there is no character synchronization, the flag pattern can start at any bit location within the stream). It does this by *bit stuffing*, inserting an extra bit in any pattern that is beginning to look like a flag. In HDLC, whenever 5 consecutive 1's are encountered in the data, a 0 is inserted after the 5th 1, regardless of the next bit in the data as shown in figure. On the receiving end, the bit stream is piped through a shift register as the receiver looks for the flag pattern. If 5 consecutive 1's followed by a 0 is seen, then the 0 is dropped before sending the data on (the receiver destuffs the stream). If 6 1's and a 0 are seen, it is a flag and either the current frame are ended or a new frame is started, depending on the current state of the receiver. If more than 6 consecutive 1's are seen, then the receiver has detected an invalid pattern, and usually the current frame, if any, is discarded.

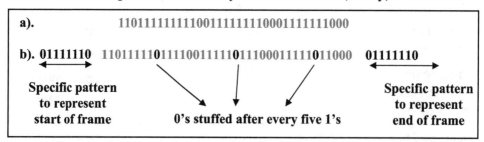

Bit oriented (a) Data to be sent to the peer, (b) Data after being bit stuffed.

With bit stuffing, the boundary between two frames can be unambiguously recognized by the flag pattern. Thus, if receiver loses track of where it is, all it has to do is to scan the input for flag sequence, since they can only occur at frame boundaries and never within data. In addition to receiving the data in logical units called frames, the receiver should have some way of determining if the data has been corrupted or not. If it has been corrupted, it is desirable not only to realize that, but also to make an attempt to obtain the correct data.

Asynchronous Communication (Word-oriented)

In asynchronous communication, small, fixed-length words (usually 5 to 9 bits long) are transferred without any clock line or clock is recovered from the signal itself. Each word has a start bit (usually as a 0) before the first data bit of the word and a stop bit (usually as a 1) after the last data bit of the word, as shown in figure. The receiver's local clock is started when the receiver detects the 1-0 transition of the start bit, and the line is sampled in the middle of the fixed bit intervals (a bit interval is the inverse of the data rate). The sender outputs the bit at the agreed-upon rate, holding the line in the appropriate state for one bit interval for each bit, but using its own local clock to determine the length of these bit intervals. The receiver's clock and the sender's clock may not run at the same speed, so that there is a relative clock drift (this may be caused by variations in the crystals used, temperature, voltage, etc.). If the receiver's clock drifts too much relative to the sender's clock, then the bits may be sampled while the line is in transition from one state to another, causing the receiver to misinterpret the received data. There can be variable amount of gap between two frames as shown in figure.

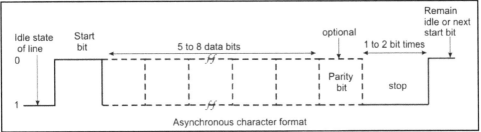

Character or word oriented format for asynchronous mode.

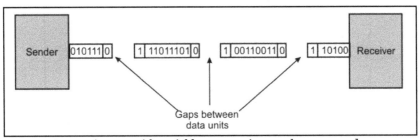

Data units sent with variable gap sent in asynchronous mode.

Advantages of asynchronous character oriented mode of communication are summarized below:

- Simple to implement.

- Self synchronization; Clock signal need not be sent.

- Tolerance in clock frequency is possible.

- The bits are sensed in the middle hence ± ½ bit tolerance is provided.

This mode of data communication, however, suffers from high overhead incurred in data transmission. Data must be sent in multiples of the data length of the word, and the two or more bits of synchronization overhead compared to the relatively short data length causes the effective data rate to be rather low. For example, 11 bits are required to transmit 8 bits of data. In other words, baud rate (number of signal elements) is higher than data rate.

Character Oriented Framing

The first framing method uses a field in the header to specify the number of characters in the frame. When the data link-layer sees the character count, it knows how many characters follow, and hence where the end of the frame is. This technique is shown in figure for frames of size 6, 4, and 8 characters, respectively. The trouble with this algorithm is that the count can be garbled by a transmission error. For example, if the character count of 4 in the second frame becomes 5, as shown in figure, the destination will get out of synchronization and will be unable to locate the start of next frame. Even if the checksum is incorrect so the destination knows that the frame is bad, it still had no way of telling where the next frame starts. Sending a frame back to the source and asking for retransmission does not help either, since the destination doesn't know how many characters to skip over to the start of retransmission. For this reason the character count method is rarely used.

Character-oriented framing assumes that character synchronization has already been achieved by the hardware. The sender uses special characters to indicate the start and end of frames, and may also use them to indicate header boundaries and to assist the receiver gain character synchronization. Frames must be of an integral character length. Data transparency must be preserved by use of character as shown in figure.

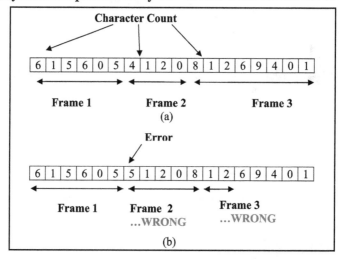

A Character Stream (a) Without error and (b) with error.

Most commonly, a DLE (data link escape) character is used to signal that the next character is a control character, with DLE SOH (start of header) used to indicate the start of the frame (it starts with a header), DLE STX (start of text) used to indicate the end of the header and start of the data portion, and DLE ETX (end of text) used to indicate the end of the frame.

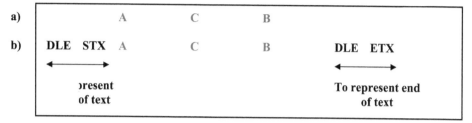

Character Oriented (a) Data to be send to the peer, (b) Data after being character stuffed.

A serious problem occurs with this method when binary data, such as object program are being transmitted. It may easily happen when the characters for DLE STX or DLE ETX occur in the data, which will interfere with the framing. One way to overcome this problem is to use character stuffing discussed below.

Character Stuffing

When a DLE character occurs in the header or the data portion of a frame, the sender must somehow let the receiver know that it is not intended to signal a control character. The sender does this by inserting an extra DLE character after the one occurring inside the frame, so that when the receiver encounters two DLEs in a row, it immediately deletes one and interpret the other as header or data. This is shown in figure. Note that since the receiver has character synchronization, it will not mistake a DLE pattern that crosses a byte boundary as a DLE signal.

a)	DLE	STX	A	DLE	B
	DLE	ETX			
b)	DLE	STX	A	DLE	B
	DLE	ETX			
c)	DLE	STX	A	DLE	B
	DLE	ETX			

Character Stuffing (a). Data send by network layer, (b) Data after being character stuffed by the data link layer. (c) Data passed to the network layer on the receiver side.

The main disadvantage of this method is that it is closely tied to 8-bit characters in general and the ASCII character code in particular. As networks grow, this disadvantage of embedding the character code in framing mechanism becomes more and more obvious, so a new technique had to be developed to allow arbitrary sized character. Bit-oriented frame synchronization and bit stuffing is used that allow data frames to contain an arbitrary number of bits and allow character code with arbitrary number of bits per character.

Data Rate Measures

- The raw data rate (the number of bits that the transmitter can per second without formatting) is only the starting point. There may be overhead for synchronization, for framing, for error checking, for headers and trailers, for retransmissions, etc.

- *Utilization* may mean more than one thing. When dealing with network monitoring and management, it refers to the fraction of the resource actually used (for useful data and for overhead, retransmissions, etc.). In this context, utilization refers to the fraction of the channel that is available for actual data transmission to the next higher layer. It is the ratio of data bits per protocol data unit (PDU) to the total size of the PDU, including synchronization, headers, etc. In other words, it is the ratio of the time spent actually sending useful data to the time it takes to transfer that data and its attendant overhead.

The *effective data rate* at a layer is the net data rate available to the next higher layer. Generally this is the utilization times the raw data rate.

DTE-DCE Interface

As two persons intending to communicate must speak in the same language, for successful communication between two computer systems or between a computer and a peripheral, a natural understanding between the two is essential. In case of two persons a common language known to both of them is used. In case of two computers or a computer and an appliance, this understanding can be ensured with the help of a *standard*, which should be followed by both the parties. Standards are usually recommended by some International bodies, such as, Electronics Industries Association (EIA), The Institution of Electrical and Electronic Engineers (IEEE), etc. The EIA and ITU-T have been involved in developing standards for the DTE-DCE interface known as EIA-232, EIA-442, etc and ITU-T standards are known as V series or X series. The standards should normally define the following four important attributes:

Mechanical: The mechanical attribute concerns the actual physical connection between the two sides. Usually various signal lines are bundled into a cable with a terminator plug, male or female at each end. Each of the systems, between which communication is to be established, provide a plug of opposite gender for connecting the terminator plugs of the cable, thus establishing the physical connection. The mechanical part specifies cables and connectors to be used to link two systems.

Electrical: The Electrical attribute relates to the voltage levels and timing of voltage changes. They in turn determine the data rates and distances that can be used for communication. So the electrical part of the standard specifies voltages, Impedances and timing requirements to be satisfied for reliable communication.

Functional: Functional attribute pertains to the function to be performed, by associating meaning to the various signal lines. Functions can be typically classified into the broad categories of data control, timing and ground. This component of standard specifies the signal pin assignments and signal definition of each of the pins used for interfacing the devices.

Procedural: The procedural attribute specifies the protocol for communication, i.e. the sequence of events that should be followed during data transfer, using the functional characteristic of the interface.

A variety of standards exist, some of the most popular interfaces are presented in this section.

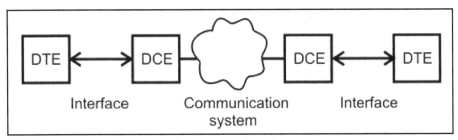

The DTE-DCE interface.

The RS-232 C

Most digital data processing devices such as computers and terminals are incapable of transmitting the digital data, which usually is in NRZ-L form, through physical transmission media over long distances. The data processing devices, commonly referred to as *Data Terminal Equipment (DTE)*, utilizes the mediation of another equipment called *Data Circuit communication Equipment (DCE)* to interface with the physical transmission media. An example of a DCE is a MODEM. On the one side, the DCE is responsible for transmitting and receiving bit-serial data in a suitable form for efficient communication through some transmission media such as telephone line. On the other side, the DCE interacts with the DTE by exchanging both data and control information. This is done over a set of wires referred to as interchange circuits. For successful operation of this scheme a high degree of cooperation is required on data processing equipment manufacturers and users, nature of interface between the DTE and DCE. The Electronic Industries Association (EIA) developed the standard RS-232C as an interface between the DTE and DCE as shown in figure. Although developed in 1960, it is still widely used for serial binary data interchange. It specifies all the four attributes mentioned above.

Mechanical: A 25-pin connector (DB-25) or 9-pin connector (DB-9) is commonly used for establishing mechanical connection. In most of the applications, however, fewer number of control lines than specified in the standard are used, as not all the systems require their use. The interface established connection between two types of systems, Data terminal Equipment (DTE) and Data communication Equipment (DCE). The equipment that generates, processes and displays the data is called DTE. Computers and monitors are considered as DTEs. A MODEM, which converts digital data into analog form by modulation and also demodulates analog signal to generate digital data, are considered as data communication equipments (DCEs). Modems are used to establish connection through (Transmission media) analog communication channel, such as a telephone line as shown in figure.

Electrical: The electrical characteristics specify the signaling between DTE and DCE. It uses single-ended, bipolar voltage and unterminated circuit. The single-ended form uses a single conductor to send and another conductor to receive a signal with the voltage reference to a common ground. The bipolar voltage levels are +3 to + 25V for logic 0 and −3 to −25V for logic 1. No termination with a resistor either at input or at output is necessary. The most striking feature is that, the voltage levels are not TTL compatible. This necessitates separate voltage supplies and extra hardware for level conversion from TTL-to-RS 232C and vice versa.

The single-ended unterminated configuration is susceptible to all forms of electromagnetic interference. Noise and cross-talk susceptibility are proportional to the cable length and bandwidth. As a result, the RS-232 C is suitable for serial binary data interchange over a short distance (up to 57 ft) and at low rates (up to 20K baud).

Functional: The functional specification of most of the important lines is given in table. There are two data lines, one for each direction, facilitating full-duplex operation. There are several control and ground lines. The pin number with respect to the connector, abbreviated name and function description of the important lines are given in the table. These nine lines are commonly used.

TABLE: Important RS-232C Pins.

Pin No.	Function	Short Name
1	Protective ground	
2	Transmit data to DCE	TxD
3	Receive data from DCE	RxD
4	Request to send to DCE	RTS
5	Clear to send from DCE	CTS
6	Data set ready from DCE	DSR
7	Signal ground	
8	Data carrier detect from DCE	DCD
20	Data terminal ready to DCE	DTR

Procedural: The procedural specification gives the protocol, is the sequence of events to be followed to accomplish data communication.

(i) When a DTE is powered on, after self-test it asserts the Data terminal ready (DTR) signal (pin) to indicate that it is ready to take part in communication. Similarly, when the DCE is powered on and gone through its own self-test, it asserts the Data set Ready (DSR) signal (pin 6) to indicate that it is ready to take part in the communication. When the MODEM detects a carrier on the telephone line, it asserts Data carrier detect (DCD) signal (pin 8).

(ii) When the DTE is ready to send data, it asserts request to send (RTS) signal (pin 4). DCE in turn responds with clear to send (CTS) signal (pin 5), when it is ready to receive data and MODEM start sending carrier over the medium indicating that data transmission is eminent. The CTS signal enables the DTE to start transmission of a data frame.

The procedural specification deals with the legal sequence of events on the action-reaction pair of signal lines. For example, the RTS-CTS control lines form an action-reaction pair. Before sending a data, the DTR-DSR pair should be active and then the DTE asserts the RTS signal. In response to this the modern should generate the CTS signal when ready; thereby indicating that data may be transmitted over the TXD. In this manner the action-reaction pairs of lines allows handshaking needed for asynchronous mode of date communication. It also leads to *flow-control*, the rate at which the two systems can communicate with each other.

Null Modem

In many situations, the distance between two DTEs may be so close that use of modems (DCE), as shown in figure, is unnecessary. In such a case the RS-232 C interface may still be used, but with out the DCEs. A scheme known as null modem is used, in which interconnection is done in such a why that both the DTEs are made to feel as if they have been connected through modems. Essentially, null modem is a cable with two connectors at both ends for interfacing with the DTEs. The reason for this behavior is apparent from the swapping interconnection shown in figure.

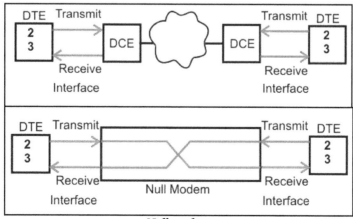

Null modem.

Modems

The DCE that is used to interface with the physical transmission media is known as MODEM, derived from MOdulator + DEModulator. The *modulator* converts digital data into an analog signal using ASK, FSK, PSK or QAM modulation techniques. A *demodulator* converts an analog signal back into a digital data. Important Parameters of the modems are the *transmission rate* and Bandwidth (Baud rate). The output of a modem has to match the bandwidth of the bandwidth of the medium, the telephone line as shown in figure.

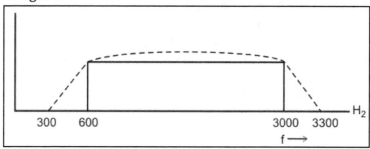

Bandwidth of the telephone line.

Error Detection and Correction

In information theory and coding theory with applications in computer science and telecommunication, error detection and correction or error control are techniques that enable reliable delivery of digital data over unreliable communication channels. Many communication channels are subject to channel noise, and thus errors may be introduced during transmission from the source to a receiver. Error detection techniques allow detecting such errors, while error correction enables reconstruction of the original data in many cases.

Definitions

The general definitions of the terms are as follows:

- *Error detection* is the detection of errors caused by noise or other impairments during transmission from the transmitter to the receiver.

- *Error correction* is the detection of errors and reconstruction of the original, error-free data.

History

The modern development of error-correcting codes in 1947 is due to Richard W. Hamming. A description of Hamming's code appeared in Claude Shannon's *A Mathematical Theory of Communication* and was quickly generalized by Marcel J. E. Golay.

Introduction

The general idea for achieving error detection and correction is to add some redundancy (i.e., some extra data) to a message, which receivers can use to check consistency of the delivered message, and to recover data that has been determined to be corrupted. Error-detection and correction schemes can be either systematic or non-systematic: In a systematic scheme, the transmitter sends the original data, and attaches a fixed number of *check bits* (or *parity data*), which are derived from the data bits by some deterministic algorithm. If only error detection is required, a receiver can simply apply the same algorithm to the received data bits and compare its output with the received check bits; if the values do not match, an error has occurred at some point during the transmission. In a system that uses a non-systematic code, the original message is transformed into an encoded message that has at least as many bits as the original message.

Good error control performance requires the scheme to be selected based on the characteristics of the communication channel. Common channel models include memory-less models where errors occur randomly and with a certain probability, and dynamic models where errors occur primarily in bursts. Consequently, error-detecting and correcting codes can be generally distinguished between *random-error-detecting/correcting* and *burst-error-detecting/correcting*. Some codes can also be suitable for a mixture of random errors and burst errors.

If the channel capacity cannot be determined, or is highly variable, an error-detection scheme may be combined with a system for retransmissions of erroneous data. This is known as automatic repeat request (ARQ), and is most notably used in the Internet. An alternate approach for error control is hybrid automatic repeat request (HARQ), which is a combination of ARQ and error-correction coding.

Implementation

Error correction may generally be realized in two different ways:

- *Automatic repeat request (ARQ)* (sometimes also referred to as *backward error correction*): This is an error control technique whereby an error detection scheme is combined with requests for retransmission of erroneous data. Every block of data received is checked using the error detection code used, and if the check fails, retransmission of the data is requested – this may be done repeatedly, until the data can be verified.

- *Forward error correction (FEC)*: The sender encodes the data using an *error-correcting code (ECC)* prior to transmission. The additional information (redundancy) added by the code is used by the receiver to recover the original data. In general, the reconstructed data is what is deemed the "most likely" original data.

ARQ and FEC may be combined, such that minor errors are corrected without retransmission, and major errors are corrected via a request for retransmission: this is called *hybrid automatic repeat-request (HARQ)*.

Error Detection Schemes

Error detection is most commonly realized using a suitable hash function (or checksum algorithm). A hash function adds a fixed-length *tag* to a message, which enables receivers to verify the delivered message by recomputing the tag and comparing it with the one provided.

There exists a vast variety of different hash function designs. However, some are of particularly widespread use because of either their simplicity or their suitability for detecting certain kinds of errors (e.g., the cyclic redundancy check's performance in detecting burst errors).

A random-error-correcting code based on minimum distance coding can provide a strict guarantee on the number of detectable errors, but it may not protect against a preimage attack. A repetition code, described in the section below, is a special case of error-correcting code: although rather inefficient, a repetition code is suitable in some applications of error correction and detection due to its simplicity.

Repetition Codes

A *repetition code* is a coding scheme that repeats the bits across a channel to achieve error-free communication. Given a stream of data to be transmitted, the data are divided into blocks of bits. Each block is transmitted some predetermined number of times. For example, to send the bit pattern "1011", the four-bit block can be repeated three times, thus producing "1011 1011 1011". However, if this twelve-bit pattern was received as "1010 1011 1011" – where the first block is unlike the other two – it can be determined that an error has occurred.

A repetition code is very inefficient, and can be susceptible to problems if the error occurs in exactly the same place for each group (e.g., "1010 1010 1010" in the previous example would be detected as correct). The advantage of repetition codes is that they are extremely simple, and are in fact used in some transmissions of numbers stations.

Parity bits

A *parity bit* is a bit that is added to a group of source bits to ensure that the number of set bits (i.e., bits with value 1) in the outcome is even or odd. It is a very simple scheme that can be used to detect single or any other odd number (i.e., three, five, etc.) of errors in the output. An even number of flipped bits will make the parity bit appear correct even though the data is erroneous.

Extensions and variations on the parity bit mechanism are horizontal redundancy checks, vertical redundancy checks, and "double," "dual," or "diagonal" parity (used in RAID-DP).

Checksums

A *checksum* of a message is a modular arithmetic sum of message code words of a fixed word length (e.g., byte values). The sum may be negated by means of a ones'-complement operation prior to transmission to detect errors resulting in all-zero messages.

Checksum schemes include parity bits, check digits, and longitudinal redundancy checks. Some checksum schemes, such as the Damm algorithm, the Luhn algorithm, and the Verhoeff algorithm, are specifically designed to detect errors commonly introduced by humans in writing down or remembering identification numbers.

Cyclic Redundancy Checks (CRCs)

A *cyclic redundancy check (CRC)* is a non-secure hash function designed to detect accidental changes to digital data in computer networks; as a result, it is not suitable for detecting maliciously introduced errors. It is characterized by specification of what is called a *generator polynomial*, which is used as the divisor in a polynomial long division over a finite field, taking the input data as the dividend, such that the remainder becomes the result.

A cyclic code has favorable properties that make it well suited for detecting burst errors. CRCs are particularly easy to implement in hardware, and are therefore commonly used in digital networks and storage devices such as hard disk drives.

Even parity is a special case of a cyclic redundancy check, where the single-bit CRC is generated by the divisor $x + 1$.

Cryptographic Hash Functions

The output of a *cryptographic hash function*, also known as a *message digest*, can provide strong assurances about data integrity, whether changes of the data are accidental (e.g., due to transmission errors) or maliciously introduced. Any modification to the data will likely be detected through a mismatching hash value. Furthermore, given some hash value, it is infeasible to find some input data (other than the one given) that will yield the same hash value. If an attacker can change not only the message but also the hash value, then a *keyed hash* or message authentication code (MAC) can be used for additional security. Without knowing the key, it is infeasible for the attacker to calculate the correct keyed hash value for a modified message.

Error-correcting Codes

Any error-correcting code can be used for error detection. A code with *minimum Hamming distance, d,* can detect up to $d - 1$ errors in a code word. Using minimum-distance-based error-correcting codes for error detection can be suitable if a strict limit on the minimum number of errors to be detected is desired.

Codes with minimum Hamming distance $d = 2$ are degenerate cases of error-correcting codes, and can be used to detect single errors. The parity bit is an example of a single-error-detecting code.

Error Correction

Automatic Repeat Request (ARQ)

Automatic Repeat Request (ARQ) is an error control method for data transmission that makes use of error-detection codes, acknowledgment and/or negative acknowledgment messages, and timeouts to achieve reliable data transmission. An *acknowledgment* is a message sent by the receiver to indicate that it has correctly received a data frame.

Usually, when the transmitter does not receive the acknowledgment before the timeout occurs (i.e., within a reasonable amount of time after sending the data frame), it retransmits the frame until it is either correctly received or the error persists beyond a predetermined number of retransmissions.

Three types of ARQ protocols are Stop-and-wait ARQ, Go-Back-N ARQ, and Selective Repeat ARQ.

ARQ is appropriate if the communication channel has varying or unknown capacity, such as is the case on the Internet. However, ARQ requires the availability of a back channel, results in possibly increased latency due to retransmissions, and requires the maintenance of buffers and timers for retransmissions, which in the case of network congestion can put a strain on the server and overall network capacity.

For example, ARQ is used on shortwave radio data links in the form of ARQ-E, or combined with multiplexing as ARQ-M.

Error-correcting Code

An error-correcting code (ECC) or forward error correction (FEC) code is a process of adding redundant data, or *parity data*, to a message, such that it can be recovered by a receiver even when a number of errors (up to the capability of the code being used) were introduced, either during the process of transmission, or on storage. Since the receiver does not have to ask the sender for retransmission of the data, a backchannel is not required in forward error correction, and it is therefore suitable for simplex communication such as broadcasting. Error-correcting codes are frequently used in lower-layer communication, as well as for reliable storage in media such as CDs, DVDs, hard disks, and RAM.

Error-correcting codes are usually distinguished between convolutional codes and block codes:

- *Convolutional codes* are processed on a bit-by-bit basis. They are particularly suitable for implementation in hardware, and the Viterbi decoder allows optimal decoding.

- *Block codes* are processed on a block-by-block basis. Early examples of block codes are repetition codes, Hamming codes and multidimensional parity-check codes. They were followed by a number of efficient codes, Reed–Solomon codes being the most notable due to their current widespread use. Turbo codes and low-density parity-check codes (LDPC) are relatively new constructions that can provide almost optimal efficiency.

Shannon's theorem is an important theorem in forward error correction, and describes the maximum information rate at which reliable communication is possible over a channel that has a certain error probability or signal-to-noise ratio (SNR). This strict upper limit is expressed in terms of the channel capacity. More specifically, the theorem says that there exist codes such that with increasing encoding length the probability of error on a discrete memoryless channel can be made arbitrarily small, provided that the code rate is smaller than the channel capacity. The code rate is defined as the fraction k/n of k source symbols and n encoded symbols.

The actual maximum code rate allowed depends on the error-correcting code used, and may be lower. This is because Shannon's proof was only of existential nature, and did not show how to construct codes which are both optimal and have efficient encoding and decoding algorithms.

Hybrid Schemes

Hybrid ARQ is a combination of ARQ and forward error correction. There are two basic approaches:

- Messages are always transmitted with FEC parity data (and error-detection redundancy). A receiver decodes a message using the parity information, and requests retransmission using ARQ only if the parity data was not sufficient for successful decoding (identified through a failed integrity check).

- Messages are transmitted without parity data (only with error-detection information). If a receiver detects an error, it requests FEC information from the transmitter using ARQ, and uses it to reconstruct the original message.

The latter approach is particularly attractive on an erasure channel when using a rate-less erasure code.

Applications

Applications that require low latency (such as telephone conversations) cannot use Automatic Repeat Request (ARQ); they must use forward error correction (FEC). By the time an ARQ system discovers an error and re-transmits it, the re-sent data will arrive too late to be any good.

Applications where the transmitter immediately forgets the information as soon as it is sent (such as most television cameras) cannot use ARQ; they must use FEC because when an error occurs, the original data is no longer available. (This is also why FEC is used in data storage systems such as RAID and distributed data store).

Applications that use ARQ must have a return channel; applications having no return channel cannot use ARQ. Applications that require extremely low error rates (such as digital money transfers) must use ARQ. Reliability and inspection engineering also make use of the theory of error-correcting codes.

Internet

In a typical TCP/IP stack, error control is performed at multiple levels:

- Each Ethernet frame carries a CRC-32 checksum. Frames received with incorrect checksums are discarded by the receiver hardware.

- The IPv4 header contains a checksum protecting the contents of the header. Packets with mismatching checksums are dropped within the network or at the receiver.

- The checksum was omitted from the IPv6 header in order to minimize processing costs in network routing and because current link layer technology is assumed to provide sufficient error detection.

- UDP has an optional checksum covering the payload and addressing information from the UDP and IP headers. Packets with incorrect checksums are discarded by the operating system network stack. The checksum is optional under IPv4, only, because the Data-Link layer checksum may already provide the desired level of error protection.

- TCP provides a checksum for protecting the payload and addressing information from the TCP and IP headers. Packets with incorrect checksums are discarded within the network stack, and eventually get retransmitted using ARQ, either explicitly (such as through triple-ack) or implicitly due to a timeout.

Deep-space Telecommunications

Development of error-correction codes was tightly coupled with the history of deep-space missions due to the extreme dilution of signal power over interplanetary distances, and the limited power availability aboard space probes. Whereas early missions sent their data uncoded, starting from 1968 digital error correction was implemented in the form of (sub-optimally decoded) convolutional codes and Reed–Muller codes. The Reed–Muller code was well suited to the noise the spacecraft was subject to (approximately matching a bell curve), and was implemented at the Mariner spacecraft for missions between 1969 and 1977.

The Voyager 1 and Voyager 2 missions, which started in 1977, were designed to deliver color imaging amongst scientific information of Jupiter and Saturn. This resulted in increased coding requirements, and thus the spacecraft were supported by (optimally Viterbi-decoded) convolutional codes that could be concatenated with an outer Golay (24,12,8) code.

The Voyager 2 craft additionally supported an implementation of a Reed–Solomon code: the concatenated Reed–Solomon–Viterbi (RSV) code allowed for very powerful error correction, and enabled the spacecraft's extended journey to Uranus and Neptune. Both craft use V2 RSV coding due to ECC system upgrades after 1989.

The CCSDS currently recommends usage of error correction codes with performance similar to the Voyager 2 RSV code as a minimum. Concatenated codes are increasingly falling out of favor with space missions, and are replaced by more powerful codes such as Turbo codes or LDPC codes.

The different kinds of deep space and orbital missions that are conducted suggest that trying to find a "one size fits all" error correction system will be an ongoing problem for some time to come. For missions close to Earth the nature of the channel noise is different from that which a spacecraft on an interplanetary mission experiences. Additionally, as a spacecraft increases its distance from Earth, the problem of correcting for noise gets larger.

Satellite Broadcasting (DVB)

The demand for satellite transponder bandwidth continues to grow, fueled by the desire to deliver television (including new channels and High Definition TV) and IP data. Transponder availability and bandwidth constraints have limited this growth, because transponder capacity is determined by the selected modulation scheme and Forward error correction (FEC) rate.

Overview

- QPSK coupled with traditional Reed Solomon and Viterbi codes have been used for nearly 20 years for the delivery of digital satellite TV.

- Higher order modulation schemes such as 8PSK, 16QAM and 32QAM have enabled the satellite industry to increase transponder efficiency by several orders of magnitude.

- This increase in the information rate in a transponder comes at the expense of an increase in the carrier power to meet the threshold requirement for existing antennas.

- Tests conducted using the latest chipsets demonstrate that the performance achieved by using Turbo Codes may be even lower than the 0.8 dB figure assumed in early designs.

Data Storage

Error detection and correction codes are often used to improve the reliability of data storage media. A "parity track" was present on the first magnetic tape data storage in 1951. The "Optimal Rectangular Code" used in group coded recording tapes not only detects but also corrects single-bit errors. Some file formats, particularly archive formats, include a checksum (most often CRC32) to detect corruption and truncation and can employ redundancy and/or parity files to recover portions of corrupted data. Reed Solomon codes are used in compact discs to correct errors caused by scratches.

Modern hard drives use CRC codes to detect and Reed–Solomon codes to correct minor errors in sector reads, and to recover data from sectors that have "gone bad" and store that data in the spare sectors. RAID systems use a variety of error correction techniques to correct errors when a hard drive completely fails. Filesystems such as ZFS or Btrfs, as well as some RAID implementations, support data scrubbing and resilvering, which allows bad blocks to be detected and (hopefully) recovered before they are used. The recovered data may be re-written to exactly the same physical location, to spare blocks elsewhere on the same piece of hardware, or to replacement hardware.

Error-correcting Memory

DRAM memory may provide increased protection against soft errors by relying on error correcting codes. Such error-correcting memory, known as *ECC* or *EDAC-protected* memory, is particularly desirable for high fault-tolerant applications, such as servers, as well as deep-space applications due to increased radiation.

Error-correcting memory controllers traditionally use Hamming codes, although some use triple modular redundancy.

Interleaving allows distributing the effect of a single cosmic ray potentially upsetting multiple physically neighboring bits across multiple words by associating neighboring bits to different words. As long as a single event upset (SEU) does not exceed the error threshold (e.g., a single error) in any particular word between accesses, it can be corrected (e.g., by a single-bit error correcting code), and the illusion of an error-free memory system may be maintained.

In addition to hardware providing features required for ECC memory to operate, operating systems usually contain related reporting facilities that are used to provide notifications when soft errors are transparently recovered. An increasing rate of soft errors might indicate that a DIMM module needs replacing, and such feedback information would not be easily available without the related reporting capabilities. An example is the Linux kernel's *EDAC* subsystem (previously known as *bluesmoke*), which collects the data from error-checking-enabled components inside a computer system; beside collecting and reporting back the events related to ECC memory, it also supports other checksumming errors, including those detected on the PCI bus. A few systems also support memory scrubbing.

Environmental interference and physical defects in the communication medium can cause random bit errors during data transmission. Error coding is a method of detecting and correcting these errors to ensure information is transferred intact from its source to its destination. Error coding is used for fault tolerant computing in computer memory, magnetic and optical data storage media, satellite and deep space communications, network communications, cellular telephone networks, and almost any other form of digital data communication. Error coding uses mathematical formulas to encode data bits at the source into longer bit words for transmission. The "code word" can then be decoded at the destination to retrieve the information. The extra bits in the code word provide *redundancy* that, according to the coding scheme used, will allow the destination to use the decoding process to determine if the communication medium introduced errors and in some cases correct them so that the data need not be retransmitted. Different error coding schemes are chosen depending on the types of errors expected, the communication medium's expected error rate, and whether or not data retransmission is possible. Faster processors and better communications technology make more complex coding schemes, with better error detecting and correcting capabilities, possible for smaller embedded systems, allowing for more robust communications. However, tradeoffs between bandwidth and coding overhead, coding complexity and allowable coding delay between transmissions, must be considered for each application.

Even if we know what type of errors can occur, we can't simple recognize them. We can do this simply by comparing this copy received with another copy of intended transmission. In this mechanism the source data block is send twice. The receiver compares them with the help of a comparator and if those two blocks differ, a request for re-transmission is made. To achieve forward error correction, three sets of the same data block are sent and majority decision selects the correct block. These methods are very inefficient and increase the traffic two or three times. Fortunately there are more efficient error detection and correction codes. There are two basic strategies for dealing with errors. One way is to include enough redundant information (extra bits are introduced into the data stream at the transmitter on a regular and logical basis) along with each block of data sent to enable the receiver to deduce what the transmitted character must have been. The other way is to include only enough redundancy to allow the receiver to deduce that error has occurred, but not which error has occurred and the receiver asks for a retransmission. The former strategy uses Error-Correcting Codes and latter uses Error-detecting Codes.

To understand how errors can be handled, it is necessary to look closely at what error really is. Normally, a frame consists of m-data bits (i.e., message bits) and r-redundant bits (or check bits). Let the total number of bits be n (m + r). An n-bit unit containing data and check-bits is often referred to as an n-bit codeword.

Given any two code-words, say 10010101 and 11010100, it is possible to determine how many corresponding bits differ, just EXCLUSIVE OR the two code-words, and count the number of 1's in the result. The number of bits position in which code words differ is called the Hamming distance. If two code words are a Hamming distance d-apart, it will require d single-bit errors to convert one code word to other. The error detecting and correcting properties depends on its Hamming distance.

- To detect d errors, you need a distance (d+1) code because with such a code there is no way that d-single bit errors can change a valid code word into another valid code word. Whenever receiver sees an invalid code word, it can tell that a transmission error has occurred.

- Similarly, to correct d errors, you need a distance 2d+1 code because that way the legal code words are so far apart that even with d changes, the original code-word is still closer than any other code-word, so it can be uniquely determined.

Types of Errors

These interferences can change the timing and shape of the signal. If the signal is carrying binary encoded data, such changes can alter the meaning of the data. These errors can be divided into two types: Single-bit error and Burst error.

Single-bit Error:

The term single-bit error means that only one bit of given data unit (such as a byte, character, or data unit) is changed from 1 to 0 or from 0 to 1 as shown in figure.

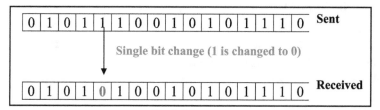

Single bit error.

Single bit errors are least likely type of errors in serial data transmission. To see why, imagine a sender sends data at 10 Mbps. This means that each bit lasts only for 0.1 µs (micro-second). For a single bit error to occur noise must have duration of only 0.1 µs (micro-second), which is very rare. However, a single-bit error can happen if we are having a parallel data transmission. For example, if 16 wires are used to send all 16 bits of a word at the same time and one of the wires is noisy, one bit is corrupted in each word.

Burst Error

The term burst error means that two or more bits in the data unit have changed from 0 to 1 or vice-versa. Note that burst error doesn't necessary means that error occurs in consecutive bits. The length of the burst error is measured from the first corrupted bit to the last corrupted bit. Some bits in between may not be corrupted.

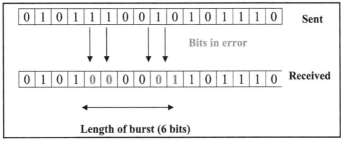

Burst Error.

Burst errors are mostly likely to happen in serial transmission. The duration of the noise is normally longer than the duration of a single bit, which means that the noise affects data; it affects a set of bits as shown in figure. The number of bits affected depends on the data rate and duration of noise.

Error Detecting Codes

Basic approach used for error detection is the use of redundancy, where additional bits are added to facilitate detection and correction of errors. Popular techniques are:

- Simple Parity check.

- Two-dimensional Parity check.

- Checksum.

- Cyclic redundancy check.

Simple Parity Checking or One-dimension Parity Check

The most common and least expensive mechanism for error- detection is the simple parity check. In this technique, a redundant bit called parity bit, is appended to every data unit so that the number of 1s in the unit (including the parity becomes even).

Blocks of data from the source are subjected to a check bit or *Parity bit* generator form, where a parity of 1 is added to the block if it contains an odd number of 1's (ON bits) and 0 is added if it contains an even number of 1's. At the receiving end the parity bit is computed from the received data bits and compared with the received parity bit, as shown in figure. This scheme makes the total number of 1's even, that is why it is called *even parity checking*. Considering a 4-bit word, different combinations of the data words and the corresponding code words are given in table.

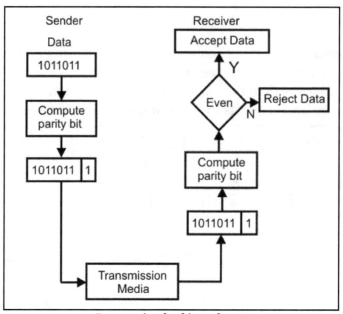

Even-parity checking scheme.

Table Possible 4-bit data words and corresponding code words.

Decimal value	Data Block	Parity bit	Code word
0	0000	0	00000
1	0001	1	00011
2	0010	1	00101
3	0011	0	00110
4	0100	1	01001
5	0101	0	01010
6	0110	0	01100
7	0111	1	01111
8	1000	1	10001
9	1001	0	10010
10	1010	0	10100
11	1011	1	10111
12	1100	0	11000
13	1101	1	11011
14	1110	1	11101
15	1111	0	11110

Note that for the sake of simplicity, we are discussing here the even-parity checking, where the number of 1's should be an even number. It is also possible to use *odd-parity* checking, where the number of 1's should be odd.

Performance

An observation of the table reveals that to move from one code word to another, at least two data bits should be changed. Hence these set of code words are said to have a minimum distance (*hamming distance*) of 2, which means that a receiver that has knowledge of the code word set can detect all single bit errors in each code word. However, if two errors occur in the code word, it becomes another valid member of the set and the decoder will see only another valid code word and know nothing of the error. Thus errors in more than one bit cannot be detected. In fact it can be shown that a single parity check code can detect only odd number of errors in a code word.

Two-dimension Parity Check

Performance can be improved by using two-dimensional parity check, which organizes the block of bits in the form of a table. Parity check bits are calculated for each row, which is equivalent to a simple parity check bit. Parity check bits are also calculated for all columns then both are sent along with the data. At the receiving end these are compared with the parity bits calculated on the received data. This is illustrated in figure.

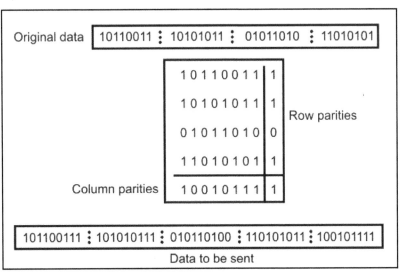

Two-dimension Parity Checking.

Performance

Two- Dimension Parity Checking increases the likelihood of detecting burst errors. As we have shown in figure that a 2-D Parity check of n bits can detect a burst error of n bits. A burst error of more than n bits is also detected by 2-D Parity check with a high-probability. There is, however, one pattern of error that remains elusive. If two bits in one data unit are damaged and two bits in exactly same position in another data unit are also damaged, the 2-D Parity check checker will not detect an error. For example, if two data units: 11001100 and 10101100. If first and second from last bits in each of them is changed, making the data units as 01001110 and 00101110, the error cannot be detected by 2-D Parity check.

Checksum

In checksum error detection scheme, the data is divided into k segments each of m bits. In the sender's end the segments are added using 1's complement arithmetic to get the sum. The sum is complemented to get the checksum. The checksum segment is sent along with the data segments as shown in figure. At the receiver's end, all received segments are added using 1's complement arithmetic to get the sum. The sum is complemented. If the result is zero, the received data is accepted; otherwise discarded, as shown in figure.

Performance

The checksum detects all errors involving an odd number of bits. It also detects most errors involving even number of bits.

Sender's end for the calculation of the checksum, Receiving end for checking the checksum.

Cyclic Redundancy Checks (CRC)

This Cyclic Redundancy Check is the most powerful and easy to implement technique. Unlike checksum scheme, which is based on addition, CRC is based on binary division. In CRC, a sequence of redundant bits, called cyclic redundancy check bits, are appended to the end of data unit so that the resulting data unit becomes exactly divisible by a second, predetermined binary number. At the destination, the incoming data unit is divided by the same number. If at this step there is no remainder, the data unit is assumed to be correct and is therefore accepted. A remainder indicates that the data unit has been damaged in transit and therefore must be rejected. The generalized technique can be explained as follows.

If a k bit message is to be transmitted, the transmitter generates an r-bit sequence, known as *Frame Check Sequence* (FCS) so that the *(k+r)* bits are actually being transmitted. Now this r-bit FCS is generated by dividing the original number, appended by r zeros, by *a* predetermined number. This number, which is *(r+1)* bit in length, can also be considered as the coefficients of a polynomial, called G*enerator Polynomial.* The remainder of this division process generates the r-bit FCS. On receiving the packet, the receiver divides the *(k+r)* bit frame by the same predetermined number and if it produces no remainder, it can be assumed that no error has occurred during the transmission. Operations at both the sender and receiver end are shown in figure.

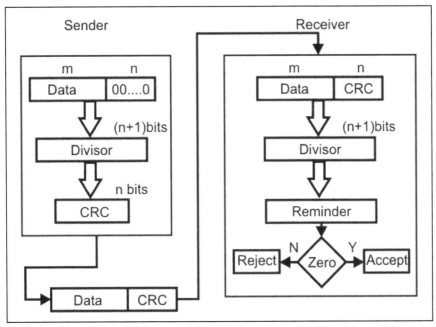

Basic scheme for Cyclic Redundancy Checking.

This mathematical operation performed is illustrated in figure by dividing a sample 4-bit number by the coefficient of the generator polynomial x^3+x+1, which is 1011, using the modulo-2 arithmetic. Modulo-2 arithmetic is a binary addition process without any carry over, which is just the Exclusive-OR operation. Consider the case where k=1101. Hence we have to divide 1101000 (i.e. k appended by 3 zeros) by 1011, which produces the remainder r=001, so that the bit frame *(k+r)* =1101001 is actually being transmitted through the communication channel. At the receiving end, if the received number, i.e., 1101001 is divided by the same generator polynomial 1011 to get the remainder as 000, it can be assumed that the data is free of errors.

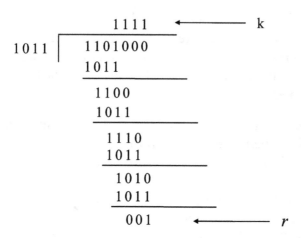

Cyclic Redundancy Checks (CRC).

The transmitter can generate the CRC by using a feedback shift register circuit. The same circuit can also be used at the receiving end to check whether any error has occurred. All the values can be expressed as polynomials of a dummy variable X. For example, for P = 11001 the corresponding polynomial is X^4+X^3+1. A polynomial is selected to have at least the following properties:

- It should not be divisible by X.

- It should not be divisible by (X+1).

The first condition guarantees that all burst errors of a length equal to the degree of polynomial are detected. The second condition guarantees that all burst errors affecting an odd number of bits are detected.

CRC process can be expressed as $XnM(X)/P(X) = Q(X) + R(X) / P(X)$

Commonly used divisor polynomials are:

- CRC-16 = $X^{16} + X^{15} + X^2 + 1$.

- CRC-CCITT = $X^{16} + X^{12} + X^5 + 1$.

- CRC-32 = $X^{32} + X^{26} + X^{23} + X^{22} + X^{16} + X^{12} + X^{11} + X^{10} + X^8 + X^7 + X^5 + X^4 + X^2 + 1$.

Performance

CRC is a very effective error detection technique. If the divisor is chosen according to the previously mentioned rules, its performance can be summarized as follows:

- CRC can detect all single-bit errors.

- CRC can detect all double-bit errors (three 1's).

- CRC can detect any odd number of errors (X+1).

- CRC can detect all burst errors of less than the degree of the polynomial.

- CRC detects most of the larger burst errors with a high probability.

- For example CRC-12 detects 99.97% of errors with a length 12 or more.

Error Correcting Codes

The techniques that we have discussed so far can detect errors, but do not correct them. Error Correction can be handled in two ways.

- One is when an error is discovered; the receiver can have the sender retransmit the entire data unit. This is known as backward error correction.

- In the other, receiver can use an error-correcting code, which automatically corrects certain errors. This is known as forward error correction.

In theory it is possible to correct any number of errors atomically. Error-correcting codes are more sophisticated than error detecting codes and require more redundant bits. The number of bits required to correct multiple-bit or burst error is so high that in most of the cases it is inefficient to do so. For this reason, most error correction is limited to one, two or at the most three-bit errors.

Single-bit Error Correction

Concept of error-correction can be easily understood by examining the simplest case of single-bit errors. As we have already seen that a single-bit error can be detected by addition of a parity bit (VRC) with the data, which needed to be send. A single additional bit can detect error, but it's not sufficient enough to correct that error too. For correcting an error one has to know the exact position of error, i.e. exactly which bit is in error (to locate the invalid bits). For example, to correct a single-bit error in an ASCII character, the error correction must determine which one of the seven bits is in error. To this, we have to add some additional redundant bits.

To calculate the numbers of redundant bits (r) required to correct d data bits, let us find out the relationship between the two. So we have (d+r) as the total number of bits, which are to be transmitted; then r must be able to indicate at least d+r+1 different values. Of these, one value means no error, and remaining d+r values indicate error location of error in each of d+r locations. So, d+r+1 states must be distinguishable by r bits, and r bits can indicates 2^r states. Hence, 2^r must be greater than d+r+1.

$$2^r >= d+r+1$$

The value of r must be determined by putting in the value of d in the relation. For example, if d is 7, then the smallest value of r that satisfies the above relation is 4. So the total bits, which are to be transmitted is 11 bits (d+r = 7+4 =11).

Now let us examine how we can manipulate these bits to discover which bit is in error. A technique developed by R.W.Hamming provides a practical solution. The solution or coding scheme he developed is commonly known as Hamming Code. Hamming code can be applied to data units of any length and uses the relationship between the data bits and redundant bits as discussed.

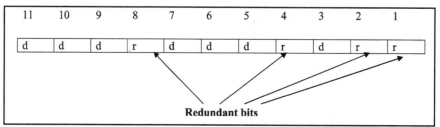

11	10	9	8	7	6	5	4	3	2	1
d	d	d	r	d	d	d	r	d	r	r

Redundant bits

Positions of redundancy bits in hamming code.

Basic approach for error detection by using Hamming code is as follows:

- To each group of m information bits k parity bits are added to form (m+k) bit code as shown in figure.

- Location of each of the (m+k) digits is assigned a decimal value.

- The k parity bits are placed in positions 1, 2, ..., 2^{k-1} positions.–K parity checks are performed on selected digits of each codeword.

- At the receiving end the parity bits are recalculated. The decimal value of the k parity bits provides the bit-position in error, if any.

	Error position	Position number $c_3 c_2 c_1$
7 6 5 4 3 2 1 $d_4 d_3 d_2 r_4 d_1 r_2 r_1$	0 (no error)	0 0 0
	1	0 0 1
$r_1 \rightarrow$ 1, 3, 5, 7	2	0 1 0
$r_2 \rightarrow$ 2, 3, 6, 7	3	0 1 1
$r_4 \rightarrow$ 4, 5, 6, 7	4	1 0 0
	5	1 0 1
7 6 5 4 3 2 1	6	1 1 0
$d_4 d_3 d_2 r_4 d_1 r_2 r_1$	7	1 1 1

1	0	1		0			Data 1010
1	0	1		0		0	Adding r_1
1	0	1		0	1	0	Adding r_2
1	0	1	0	0	1	0	Adding r_4
1	0	1	0	0	1	0	Data sent

corrupted

| 1 | 1 | 1 | 0 | 0 | 1 | 0 | Received Data |

Error position = 6 $C_3 C_2 C_1$
                          1 1 0

| 1 | 0 | 1 | 0 | 0 | 1 | 0 | corrected data |

Use of Hamming code for error correction for a 4-bit data.

Figure shows how hamming code is used for correction for 4-bit numbers $(d_4d_3d_2d_1)$ with the help of three redundant bits $(r_3r_2r_1)$. For the example data 1010, first r1 (0) is calculated considering the parity of the bit positions, 1, 3, 5 and 7. Then the parity bits r_2 is calculated considering bit positions 2, 3, 6 and 7. Finally, the parity bits r_4 is calculated considering bit positions 4, 5, 6 and 7 as shown. If any corruption occurs in any of the transmitted code 1010010, the bit position in error can be found out by calculating $r_3r_2r_1$ at the receiving end. For example, if the received code word is 1110010, the recalculated value of $r_3r_2r_1$ is 110, which indicates that bit position in error is 6, the decimal value of 110.

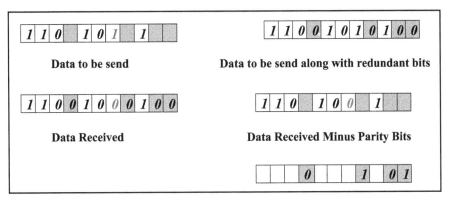

Calculations:

Parity recalculated (r8, r4, r2, r1) = 01012 = 510.

Hence, bit 5th is in error i.e. d5 is in error.

So, correct code-word which was transmitted is:

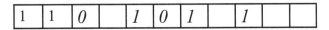

Figure: Use of Hamming code for error correction for a 5-bit data.

Flow Control and Error Control

As we have mentioned earlier, for reliable and efficient data communication a great deal of coordination is necessary between at least two machines. Some of these are necessary because of the following constraints:

- Both sender and receiver have limited speed.

- Both sender and receiver have limited memory.

It is necessary to satisfy the following requirements:

- A fast sender should not overwhelm a slow receiver, which must perform a certain amount of processing before passing the data on to the higher-level software.

- If error occur during transmission, it is necessary to devise mechanism to correct it.

The most important functions of Data Link layer to satisfy the above requirements are error control and flow control. Collectively, these functions are known as data link control, as discussed in this lesson.

Flow Control is a technique so that transmitter and receiver with different speed characteristics can communicate with each other. Flow control ensures that a transmitting station, such as a server with higher processing capability, does not overwhelm a receiving station, such as a desktop system, with lesser processing capability. This is where there is an orderly flow of transmitted data between the source and the destination.

Error Control involves both error detection and error correction. It is necessary because errors are inevitable in data communication, in spite of the use of better equipment and reliable transmission media based on the current technology. In the preceding lesson we have already discussed how errors can be detected. In this lesson we shall discuss how error control is performed based on retransmission of the corrupted data. When an error is detected, the receiver can have the specified frame retransmitted by the sender. This process is commonly known as Automatic Repeat Request (ARQ). For example, Internet's Unreliable Delivery Model allows packets to be discarded if network resources are not available, and demands that ARQ protocols make provisions for retransmission.

In data communications, flow control is the process of managing the rate of data transmission between two nodes to prevent a fast sender from overwhelming a slow receiver. It provides a mechanism for the receiver to control the transmission speed, so that the receiving node is not overwhelmed with data from transmitting node. Flow control should be distinguished from congestion control, which is used for controlling the flow of data when congestion has actually occurred. Flow control mechanisms can be classified by whether or not the receiving node sends feedback to the sending node.

Flow control is important because it is possible for a sending computer to transmit information at a faster rate than the destination computer can receive and process it. This can happen if the receiving computers have a heavy traffic load in comparison to the sending computer, or if the receiving computer has less processing power than the sending computer.

Stop-and-wait

Stop-and-wait flow control is the simplest form of flow control. In this method, the receiver indicates its readiness to receive data for each frame, the message is broken into multiple frames. The sender waits for an ACK (acknowledgement) after every frame for specified time (called time out). It is sent to ensure that the receiver has received the frame correctly. It will then send the next frame only after the ACK has been received.

Operations

1. Sender: Transmits a single frame at a time.

2. Receiver: Transmits acknowledgement (ACK) as it receives a frame.

3. Sender receive ACK within time out.

4. Go to step 1.

If a frame or ACK is lost during transmission then it has to be transmitted again by sender. This re-transmission process is known as ARQ (automatic repeat request).

The problem with Stop-and wait is that only one frame can be transmitted at a time, and that often leads to inefficient transmission, because until the sender receives the ACK it cannot transmit any new packet. During this time both the sender and the channel are unutilised.

Pros and Cons of Stop and Wait

Pros

The only advantage of this method of flow control is its simplicity.

Cons

The sender needs to wait for the ACK after every frame it transmits. This is a source of inefficiency, and is particularly bad when the propagation delay is much longer than the transmission delay.

Stop and wait can also create inefficiencies when sending longer transmissions. When longer transmissions are sent there is more likely chance for error in this protocol. If the messages are short the errors are more likely to be detected early. More inefficiency is created when single messages are broken into separate frames because it makes the transmission longer.

Sliding Window

A method of flow control in which a receiver gives a transmitter permission to transmit data until a window is full. When the window is full, the transmitter must stop transmitting until the receiver advertises a larger window.

Sliding-window flow control is best utilized when the buffer size is limited and pre-established. During a typical communication between a sender and a receiver the receiver allocates buffer space for n frames (n is the buffer size in frames). The sender can send and the receiver can accept n frames without having to wait for an acknowledgement. A sequence number is assigned to frames in order to help keep track of those frames which did receive an acknowledgement. The receiver acknowledges a frame by sending an acknowledgement that includes the sequence number of the next frame expected. This acknowledgement announces that the receiver is ready to receive n frames, beginning with the number specified. Both the sender and receiver maintain what is called a window. The size of the window is less than or equal to the buffer size.

Sliding window flow control has a far better performance than stop-and-wait flow control. For example, in a wireless environment if data rates are low and noise level is very high, waiting for an acknowledgement for every packet that is transferred is not very feasible. Therefore, transferring data as a bulk would yield a better performance in terms of higher throughput.

Sliding window flow control is a point to point protocol assuming that no other entity tries to communicate until the current data transfer is complete. The window maintained by the sender indicates which frames he can send. The sender sends all the frames in the window and waits for an acknowledgement (as opposed to acknowledging after every frame). The sender then shifts the window to the corresponding sequence number, thus indicating that frames within the window starting from the current sequence number can be sent.

Go Back N

An automatic repeat request (ARQ) algorithm, used for error correction, in which a negative acknowledgement (NAK) causes retransmission of the word in error as well as the previous N−1 words. The value of N is usually chosen such that the time taken to transmit the N words is less than the round trip delay from transmitter to receiver and back again. Therefore, a buffer is not needed at the receiver.

The normalized propagation delay $(a) = \frac{\text{propagation time (Tp)}}{\text{transmission time (Tt)}}$, where Tp = Length (L) over propagation velocity (V) and Tt = bitrate (r) over Framerate (F). So that a $= \frac{LF}{Vr}$.

To get the utilization you must define a window size (N). If N is greater than or equal to $2a + 1$ then the utilization is 1 (full utilization) for the transmission channel. If it is less than $2a + 1$ then the equation $\frac{N}{1+2a}$ must be used to compute utilization.

Selective Repeat

Selective Repeat is a connection oriented protocol in which both transmitter and receiver have a window of sequence numbers. The protocol has a maximum number of messages that can be sent without acknowledgement. If this window becomes full, the protocol is blocked until an acknowledgement is received for the earliest outstanding message. At this point the transmitter is clear to send more messages.

Comparison

This section is geared towards the idea of comparing Stop-and-wait, Sliding Window with the subsets of Go Back N and Selective Repeat.

Stop-and-wait

Error free: $\dfrac{1}{2a+1}$.

With errors: $\dfrac{1-P}{2a+1}$.

Selective Repeat

We define throughput T as the average number of blocks communicated per transmitted block. It is more convenient to calculate the average number of transmissions necessary to communicate a block, a quantity we denote by o, and then to determine T from the equation $T = \dfrac{1}{b}$.

Transmit Flow Control

Transmit flow control may occur:

- Between data terminal equipment (DTE) and a switching center, via data circuit-terminating equipment (DCE), the opposite types interconnected straightforwardly.

- Or between two devices of the same type (two DTEs, or two DCEs), interconnected by a crossover cable.

The transmission rate may be controlled because of network or DTE requirements. Transmit flow control can occur independently in the two directions of data transfer, thus permitting the transfer rates in one direction to be different from the transfer rates in the other direction. Transmit flow control can be:

- Either stop-and-wait.

- Or use a sliding window.

Flow control can be performed:

- Either by control signal lines in a data communication interface.

- Or by reserving in-band control characters to signal flow start and stop (such as the ASCII codes for XON/XOFF).

Hardware Flow Control

In common RS-232 there are pairs of control lines which are usually referred to as *hardware flow control*:

- RTS (Request To Send) and CTS (Clear To Send), used in RTS flow control.

- DTR (Data Terminal Ready) and DSR (Data Set Ready), DTR flow control.

Hardware flow control is typically handled by the DTE or "master end", as it is first raising or asserting its line to command the other side:

- In the case of RTS control flow, DTE sets its RTS, which signals the opposite end (the slave end such as a DCE) to begin monitoring its data input line. When ready for data, the slave end will raise its complementary line, CTS in this example, which signals the master to start sending data, and for the master to begin monitoring the slave's data output line. If either end needs to stop the data, it lowers its respective "data readyness" line.

- For PC-to-modem and similar links, in the case of DTR flow control, DTR/DSR are raised for the entire modem session (say a dialup internet call where DTR is raised to signal the modem to dial, and DSR is raised by the modem when the connection is complete), and RTS/CTS are raised for each block of data.

An example of hardware flow control is a Half-duplex radio modem to computer interface. In this case, the controlling software in the modem and computer may be written to give priority to incoming radio signals such that outgoing data from the computer is paused by lowering CTS if the modem detects a reception.

Polarity

- RS-232 level signals are inverted by the driver ICs, so line is TxD-, RxD-, CTS+, RTS+ (Clear to send when HI, Data 1 is a LO).

- For microprocessor pins the signals are TxD+, RxD+, CTS-, RTS- (Clear to send when LO, Data 1 is a HI).

Software Flow Control

Conversely, XON/XOFF is usually referred to as software flow control.

Open-loop Flow Control

The open-loop flow control mechanism is characterized by having no feedback between the receiver and the transmitter. This simple means of control is widely used. The allocation of resources must be a "prior reservation" or "hop-to-hop" type.

Open-loop flow control has inherent problems with maximizing the utilization of network resources. Resource allocation is made at connection setup using a CAC (Connection Admission Control) and this allocation is made using information that is already "old news" during the lifetime of the connection. Often there is an over-allocation of resources and reserved but unused capacities are wasted. Open-loop flow control is used by ATM in its CBR, VBR and UBR services.

Open-loop flow control incorporates two controls; the controller and a regulator. The regulator is able to alter the input variable in response to the signal from the controller. An open-loop system has no feedback or feed forward mechanism, so the input and output signals are not directly related and there is increased traffic variability. There is also a lower arrival rate in such system and a higher loss rate. In an open control system, the controllers can operate the regulators at regular intervals, but there is no assurance that the output variable can be maintained at the desired level. While it may be cheaper to use this model, the open-loop model can be unstable.

Closed-loop Flow Control

The closed-loop flow control mechanism is characterized by the ability of the network to report pending network congestion back to the transmitter. This information is then used by the transmitter in various ways to adapt its activity to existing network conditions. Closed-loop flow control is used by ABR (see traffic contract and congestion control). Transmit flow control described above is a form of closed-loop flow control.

This system incorporates all the basic control elements, such as, the sensor, transmitter, controller and the regulator. The sensor is used to capture a process variable. The process variable is sent to a transmitter which translates the variable to the controller. The controller examines the information with respect to a desired value and initiates a correction action if required. The controller then communicates to the regulator what action is needed to ensure that the output variable value is matching the desired value. Therefore, there is a high degree of assurance that the output variable can be maintained at the desired level. The closed-loop control system can be a feedback or a feed forward system:

A feedback closed-loop system has a feed-back mechanism that directly relates the input and output signals. The feed-back mechanism monitors the output variable and determines if additional correction is required. The output variable value that is fed backward is used to initiate that corrective action on a regulator. Most control loops in the industry are of the feedback type.

In a feed-forward closed loop system, the measured process variable is an input variable. The measured signal is then used in the same fashion as in a feedback system.

The closed-loop model produces lower loss rate and queuing delays, as well as it results in congestion-responsive traffic. The closed-loop model is always stable, as the number of active lows is bounded.

Error Control Techniques

When an error is detected in a message, the receiver sends a request to the transmitter to retransmit the ill-fated message or packet. The most popular retransmission scheme is known as Automatic-Repeat-Request (ARQ). Such schemes, where receiver asks transmitter to re-transmit if it detects an error, are known as reverse error correction techniques. There exist three popular ARQ techniques, as shown in figure.

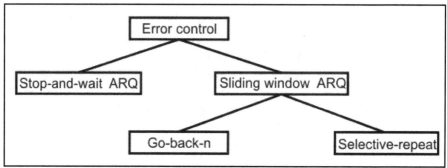

Error control techniques.

Stop-and-Wait ARQ

In Stop-and-Wait ARQ, which is simplest among all protocols, the sender (say station A) transmits a frame and then waits till it receives positive acknowledgement (ACK) or negative acknowledgement (NACK) from the receiver (say station B). Station B sends an ACK if the frame is received correctly, otherwise it sends NACK. Station A sends a new frame after receiving ACK; otherwise it retransmits the old frame, if it receives a NACK. This is illustrated in figure.

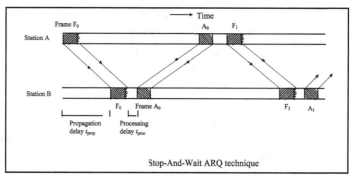

To tackle the problem of a lost or damaged frame, the sender is equipped with a timer. In case of a lost ACK, the sender transmits the old frame. In the figure, the second PDU of Data is lost during transmission. The sender is unaware of this loss, but starts a timer after sending each PDU. Normally an ACK PDU is received before the timer expires. In this case no ACK is received, and the timer counts down to zero and triggers retransmission of the same PDU by the sender. The sender always starts a timer following transmission, but in the second transmission receives an ACK PDU before the timer expires, finally indicating that the data has now been received by the remote node.

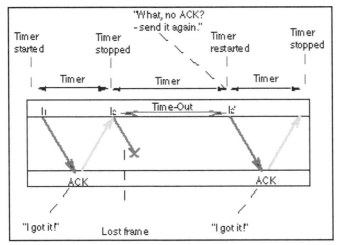

Retransmission due to lost frame.

The receiver now can identify that it has received a duplicate frame from the label of the frame and it is discarded.

To tackle the problem of damaged frames, say a frame that has been corrupted during the transmission due to noise, there is a concept of NACK frames, i.e. Negative Acknowledge frames. Receiver transmits a NACK frame to the sender if it founds the received frame to be corrupted. When a NACK is received by a transmitter before the time-out, the old frame is sent again as shown in figure.

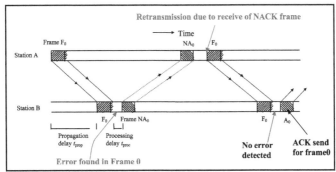

Retransmission due to damaged frame.

The main advantage of stop-and-wait ARQ is its simplicity. It also requires minimum buffer size. However, it makes highly inefficient use of communication links, particularly when 'a' is large.

Go-back-N ARQ

The most popular ARQ protocol is the go-back-N ARQ, where the sender sends the frames continuously without waiting for acknowledgement. That is why it is also called as *continuous ARQ*. As the receiver receives the frames, it keeps on sending ACKs or a NACK, in case a frame is incorrectly received. When the sender receives a NACK, it retransmits the frame in error plus all the succeeding frames as shown in figure. Hence, the name of the protocol is go-back-N ARQ. If a frame is lost, the receiver sends NAK after receiving the next frame as shown in figure. In case there is long delay before sending the NAK, the sender will resend the lost frame after its timer times out. If the ACK frame sent by the receiver is lost, the sender resends the frames after its timer times out as shown in figure.

Assuming full-duplex transmission, the receiving end sends piggybacked acknowledgement by using some number in the ACK field of its data frame. Let us assume that a 3-bit sequence number is used and suppose that a station sends frame 0 and gets back an RR1, and then sends frames 1, 2, 3, 4, 5, 6, 7, 0 and gets another RR1. This might either mean that RR1 is a cumulative ACK or all 8 frames were damaged. This ambiguity can be overcome if the maximum window size is limited to 7, i.e. for a k-bit sequence number field it is limited to 2^k-1. The number N (=2^k-1) specifies how many frames can be sent without receiving acknowledgement.

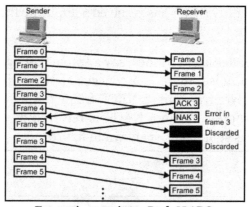

Frames in error in go-Back-N ARQ.

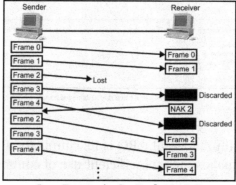

Lost Frames in Go-Back-N ARQ.

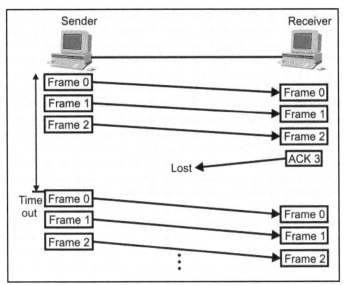

Lost ACK in Go-Back-N ARQ.

If no acknowledgement is received after sending N frames, the sender takes the help of a timer. After the time-out, it resumes retransmission. The go-back-N protocol also takes care of damaged frames and damaged ACKs. This scheme is little more complex than the previous one but gives much higher throughput.

Assuming full-duplex transmission, the receiving end sends piggybacked acknowledgement by using some number in the ACK field of its data frame. Let us assume that a 3-bit sequence number is used and suppose that a station sends frame 0 and gets back an RR1, and then sends frames 1, 2, 3, 4, 5, 6, 7, 0 and gets another RR1.This might either mean that RR1 is a cumulative ACK or all 8 frames were damaged. This ambiguity can be overcome if the maximum window size is limited to 7, i.e. for a k-bit sequence number field it is limited to 2^k-1. The number N $(=2^k-1)$ specifies how many frames can be sent without receiving acknowledgement. If no acknowledgement is received after sending N frames, the sender takes the help of a timer. After the time-out, it resumes retransmission. The go-back-N protocol also takes care of damaged frames and damaged ACKs. This scheme is little more complex than the previous one but gives much higher throughput.

High-Level Data Link Control

HDLC is a bit-oriented protocol. It was developed by the International Organization for Standardization (ISO). It falls under the ISO standards ISO 3309 and ISO 4335. It specifies a packitization standard for serial links. It has found itself being used throughout the world. It has been so widely implemented because it supports both half-duplex and full-duplex communication lines, point-to-point (peer to peer) and multi-point networks, and switched or non-switched channels. HDLC supports several modes of operation, including a simple sliding-window mode for reliable delivery. Since Internet provides retransmission at higher levels (i.e., TCP), most Internet applications use HDLC's unreliable delivery mode, Unnumbered Information.

Other benefits of HDLC are that the control information is always in the same position, and specific bit patterns used for control differ dramatically from those in representing data, which reduces the chance of errors. It has also led to many subsets. Two subsets widely in use are Synchronous Data Link Control (SDLC) and Link Access Procedure-Balanced (LAP-B).

In this lesson we shall consider the following aspects of HDLC:

- Stations and Configurations.

- Operational Modes.

- Non-Operational Modes.

- Frame Structure.

- Commands and Responses.

- HDLC Subsets (SDLC and LAPB).

HDLC Stations and Configurations

HDLC specifies the following three types of stations for data link control:

- Primary Station.

- Secondary Station.

- Combined Station.

Primary Station

Within a network using HDLC as its data link protocol, if a configuration is used in which there is a primary station, it is used as the controlling station on the link. It has the responsibility of controlling all other stations on the link (usually secondary stations). A primary issues *commands* and secondary issues *responses*. Despite this important aspect of being on the link, the primary station is also responsible for the organization of data flow on the link. It also takes care of error recovery at the data link level (layer 2 of the OSI model).

Secondary Station

If the data link protocol being used is HDLC, and a primary station is present, a secondary station must also be present on the data link. The secondary station is under the control of the primary station. It has no ability, or direct responsibility for controlling the link. It is only activated when requested by the primary station. It only responds to the primary station. The secondary station's frames are called responses. It can only send response frames when requested by the primary station. A primary station maintains a separate logical link with each secondary station.

Combined Station

A combined station is a combination of a primary and secondary station. On the link, all combined stations are able to send and receive commands and responses without any permission from any other stations on the link. Each combined station is in full control of itself, and does not rely on any other stations on the link. No other stations can control any combined station. May issue both commands and responses.

HDLC also defines three types of configurations for the three types of stations. The word configuration refers to the relationship between the hardware devices on a link. Following are the three configurations defined by HDLC:

- Unbalanced Configuration.

- Balanced Configuration.

- Symmetrical Configuration.

Unbalanced Configuration

The unbalanced configuration in an HDLC link consists of a primary station and one or more secondary stations. The unbalanced condition arises because one station controls the other stations. In an unbalanced configuration, any of the following can be used:

- Full-Duplex or Half-Duplex operation.

- Point to Point or Multi-point networks.

An example of an unbalanced configuration can be found below in figure.

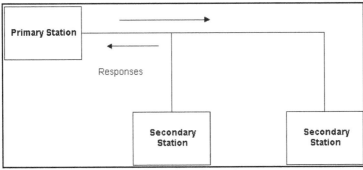

Unbalanced configuration.

Balanced Configuration

The balanced configuration in an HDLC link consists of two or more combined stations. Each of the stations has equal and complimentary responsibility compared to each other. Balanced configurations can use only the following:

- Full - Duplex or Half - Duplex operation.

- Point to Point networks.

An example of a balanced configuration can be found below in figure.

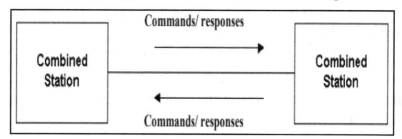

balanced configuration.

Symmetrical Configuration

This third type of configuration is not widely in use today. It consists of two independent point-to-point, unbalanced station configurations as shown in figure. In this configuration, each station has a primary and secondary status. Each station is logically considered as two stations.

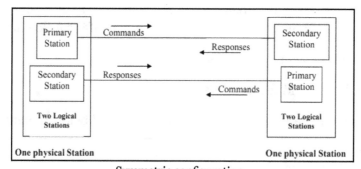

Symmetric configuration.

HDLC Operational Modes

A mode in HDLC is the relationship between two devices involved in an exchange; the mode describes who controls the link. Exchanges over unbalanced configurations are always conducted in normal response mode. Exchanges over symmetric or balanced configurations can be set to specific mode using a frame design to deliver the command. HDLC offers three different modes of operation. These three modes of operations are:

- Normal Response Mode (NRM).

- Asynchronous Response Mode (ARM).

- Asynchronous Balanced Mode (ABM).

Normal Response Mode

This is the mode in which the primary station initiates transfers to the secondary station. The secondary station can only transmit a response when, and only when, it is instructed to do so by the primary station. In other words, the secondary station must receive explicit permission from the primary station to transfer a response. After receiving permission from the primary station, the secondary station initiates its transmission. This transmission from the secondary station to the primary station may be much more than just an acknowledgment of a frame. It may in fact be more than one information frame. Once the last frame is transmitted by the secondary station, it must wait once again from explicit permission to transfer anything, from the primary station. Normal Response Mode is only used within an unbalanced configuration.

Asynchronous Response Mode

In this mode, the primary station doesn't initiate transfers to the secondary station. In fact, the secondary station does not have to wait to receive explicit permission from the primary station to transfer any frames. The frames may be more than just acknowledgment frames. They may contain data, or control information regarding the status of the secondary station. This mode can reduce overhead on the link, as no frames need to be transferred in order to give the secondary station permission to initiate a transfer. However, some limitations do exist. Due to the fact that this mode is asynchronous, the secondary station must wait until it detects and idle channel before it can transfer any frames. This is when the ARM link is operating at half-duplex. If the ARM link is operating at full duplex, the secondary station can transmit at any time. In this mode, the primary station still retains responsibility for error recovery, link setup, and link disconnection.

Synchronous Balanced Mode

This mode is used in case of combined stations. There is no need for permission on the part of any station in this mode. This is because combined stations do not require any sort of instructions to perform any task on the link.

Normal Response Mode is used most frequently in multi-point lines, where the primary station controls the link. Asynchronous Response Mode is better for point-to-point links, as it reduces overhead. Asynchronous Balanced Mode is not used widely today. The "asynchronous" in both ARM and ABM does not refer to the format of the data on the link. It refers to the fact that any given station can transfer frames without explicit permission or instruction from any other station.

HDLC Non-Operational Modes

HDLC also defines three non-operational modes. These three non-operational modes are:

- Normal Disconnected Mode (NDM).

- Asynchronous Disconnected Mode (ADM).

- Initialization Mode (IM).

The two disconnected modes (NDM and ADM) differ from the operational modes in that the secondary station is logically disconnected from the link (note the secondary station is not physically disconnected from the link). The IM mode is different from the operations modes in that the secondary station's data link control program is in need of regeneration or it is in need of an exchange of parameters to be used in an operational mode.

HDLC Frame Structure

There are three different types of frames as shown in figure and the size of different fields are shown table.

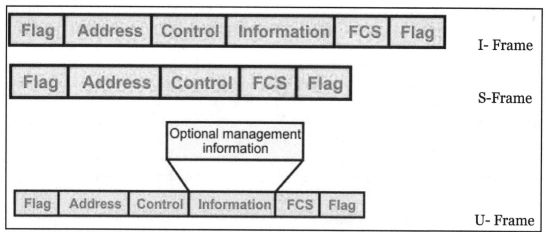

Different types of frames used in HDLC

Table: Size of different fields Field Name	Size(in bits)
Flag Field(F)	8 bits
Address Field(A)	8 bits
Control Field(C)	8 or 16 bits
Information Field(I) OR Data	Variable; Not used in some frames
Frame Check Sequence(FCS)	16 or 32 bits
Closing Flag Field(F)	8 bits

The Flag Field

Every frame on the link must begin and end with a flag sequence field (F). Stations attached to the data link must continually listen for a flag sequence. The flag sequence is an octet looking like 01111110. Flags are continuously transmitted on the link between frames to keep the link active. Two other bit sequences are used in HDLC as signals for the stations on the link. These two bit sequences are:

- Seven 1's, but less than 15 signal an abort signal. The stations on the link know there is a problem on the link.

- 15 or more 1's indicate that the channel is in an idle state.

The time between the transmissions of actual frames is called the interframe time fill. The interframe time fill is accomplished by transmitting continuous flags between frames. The flags may be in 8 bit multiples.

HDLC is a code-transparent protocol. It does not rely on a specific code for interpretation of line control. This means that if a bit at position N in an octet has a specific meaning, regardless of the other bits in the same octet. If an octet has a bit sequence of 01111110, but is not a flag field, HLDC uses a technique called bit-stuffing to differentiate this bit sequence from a flag field.

At the receiving end, the receiving station inspects the incoming frame. If it detects 5 consecutive 1's it looks at the next bit. If it is a 0, it pulls it out. If it is a 1, it looks at the 8th bit. If the 8th bit is a 0, it knows an abort or idle signal has been sent. It then proceeds to inspect the following bits to determine appropriate action. This is the manner in which HDLC achieves code-transparency. HDLC is not concerned with any specific bit code inside the data stream. It is only concerned with keeping flags unique.

The Address Field

The address field (A) identifies the primary or secondary stations involvement in the frame transmission or reception. Each station on the link has a unique address. In an unbalanced configuration, the A field in both commands and responses refer to the secondary station. In a balanced configuration, the command frame contains the destination station address and the response frame has the sending station's address.

The Control Field

HDLC uses the control field (C) to determine how to control the communications process. This field contains the commands, responses and sequences numbers used to maintain the data flow accountability of the link, defines the functions of the frame and initiates the logic to control the movement of traffic between sending and receiving stations. There three control field formats.

- Information Transfer Format: The frame is used to transmit end-user data between two devices.

- Supervisory Format: The control field performs control functions such as acknowledgment of frames, requests for re-transmission, and requests for temporary suspension of frames being transmitted. Its use depends on the operational mode being used.

- Unnumbered Format: This control field format is also used for control purposes. It is used to perform link initialization, link disconnection and other link control functions.

The Poll/Final Bit (P/F)

The 5th bit position in the control field is called the poll/final bit, or P/F bit. It can only be recognized when it is set to 1. If it is set to 0, it is ignored. The poll/final bit is used to provide dialogue between the primary station and secondary station. The primary station uses P=1 to acquire a status response from the secondary station. The P bit signifies a poll. The secondary station responds to the P bit by transmitting a data or status frame to the primary station with the P/F bit set to F=1. The F bit can also be used to signal the end of a transmission from the secondary station under Normal Response Mode.

The Information Field or Data Field

This field is not always present in a HDLC frame. It is only present when the Information Transfer Format is being used in the control field. The information field contains the actually data the sender is transmitting to the receiver in an I-Frame and network management information in U-Frame.

The Frame Check Sequence Field

This field contains a 16-bit, or 32-bit cyclic redundancy check bits.

HDLC Commands and Responses

The set of commands and responses in HDLC is summarized in table.

Information Transfer Format Command and Response (I-Frame)

The function of the information command and response is to transfer sequentially numbered frames, each containing an information field, across the data link.

Supervisory Format Command and Responses (S-Frame)

Supervisory (S) commands and responses are used to perform numbered supervisory functions such as acknowledgment, polling, temporary suspension of information transfer, or error recovery. Frames with the S format control field cannot contain an information field. A primary station may use the S format command frame with the P bit set to 1 to request a response from a secondary station regarding its status. Supervisory Format commands and responses are as follows:

- Receive Ready (RR) is used by the primary or secondary station to indicate that it is ready to receive an information frame and/or acknowledge previously received frames.

- Receive Not Ready (RNR) is used to indicate that the primary or secondary station is not ready to receive any information frames or acknowledgments.

- Reject (REJ) is used to request the retransmission of frames.

- Selective Reject (SREJ) is used by a station to request retransmission of specific frames. An SREJ must be transmitted for each erroneous frame; each frame is treated as a separate error. Only one SREJ can remain outstanding on the link at any one time.

TABLE: HDLC Commands and Responses **Information Transfer**	**Information Transfer**
Format Commands	**Format Responses**
I - Information	I - Information
Supervisory Format	**Supervisory Format**
Commands	**Responses**
RR - Receive ready	RR - Receive ready
RNR - Receive not ready	RNR - Receive not ready
REJ - Reject	REJ - Reject
SREJ - Selective reject	SREJ - Selective reject
Unnumbered Format	**Unnumbered Format**
Commands	**Commands**
SNRM - Set Normal Response Mode	UA - Unnumbered Acknowledgment
SARM - Set Asynchronous Response Mode	DM - Disconnected Mode
SABM - Set Asynchronous Balanced Mode	RIM - Request Initialization Mode
DISC - Disconnect	RD - Request Disconnect
SNRME - Set Normal Response Mode Extended	UI - Unnumbered Information
SARME - Set Asynchronous Response Mode Extended	XID - Exchange Identification
SABME - Set Asynchronous Balanced Mode Extended	FRMR - Frame Reject
SIM - Set Initialization Mode	TEST - Test

UP - Unnumbered Poll
UI - Unnumbered Information
XID - Exchange identification
RSET - Reset
TEST - Test

Unnumbered Format Commands and Responses (U-Frame)

The unnumbered format commands and responses are used to extend the number of data link control functions. The unnumbered format frames have 5 modifier bits, which allow for up to 32 additional commands and 32 additional response functions. Below, 13 command functions, and 8 response functions are described.

- Set Normal Response Mode (SNRM) places the secondary station into NRM. NRM does not allow the secondary station to send any unsolicited frames. Hence the primary station has control of the link.

- Set Asynchronous Response Mode (SARM) allows a secondary station to transmit frames without a poll from the primary station.

- Set Asynchronous Balanced Mode (SABM) sets the operational mode of the link to ABM.

- Disconnect (DISC) places the secondary station in to a disconnected mode.

- Set Normal Response Mode Extended (SNRME) increases the size of the control field to 2 octets instead of one in NRM. This is used for extended sequencing. The same applies for *SARME* and *SABME*.

- Set Initialization Mode (SIM) is used to cause the secondary station to initiate a station-specific procedure(s) to initialize its data link level control functions.

- Unnumbered Poll (UP) polls a station without regard to sequencing or acknowledgment.

- Unnumbered Information (UI) is used to send information to a secondary station.

- Exchange Identification (XID) is used to cause the secondary station to identify itself and provide the primary station identifications characteristics of itself.

- Reset (RSET) is used to reset the receive state variable in the addressed station.

- Test (TEST) is used to cause the addressed secondary station to respond with a TEST response at the first response opportunity. It performs a basic test of the data link control.

- Unnumbered Acknowledgment (UA) is used by the secondary station to acknowledge the receipt and acceptance of an *SNRM, SARM, SABM, SNRME, SARME, SABME, RSET, SIM,* or *DISC* commands.

- Disconnected Mode (DM) is transmitted from a secondary station to indicate it is in disconnected mode(non-operational mode.)

- Request Initialization Mode (RIM) is a request from a secondary station for initialization to a primary station. Once the secondary station sends *RIM*, it can only respond to *SIM, DSIC, TEST* or *XID* commands.

- Request Disconnect (RD) is sent by the secondary station to inform the primary station that it wishes to disconnect from the link and go into a non-operational mode(NDM or ADM).

- Frame Reject (FRMR) is used by the secondary station in an operation mode to report that a condition has occurred in transmission of a frame and retransmission of the frame will not correct the condition.

References

- Gary Cutlack (25 August 2010). "Mysterious Russian 'Numbers Station' Changes Broadcast After 20 Years". Gizmodo. Retrieved 12 March 2012

- Huffman, William Cary; Pless, Vera S. (2003). Fundamentals of Error-Correcting Codes. Cambridge University Press. ISBN 978-0-521-78280-7

- Shannon, C.E. (1948), "A Mathematical Theory of Communication", Bell System Tech. Journal, p. 418, 27

- Thompson, Thomas M. (1983), From Error-Correcting Codes through Sphere Packings to Simple Groups, The Carus Mathematical Monographs (#21), The Mathematical Association of America, p. vii, ISBN 0-88385-023-0

- "Using StrongArm SA-1110 in the On-Board Computer of Nanosatellite". Tsinghua Space Center, Tsinghua University, Beijing. Retrieved 2009-02-16

6

Understanding Internet Security and Network Security

Network security is a broad term that covers a multitude of processes designed to protect the integrity and confidentiality of computer networks and data, using both software and hardware technologies. Internet security comprises the various means used to ensure the security of data transmission and transactions online. Network and internet security along with the various methods employed by them are examined and explained in an easy to understand manner in this chapter.

Network Security

Network security consists of the policies and practices adopted to prevent and monitor unauthorized access, misuse, modification, or denial of a computer network and network-accessible resources. Only network security can remove trojan horse viruses if it is activated. Network security involves the authorization of access to data in a network, which is controlled by the network administrator. Users choose or are assigned an ID and password or other authenticating information that allows them access to information and programs within their authority. Network security covers a variety of computer networks, both public and private, that are used in everyday jobs; conducting transactions and communications among businesses, government agencies and individuals. Networks can be private, such as within a company, and others which might be open to public access. Network security is involved in organizations, enterprises, and other types of institutions. It does as its title explains: It secures the network, as well as protecting and overseeing operations being done. The most common and simple way of protecting a network resource is by assigning it a unique name and a corresponding password.

Network Security Concept

Network security starts with Authentication, commonly with a username and a password. Since this requires just one detail authenticating the user name—i.e., the password—this is sometimes termed one-factor authentication. With two-factor authentication, something the user 'has' is also used (e.g., a security token or 'dongle', an ATM card, or a mobile phone); and with three-factor authentication, something the user 'is' is also used (e.g., a fingerprint or retinal scan).

Once authenticated, a firewall enforces access policies such as what services are allowed to be accessed by the network users. Though effective to prevent unauthorized access, or Trojans being transmitted over the network. Anti-virus software or an intrusion prevention system (IPS) help detect and inhibit the action of such malware. An anomaly-based intrusion detection system may also monitor the network like wireshark traffic and may be logged for audit purposes and for later high-level analysis. Newer systems combining unsupervised machine learning with full network traffic analysis can detect active network attackers from malicious insiders or targeted external attackers that have compromised a user machine or account.

Communication between two hosts using a network may be encrypted to maintain privacy.

Honeypots, essentially decoy network-accessible resources, may be deployed in a network as surveillance and early-warning tools, as the honeypots are not normally accessed for legitimate purposes. Techniques used by the attackers that attempt to compromise these decoy resources are studied during and after an attack to keep an eye on new exploitation techniques. Such analysis may be used to further tighten security of the actual network being protected by the honeypot. A honeypot can also direct an attacker's attention away from legitimate servers. A honeypot encourages attackers to spend their time and energy on the decoy server while distracting their attention from the data on the real server. Similar to a honeypot, a honeynet is a network set up with intentional vulnerabilities. Its purpose is also to invite attacks so that the attacker's methods can be studied and that information can be used to increase network security. A honeynet typically contains one or more honeypots.

Firewall

In computing, a firewall is a network security system that monitors and controls incoming and outgoing network traffic based on predetermined security rules. A firewall typically establishes a barrier between a trusted internal network and untrusted external network, such as the Internet.

Firewalls are often categorized as either network firewalls or host-based firewalls. Network firewalls filter traffic between two or more networks and run on network hardware. Host-based firewalls run on host computers and control network traffic in and out of those machines.

Types

Firewalls are generally categorized as network-based or host-based. Network-based firewalls are positioned on the gateway computers of LANs, WANs and intranets. They are either software appliances running on general-purpose hardware, or hardware-based firewall computer appliances. Firewall appliances may also offer other functionality to the internal network they protect, such as acting as a DHCP or VPN server for that network. Host-based firewalls are positioned on the network node itself and control network traffic in and out of those machines.. The host-based firewall may be a daemon or service as a part of the operating system or an agent application such as endpoint security or protection. Each has advantages and disadvantages. However, each has a role in layered security.

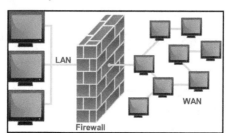

An illustration of where a firewall would be located in a network.

Firewalls also vary in type depending on where communication originates, where it is intercepted, and the state of communication being traced.

Network Layer or Packet Filters

Network layer firewalls, also called packet filters, operate at a relatively low level of the TCP/IP protocol stack, not allowing packets to pass through the firewall unless they match the established rule set. The firewall administrator may define the rules; or default rules may apply. The term "packet filter" originated in the context of BSD operating systems.

Network layer firewalls generally fall into two sub-categories, stateful and stateless.

Stateful firewalls maintain context about active sessions, and use that "state information" to speed packet processing. Any existing network connection can be described by several properties, including source and destination IP address, UDP or TCP ports, and the current stage of the connection's lifetime (including session initiation, handshaking, data transfer, or completion connection). If a packet does not match an existing connection, it will be evaluated according to the ruleset for new connections. If a packet matches an existing connection based on comparison with the firewall's state table, it will be allowed to pass without further processing.

Stateless firewalls require less memory, and can be faster for simple filters that require less time to filter than to look up a session. They may also be necessary for filtering stateless network protocols that have no concept of a session. However, they cannot make more complex decisions based on what stage communications between hosts have reached.

Newer firewalls can filter traffic based on many packet attributes like source IP address, source port, destination IP address or port, destination service like HTTP or FTP. They can filter based on protocols, TTL values, network block of the originator, of the source, and many other attributes.

Commonly used packet filters on various versions of Unix are *ipfw* (FreeBSD, Mac OS X (< 10.7)), *NPF* (NetBSD), *PF* (Mac OS X (> 10.4), OpenBSD, and some other BSDs), *iptables/ipchains* (Linux) and *IPFilter*.

Application-layer

Application-layer firewalls work on the application level of the TCP/IP stack (i.e., all browser traffic, or all telnet or FTP traffic), and may intercept all packets traveling to or from an application. They block other packets (usually dropping them without acknowledgment to the sender).

On inspecting all packets for improper content, firewalls can restrict or prevent outright the spread of networked computer worms and Trojans. The additional inspection criteria can add extra latency to the forwarding of packets to their destination.

Application firewalls function by determining whether a process should accept any given connection. Application firewalls accomplish their function by hooking into socket calls to filter the connections between the application layer and the lower layers of the OSI model. Application firewalls that hook into socket calls are also referred to as socket filters. Application firewalls work much like a packet filter but application filters apply filtering rules (allow/block) on a per process basis instead of filtering connections on a per port basis. Generally, prompts are used to define rules for processes that have not yet received a connection. It is rare to find application firewalls not combined or used in conjunction with a packet filter.

Also, application firewalls further filter connections by examining the process ID of data packets against a rule set for the local process involved in the data transmission. The extent of the filtering that occurs is defined by the provided rule set. Given the variety of software that exists, application firewalls only have more complex rule sets for the standard services, such as sharing services. These per-process rule sets have limited efficacy in filtering every possible association that may occur with other processes. Also, these per-process rule sets cannot defend against modification of the process via exploitation, such as memory corruption exploits. Because of these limitations, application firewalls are beginning to be supplanted by a new generation of application firewalls that rely on mandatory access control (MAC), also referred to as sandboxing, to protect vulnerable services.

Proxies

A proxy server (running either on dedicated hardware or as software on a general-purpose machine) may act as a firewall by responding to input packets (connection requests, for example) in the manner of an application, while blocking other packets. A proxy server is a gateway from one network to another for a specific network application, in the sense that it functions as a proxy on behalf of the network user.

Proxies make tampering with an internal system from the external network more difficult, so that misuse of one internal system would not necessarily cause a security breach exploitable from outside the firewall (as long as the application proxy remains intact and properly configured). Conversely, intruders may hijack a publicly reachable system and use it as a proxy for their own purposes; the proxy then masquerades as that system to other internal machines. While use of internal address spaces enhances security, crackers may still employ methods such as IP spoofing to attempt to pass packets to a target network.

Network Address Translation

Firewalls often have network address translation (NAT) functionality, and the hosts protected behind a firewall commonly have addresses in the "private address range", as defined in RFC 1918. Firewalls often have such functionality to hide the true address of computer which is connected to the network. Originally, the NAT function was developed to address the limited number of IPv4 routable addresses that could be used or assigned to companies or individuals as well as reduce both the amount and therefore cost of obtaining enough public addresses for every computer in an organization. Although NAT on its own is not considered a security feature, hiding the addresses of protected devices has become an often used defense against network reconnaissance.

Intrusion Detection System

An intrusion detection system (IDS) is a device or software application that monitors a network or systems for malicious activity or policy violations. Any detected activity or violation is typically reported either to an administrator or collected centrally using a security information and event management (SIEM) system. A SIEM system combines outputs from multiple sources, and uses alarm filtering techniques to distinguish malicious activity from false alarms.

There is a wide spectrum of IDS, varying from antivirus software to hierarchical systems that monitor the traffic of an entire backbone network. The most common classifications are network intrusion detection systems (NIDS) and host-based intrusion detection systems (HIDS). A system that monitors important operating system files is an example of a HIDS, while a system that analyzes incoming network traffic is an example of a NIDS. It is also possible to classify IDS by detection approach: the most well-known variants are signature-based detection (recognizing bad patterns, such as malware) and anomaly-based detection (detecting deviations from a model of "good" traffic, which often relies on machine learning). Some IDS have the ability to respond to detected intrusions. Systems with response capabilities are typically referred to as an intrusion prevention system.

Comparison with Firewalls

Though they both relate to network security, an IDS differs from a firewall in that a firewall looks outwardly for intrusions in order to stop them from happening. Firewalls limit access between networks to prevent intrusion and do not signal an attack from inside the network. An IDS describes a suspected intrusion once it has taken place and signals an alarm. An IDS also watches for attacks that originate from within a system. This is traditionally achieved by examining network communications, identifying heuristics and patterns (often known as signatures) of common computer attacks, and taking action to alert operators. A system that terminates connections is called an intrusion prevention system, and is another form of an application layer firewall.

Intrusion Detection

IDS can be classified by where detection takes place (network or host) and the detection method that is employed.

Analyzed Activity

Network Intrusion Detection Systems

Network intrusion detection systems (NIDS) are placed at a strategic point or points within the network to monitor traffic to and from all devices on the network. It performs an analysis of passing traffic on the entire subnet, and matches the traffic that is passed on the subnets to the library of known attacks. Once an attack is identified, or abnormal behavior is sensed, the alert can be sent to the administrator. An example of an NIDS would be installing it on the subnet where firewalls are located in order to see if someone is trying to break into the firewall. Ideally one would scan all inbound and outbound traffic, however doing so might create a bottleneck that would impair the overall speed of the network. OPNET and NetSim are commonly used tools for simulating network intrusion detection systems. NID Systems are also capable of comparing signatures for similar packets to link and drop harmful detected packets which have a signature matching the records in the NIDS. When we classify the design of the NIDS according to the system interactivity property, there are two types: on-line and off-line NIDS, often referred to as inline and tap mode, respectively. On-line NIDS deals with the network in real time. It analyses the Ethernet packets and applies some rules, to decide if it is an attack or not. Off-line NIDS deals with stored data and passes it through some processes to decide if it is an attack or not.

Host Intrusion Detection Systems

Host intrusion detection systems (HIDS) run on individual hosts or devices on the network. A HIDS monitors the inbound and outbound packets from the device only and will alert the user or administrator if suspicious activity is detected. It takes a snapshot of existing system files and matches it to the previous snapshot. If the critical system files were modified or deleted, an alert is sent to the administrator to investigate. An example of HIDS usage can be seen on mission critical machines, which are not expected to change their configurations.

Intrusion detection systems can also be system-specific using custom tools and honey-pots.

Detection Method

Signature-based

Signature-based IDS refers to the detection of attacks by looking for specific patterns, such as byte sequences in network traffic, or known malicious instruction sequences used by malware. This terminology originates from anti-virus software, which refers to these detected patterns as signatures. Although signature-based IDS can easily detect known attacks, it is impossible to detect new attacks, for which no pattern is available.

Anomaly-based

Anomaly-based intrusion detection systems were primarily introduced to detect unknown attacks, in part due to the rapid development of malware. The basic approach is to use machine learning to create a model of trustworthy activity, and then compare new behavior against this model. Although this approach enables the detection of previously unknown attacks, it may suffer from false positives: previously unknown legitimate activity may also be classified as malicious.

New types of what could be called anomaly-based intrusion detection systems are being viewed by Gartner as User and Entity Behavior Analytics (UEBA) (an evolution of the user behavior analytics category) and network traffic analysis (NTA). In particular, NTA deals with malicious insiders as well as targeted external attacks that have compromised a user machine or account. Gartner has noted that some organizations have opted for NTA over more traditional IDS.

Intrusion Prevention

Some systems may attempt to stop an intrusion attempt but this is neither required nor expected of a monitoring system. Intrusion detection and prevention systems (IDPS) are primarily focused on identifying possible incidents, logging information about them, and reporting attempts. In addition, organizations use IDPS for other purposes, such as identifying problems with security policies, documenting existing threats and deterring individuals from violating security policies. IDPS have become a necessary addition to the security infrastructure of nearly every organization.

IDPS typically record information related to observed events, notify security administrators of important observed events and produce reports. Many IDPS can also respond to a detected threat by attempting to prevent it from succeeding. They use several response techniques, which involve the IDPS stopping the attack itself, changing the security environment (e.g. reconfiguring a firewall) or changing the attack's content.

Intrusion prevention systems (IPS), also known as intrusion detection and prevention systems (IDPS), are network security appliances that monitor network or system activities for malicious activity. The main functions of intrusion prevention systems are to identify malicious activity, log information about this activity, report it and attempt to block or stop it.

Intrusion prevention systems are considered extensions of intrusion detection systems because they both monitor network traffic and/or system activities for malicious activity. The main differences are, unlike intrusion detection systems, intrusion prevention systems are placed in-line and are able to actively prevent or block intrusions that are detected. IPS can take such actions as sending an alarm, dropping detected malicious packets, resetting a connection or blocking traffic from the offending IP address. An IPS also can correct cyclic redundancy check (CRC) errors, defragment packet streams, mitigate TCP sequencing issues, and clean up unwanted transport and network layer options.

Classification

Intrusion prevention systems can be classified into four different types:

- Network-based intrusion prevention system (NIPS): monitors the entire network for suspicious traffic by analyzing protocol activity.

- Wireless intrusion prevention system (WIPS): monitor a wireless network for suspicious traffic by analyzing wireless networking protocols.

- Network behavior analysis (NBA): examines network traffic to identify threats that generate unusual traffic flows, such as distributed denial of service (DDoS) attacks, certain forms of malware and policy violations.

- Host-based intrusion prevention system (HIPS): an installed software package which monitors a single host for suspicious activity by analyzing events occurring within that host.

Detection Methods

The majority of intrusion prevention systems utilize one of three detection methods: signature-based, statistical anomaly-based, and stateful protocol analysis.

- Signature-based detection: Signature-based IDS monitors packets in the

Network and compares with pre-configured and pre-determined attack patterns known as signatures.

- Statistical anomaly-based detection: An IDS which is anomaly-based will monitor network traffic and compare it against an established baseline. The baseline will identify what is "normal" for that network – what sort of bandwidth is generally used and what protocols are used. It may however, raise a False Positive alarm for legitimate use of bandwidth if the baselines are not intelligently configured.

- Stateful protocol analysis detection: This method identifies deviations of protocol states by comparing observed events with "pre-determined profiles of generally accepted definitions of benign activity".

Limitations

- Noise can severely limit an intrusion detection system's effectiveness. Bad packets generated from software bugs, corrupt DNS data, and local packets that escaped can create a significantly high false-alarm rate.

- It is not uncommon for the number of real attacks to be far below the number of false-alarms. Number of real attacks is often so far below the number of false-alarms that the real attacks are often missed and ignored.

- Many attacks are geared for specific versions of software that are usually outdated. A constantly changing library of signatures is needed to mitigate threats. Outdated signature databases can leave the IDS vulnerable to newer strategies.

- For signature-based IDS, there will be lag between a new threat discovery and its signature being applied to the IDS. During this lag time, the IDS will be unable to identify the threat.

- It cannot compensate for weak identification and authentication mechanisms or for weaknesses in network protocols. When an attacker gains access due to weak authentication mechanisms then IDS cannot prevent the adversary from any malpractice.

- Encrypted packets are not processed by most intrusion detection devices. Therefore, the encrypted packet can allow an intrusion to the network that is undiscovered until more significant network intrusions have occurred.

- Intrusion detection software provides information based on the network address that is associated with the IP packet that is sent into the network. This is beneficial if the network address contained in the IP packet is accurate. However, the address that is contained in the IP packet could be faked or scrambled.

- Due to the nature of NIDS systems, and the need for them to analyse protocols as they are captured, NIDS systems can be susceptible to the same protocol-based attacks to which network hosts may be vulnerable. Invalid data and TCP/IP stack attacks may cause an NIDS to crash.

Evasion Techniques

There are a number of techniques which attackers are using, the following are considered 'simple' measures which can be taken to evade IDS:

- Fragmentation: by sending fragmented packets, the attacker will be under the radar and can easily bypass the detection system's ability to detect the attack signature.

- Avoiding defaults: The TCP port utilised by a protocol does not always provide an indication to the protocol which is being transported. For example, an IDS may expect to detect a trojan on port 12345. If an attacker had reconfigured it to use a different port, the IDS may not be able to detect the presence of the trojan.

- Coordinated, low-bandwidth attacks: coordinating a scan among numerous attackers (or agents) and allocating different ports or hosts to different attackers makes it difficult for the IDS to correlate the captured packets and deduce that a network scan is in progress.

- Address spoofing/proxying: attackers can increase the difficulty of the ability of Security Administrators to determine the source of the attack by using poorly secured or incorrectly configured proxy servers to bounce an attack. If the source is spoofed and bounced by a server, it makes it very difficult for IDS to detect the origin of the attack.

- Pattern change evasion: IDS generally rely on 'pattern matching' to detect an attack. By changing the data used in the attack slightly, it may be possible to evade detection. For example, an Internet Message Access Protocol (IMAP) server may be vulnerable to a buffer overflow, and an IDS is able to detect the attack signature of 10 common attack tools. By modifying the payload sent by the tool, so that it does not resemble the data that the IDS expects, it may be possible to evade detection.

Development

The earliest preliminary IDS concept was delineated in 1980 by James Anderson at the National Security Agency and consisted of a set of tools intended to help administrators review audit trails. User access logs, file access logs, and system event logs are examples of audit trails.

Fred Cohen noted in 1987 that it is impossible to detect an intrusion in every case, and that the resources needed to detect intrusions grow with the amount of usage.

Dorothy E. Denning, assisted by Peter G. Neumann, published a model of an IDS in 1986 that formed the basis for many systems today. Her model used statistics for anomaly detection, and resulted in an early IDS at SRI International named the Intrusion Detection Expert System (IDES), which ran on Sun workstations and could consider both user and network level data. IDES had a dual approach with a rule-based Expert System to detect known types of intrusions plus a statistical anomaly detection component based on profiles of users, host systems, and target systems. Lunt proposed adding an Artificial neural network as a third component. She said all three components could then report to a resolver. SRI followed IDES in 1993 with the Next-generation Intrusion Detection Expert System (NIDES).

The Multics intrusion detection and alerting system (MIDAS), an expert system using P-BEST and Lisp, was developed in 1988 based on the work of Denning and Neumann. Haystack was also developed in that year using statistics to reduce audit trails.

In 1986 the National Security Agency started an IDS research transfer program under Rebecca Bace. Bace later published the seminal text on the subject, *Intrusion Detection*, in 2000.

Wisdom & Sense (W&S) was a statistics-based anomaly detector developed in 1989 at the Los Alamos National Laboratory. W&S created rules based on statistical analysis, and then used those rules for anomaly detection.

In 1990, the Time-based Inductive Machine (TIM) did anomaly detection using inductive learning of sequential user patterns in Common Lisp on a VAX 3500 computer. The Network Security Monitor (NSM) performed masking on access matrices for anomaly detection on a Sun-3/50 workstation. The Information Security Officer's Assistant (ISOA) was a 1990 prototype that considered a variety of strategies including statistics, a profile checker, and an expert system. ComputerWatch at AT&T Bell Labs used statistics and rules for audit data reduction and intrusion detection.

Then, in 1991, researchers at the University of California, Davis created a prototype Distributed Intrusion Detection System (DIDS), which was also an expert system. The Network Anomaly Detection and Intrusion Reporter (NADIR), also in 1991, was a prototype IDS developed at the Los Alamos National Laboratory's Integrated Computing Network (ICN), and was heavily influenced by the work of Denning and Lunt. NADIR used a statistics-based anomaly detector and an expert system.

The Lawrence Berkeley National Laboratory announced Bro in 1998, which used its own rule language for packet analysis from libpcap data. Network Flight Recorder (NFR) in 1999 also used libpcap.

APE was developed as a packet sniffer, also using libpcap, in November, 1998, and was renamed Snort one month later. Snort has since become the world's largest used IDS/IPS system with over 300,000 active users. It can monitor both local systems, and remote capture points using the TZSP protocol.

The Audit Data Analysis and Mining (ADAM) IDS in 2001 used tcpdump to build profiles of rules for classifications. In 2003, Yongguang Zhang and Wenke Lee argue for the importance of IDS in networks with mobile nodes.

In 2015, Viegas and his colleagues proposed an anomaly-based intrusion detection engine, aiming System-on-Chip (SoC) for applications in Internet of Things (IoT), for instance. The proposal applies machine learning for anomaly detection, providing energy-efficiency to a Decision Tree, Naive-Bayes, and k-Nearest Neighbors classifiers implementation in an Atom CPU and its hardware-friendly implementation in a FPGA. In the literature, this was the first work that implement each classifier equivalently in software and hardware and measures its energy consumption on both. Additionally, it was the first time that was measured the energy consumption for extracting each features used to make the network packet classification, implemented in software and hardware.

Anomaly-based Intrusion Detection System

An anomaly-based intrusion detection system, is an intrusion detection system for detecting both network and computer intrusions and misuse by monitoring system activity and classifying it as either *normal* or *anomalous*. The classification is based on heuristics or rules, rather than patterns or signatures, and attempts to detect any type of misuse that falls out of normal system operation. This is as opposed to signature-based systems, which can only detect attacks for which a signature has previously been created.

In order to positively identify attack traffic, the system must be taught to recognize normal system activity. The two phases of a majority of anomaly detection systems consist of the training phase (where a profile of normal behaviors is built) and testing phase (where current traffic is compared with the profile created in the training phase). Anomalies are detected in several ways, most often with artificial intelligence type techniques. Systems using artificial neural networks have been used to great effect. Another method is to define what normal usage of the system comprises using a strict mathematical model, and flag any deviation from this as an attack. This is known as strict anomaly detection. Other techniques used to detect anomalies include data mining methods, grammar based methods, and Artificial Immune System.

Network-based anomalous intrusion detection systems often provide a second line of defense to detect anomalous traffic at the physical and network layers after it has passed through a firewall or other security appliance on the border of a network. Host-based anomalous intrusion detection systems are one of the last layers of defense and reside on computer end points. They allow for fine-tuned, granular protection of end points at the application level.

Anomaly-based Intrusion Detection at both the network and host levels have a few shortcomings; namely a high false-positive rate and the ability to be fooled by a correctly delivered attack. Attempts have been made to address these issues through techniques used by PAYL and MCPAD.

Honeypot

In computer terminology, a honeypot is a computer security mechanism set to detect, deflect, or, in some manner, counteract attempts at unauthorized use of information systems. Generally, a honeypot consists of data (for example, in a network site) that appears to be a legitimate part of the site, but is actually isolated and monitored, and that seems to contain information or a resource of value to attackers, who are then blocked. This is similar to police sting operations, colloquially known as "baiting," a suspect.

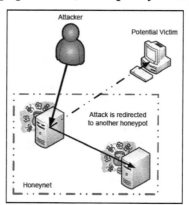

Honeypot diagram to help understand the topic.

Types

Honeypots can be classified based on their deployment (use/action) and based on their level of involvement. Based on deployment, honeypots may be classified as:

- Production honeypots.

- Research honeypots.

Production honeypots are easy to use, capture only limited information, and are used primarily by corporations. Production honeypots are placed inside the production network with other production servers by an organization to improve their overall state of security. Normally, production honeypots are low-interaction honeypots, which are easier to deploy. They give less information about the attacks or attackers than research honeypots.

Research honeypots are run to gather information about the motives and tactics of the black hat community targeting different networks. These honeypots do not add direct value to a specific organization; instead, they are used to research the threats that organizations face and to learn how to better protect against those threats. Research honeypots are complex to deploy and maintain, capture extensive information, and are used primarily by research, military, or government organizations.

Based on design criteria, honeypots can be classified as:

- Pure honeypots.

- High-interaction honeypots.

- Low-interaction honeypots.

Pure honeypots are full-fledged production systems. The activities of the attacker are monitored by using a bug tap that has been installed on the honeypot's link to the network. No other software needs to be installed. Even though a pure honeypot is useful, stealthiness of the defense mechanisms can be ensured by a more controlled mechanism.

High-interaction honeypots imitate the activities of the production systems that host a variety of services and, therefore, an attacker may be allowed a lot of services to waste his time. By employing virtual machines, multiple honeypots can be hosted on a single physical machine. Therefore, even if the honeypot is compromised, it can be restored more quickly. In general, high-interaction honeypots provide more security by being difficult to detect, but they are expensive to maintain. If virtual machines are not available, one physical computer must be maintained for each honeypot, which can be exorbitantly expensive. Example: Honeynet.

Low-interaction honeypots simulate only the services frequently requested by attackers. Since they consume relatively few resources, multiple virtual machines can easily be hosted on one physical system, the virtual systems have a short response time, and less code is required, reducing the complexity of the virtual system's security. Example: Honeyd.

Deception Technology

Recently, a new market segment called deception technology has emerged using basic honeypot technology with the addition of advanced automation for scale. Deception technology addresses the automated deployment of honeypot resources over a large commercial enterprise or government institution.

Malware Honeypots

Malware honeypots are used to detect malware by exploiting the known replication and attack vectors of malware. Replication vectors such as USB flash drives can easily be verified for evidence of modifications, either through manual means or utilizing special-purpose honeypots that emulate drives. Malware increasingly is used to search for and steal cryptocurrencies, which provides opportunities for services such as Bitcoin Vigil to create and monitor honeypots by using small amount of money to provide early warning alerts of malware infection.

Spam Versions

Spammers abuse vulnerable resources such as open mail relays and open proxies. Some system administrators have created honeypot programs that masquerade as these abusable resources to discover spammer activity. There are several capabilities such honeypots provide to these administrators and the existence of such fake abusable systems makes abuse more difficult or risky. Honeypots can be a powerful countermeasure to abuse from those who rely on very high volume abuse (e.g., spammers).

These honeypots can reveal the abuser's IP address and provide bulk spam capture (which enables operators to determine spammers' URLs and response mechanisms). For open relay honeypots, it is possible to determine the e-mail addresses ("dropboxes") spammers use as targets for their test messages, which are the tool they use to detect open relays. It is then simple to deceive the spammer: transmit any illicit relay e-mail received addressed to that dropbox e-mail address. That tells the spammer the honeypot is a genuine abusable open relay, and they often respond by sending large quantities of relay spam to that honeypot, which stops it. The apparent source may be another abused system—spammers and other abusers may use a chain of abused systems to make detection of the original starting point of the abuse traffic difficult.

This in itself is indicative of the power of honeypots as anti-spam tools. In the early days of anti-spam honeypots, spammers, with little concern for hiding their location, felt safe testing for vulnerabilities and sending spam directly from their own systems. Honeypots made the abuse riskier and more difficult.

Spam still flows through open relays, but the volume is much smaller than in 2001 to 2002. While most spam originates in the U.S., spammers hop through open relays across political boundaries to mask their origin. Honeypot operators may use intercepted relay tests to recognize and thwart attempts to relay spam through their honeypots. "Thwart" may mean "accept the relay spam but decline to deliver it." Honeypot operators may discover other details concerning the spam and the spammer by examining the captured spam messages.

Open relay honeypots include Jackpot, written in Java by Jack Cleaver; *smtpot.py*, written in Python by Karl A. Krueger; and *spamhole (honeypot)|spamhole*, written in C. The *Bubblegum Proxypot* is an open source honeypot (or "proxypot").

Email Trap

An email address that is not used for any other purpose than to receive spam can also be considered a spam honeypot. Compared with the term "spamtrap", the term "honeypot" might be more suitable for systems and techniques that are used to detect or counterattacks and probes. With a spamtrap, spam arrives at its destination "legitimately"—exactly as non-spam email would arrive.

An amalgam of these techniques is Project Honey Pot, a distributed, open source project that uses honeypot pages installed on websites around the world. These honeypot pages disseminate uniquely tagged spamtrap email addresses and spammers can then be tracked—the corresponding spam mail is subsequently sent to these spamtrap e-mail addresses.

Database Honeypot

Databases often get attacked by intruders using SQL injection. As such activities are not recognized by basic firewalls, companies often use database firewalls for protection. Some of the available SQL database firewalls provide/support honeypot architectures so that the intruder runs against a trap database while the web application remains functional.

Detection

Just as honeypots are weapons against spammers, honeypot detection systems are spammer-employed counter-weapons. As detection systems would likely use unique characteristics of specific honeypots to identify them, a great deal of honeypots in use makes the set of unique characteristics larger and more daunting to those seeking to detect and thereby identify them. This is an unusual circumstance in software: a situation in which "versionitis" (a large number of versions of the same software, all differing slightly from each other) can be beneficial. There's also an advantage in having some easy-to-detect honeypots deployed. Fred Cohen, the inventor of the Deception Toolkit, even argues that every system running his honeypot should have a deception port that adversaries can use to detect the honeypot. Cohen believes that this might deter adversaries.

Honey Nets

"A 'honey net' is a network of high interaction honeypots that simulates a production network and configured such that all activity is monitored, recorded and in a degree, discreetly regulated."

-Lance Spitzner,
Honeynet Project

Two or more honeypots on a network form a *honey net*. Typically, a honey net is used for monitoring a larger and/or more diverse network in which one honeypot may not be sufficient. Honey nets and honeypots are usually implemented as parts of larger network intrusion detection systems. A *honey farm* is a centralized collection of honeypots and analysis tools.

The concept of the honey net first began in 1999 when Lance Spitzner, founder of the Honeynet Project, published the paper "To Build a Honeypot".

Metaphor

The metaphor of a bear being attracted to and stealing honey is common in many traditions, including Germanic and Slavic. A common Germanic kenning for the bear was "honey eater". The tradition of bears stealing honey has been passed down through stories and folklore, especially the well known Winnie the Pooh.

Internet Security

Example of Webtitan Web Filter by TitanHQ blocking a restricted site.

Internet security is a branch of computer security specifically related to the Internet, often involving browser security but also network security on a more general level, as it applies to other applications or operating systems as a whole. Its objective is to establish rules and measures to use against attacks over the Internet. The Internet represents an insecure channel for exchanging information leading to a high risk of intrusion or fraud, such as phishing, online viruses, trojans, worms and more.

Many methods are used to protect the transfer of data, including encryption and from-the-ground-up engineering. The current focus is on prevention as much as on real time protection against well known and new threats.

Threats

Malicious Software

A computer user can be tricked or forced into downloading software onto a computer that is of malicious intent. Such software comes in many forms, such as viruses, Trojan horses, spyware, and worms.

- Malware, short for malicious software, is any software used to disrupt computer operation, gather sensitive information, or gain access to private computer systems. Malware is defined by its malicious intent, acting against the requirements of the computer user, and does not include software that causes unintentional harm due to some deficiency. The term badware is sometimes used, and applied to both true (malicious) malware and unintentionally harmful software.

- A botnet is a network of zombie computers that have been taken over by a robot or bot that performs large-scale malicious acts for the creator of the botnet.

- Computer Viruses are programs that can replicate their structures or effects by infecting other files or structures on a computer. The common use of a virus is to take over a computer to steal data.

- Computer worms are programs that can replicate themselves throughout a computer network, performing malicious tasks throughout.

- Ransomware is a type of malware which restricts access to the computer system that it infects, and demands a ransom paid to the creator(s) of the malware in order for the restriction to be removed.

- Scareware is scam software with malicious payloads, usually of limited or no benefit, that are sold to consumers via certain unethical marketing practices. The selling approach uses social engineering to cause shock, anxiety, or the perception of a threat, generally directed at an unsuspecting user.

- Spyware refers to programs that surreptitiously monitor activity on a computer system and report that information to others without the user's consent.

- A Trojan horse, commonly known as a *Trojan*, is a general term for malicious software that pretends to be harmless, so that a user willingly allows it to be downloaded onto the computer.

- KeyLogger, Keystroke logging, often referred to as keylogging or keyboard capturing, is the action of recording (logging) the keys struck on a keyboard.

Denial-of-service Attacks

A denial-of-service attack (DoS attack) or distributed denial-of-service attack (DDoS attack) is an attempt to make a computer resource unavailable to its intended users. Another way of understanding DDoS is seeing it as attacks in cloud computing environment that are growing due to the essential characteristics of cloud computing. Although the means to carry out, motives for, and targets of a DoS attack may vary, it generally consists of the concerted efforts to prevent an Internet site or service from functioning efficiently or at all, temporarily or indefinitely. According to businesses who participated in an international business security survey, 25% of respondents experienced a DoS attack in 2007 and 16.8% experienced one in 2010.

Phishing

Phishing is an attack which targets online users for extraction of their sensitive information such as username, password and credit card information. Phishing occurs when the attacker pretends to be a trustworthy entity, either via email or web page. Victims are directed to fake web pages, which are dressed to look legitimate, via spoof emails, instant messenger/social media or other avenues. Often tactics such as email spoofing are used to make emails appear to be from legitimate senders, or long complex subdomains hide the real website host. Insurance group RSA said that phishing accounted for worldwide losses of $1.5 billion in 2012.

Application Vulnerabilities

Applications used to access Internet resources may contain security vulnerabilities such as memory safety bugs or flawed authentication checks. The most severe of these bugs can give network attackers full control over the computer. Most security applications and suites are incapable of adequate defense against these kinds of attacks.

Remedies

Network Layer Security

TCP/IP protocols may be secured with cryptographic methods and security protocols. These protocols include Secure Sockets Layer (SSL), succeeded by Transport Layer Security (TLS) for web traffic, Pretty Good Privacy (PGP) for email, and IPsec for the network layer security.

Internet Protocol Security (IPsec)

IPsec is designed to protect TCP/IP communication in a secure manner. It is a set of security extensions developed by the Internet Task Force (IETF). It provides security and authentication at the IP layer by transforming data using encryption. Two main types of transformation that form the basis of IPsec: the Authentication Header (AH) and ESP. These two protocols provide data integrity, data origin authentication, and anti-replay service. These protocols can be used alone or in combination to provide the desired set of security services for the Internet Protocol (IP) layer.

The basic components of the IPsec security architecture are described in terms of the following functionalities:

- Security protocols for AH and ESP.

- Security association for policy management and traffic processing.

- Manual and automatic key management for the Internet key exchange (IKE).

- Algorithms for authentication and encryption.

The set of security services provided at the IP layer includes access control, data origin integrity, protection against replays, and confidentiality. The algorithm allows these sets to work independently without affecting other parts of the implementation. The IPsec implementation is operated in a host or security gateway environment giving protection to IP traffic.

Multi-factor Authentication

Multi-factor authentication (MFA) is a method of computer access control in which a user is granted access only after successfully presenting several separate pieces of evidence to an authentication mechanism – typically at least two of the following categories: knowledge (something they know), possession (something they have), and inherence (something they are). Internet resources, such as websites and email, may be secured using multi-factor authentication.

Security Token

Some online sites offer customers the ability to use a six-digit code which randomly changes every 30–60 seconds on a security token. The keys on the security token have built in mathematical computations and manipulate numbers based on the current time built into the device. This means that every thirty seconds there is only a certain array of numbers possible which would be correct to validate access to the online account. The website that the user is logging into would be made aware of that device's serial number and would know the computation and correct time built into the device to verify that the number given is indeed one of the handful of six-digit numbers that works in that given 30-60 second cycle. After 30–60 seconds the device will present a new random six-digit number which can log into the website.

Electronic Mail Security

Background

Email messages are composed, delivered, and stored in a multiple step process, which starts with the message's composition. When the user finishes composing the message and sends it, the message is transformed into a standard format: an RFC 2822 formatted message. Afterwards, the message can be transmitted. Using a network connection, the mail client, referred to as a mail user agent (MUA), connects to a mail transfer agent (MTA) operating on the mail server. The mail client then provides the sender's identity to the server. Next, using the mail server commands, the client sends the recipient list to the mail server. The client then supplies the message. Once the mail server receives and processes the message, several events occur: recipient server identification, connection establishment, and message transmission. Using Domain Name System (DNS) services, the sender's mail server determines the mail server(s) for the recipient(s). Then, the server opens up a connection(s) to the recipient mail server(s) and sends the message employing a process similar to that used by the originating client, delivering the message to the recipient(s).

Pretty Good Privacy (PGP)

Pretty Good Privacy provides confidentiality by encrypting messages to be transmitted or data files to be stored using an encryption algorithm such as Triple DES or CAST-128. Email messages can be protected by using cryptography in various ways, such as the following:

- Signing an email message to ensure its integrity and confirm the identity of its sender.

- Encrypting the body of an email message to ensure its confidentiality.

- Encrypting the communications between mail servers to protect the confidentiality of both message body and message header.

The first two methods, message signing and message body encryption, are often used together; however, encrypting the transmissions between mail servers is typically used only when two organizations want to protect emails regularly sent between each other. For example, the organizations could establish a virtual private network (VPN) to encrypt the communications between their mail servers over the Internet. Unlike methods that can only encrypt a message body, a VPN can encrypt entire messages, including email header information such as senders, recipients, and subjects. In some cases, organizations may need to protect header information. However, a VPN solution alone cannot provide a message signing mechanism, nor can it provide protection for email messages along the entire route from sender to recipient.

Multipurpose Internet Mail Extensions (MIME)

MIME transforms non-ASCII data at the sender's site to Network Virtual Terminal (NVT) ASCII data and delivers it to client's Simple Mail Transfer Protocol (SMTP) to be sent through the Internet. The server SMTP at the receiver's side receives the NVT ASCII data and delivers it to MIME to be transformed back to the original non-ASCII data.

Message Authentication Code

A Message authentication code (MAC) is a cryptography method that uses a secret key to encrypt a message. This method outputs a MAC value that can be decrypted by the receiver, using the same secret key used by the sender. The Message Authentication Code protects both a message's data integrity as well as its authenticity.

Firewalls

A computer firewall controls access between networks. It generally consists of gateways and filters which vary from one firewall to another. Firewalls also screen network traffic and are able to block traffic that is dangerous. Firewalls act as the intermediate server between SMTP and Hypertext Transfer Protocol (HTTP) connections.

Role of Firewalls in Web Security

Firewalls impose restrictions on incoming and outgoing Network packets to and from private networks. Incoming or outgoing traffic must pass through the firewall; only authorized traffic is allowed to pass through it. Firewalls create checkpoints between an internal private network and the public Internet, also known as *choke points* (borrowed from the identical military term of a combat limiting geographical feature). Firewalls can create choke points based on IP source and TCP port number. They can also serve as the platform for IPsec. Using tunnel mode capability, firewall can be used to implement VPNs. Firewalls can also limit network exposure by hiding the internal network system and information from the public Internet.

Types of Firewall

Packet Filter

A packet filter is a first generation firewall that processes network traffic on a packet-by-packet basis. Its main job is to filter traffic from a remote IP host, so a router is needed to connect the internal network to the Internet. The router is known as a screening router, which screens packets leaving and entering the network.

Stateful Packet Inspection

In a stateful firewall the circuit-level gateway is a proxy server that operates at the network level of an Open Systems Interconnection (OSI) model and statically defines what traffic will be allowed. Circuit proxies will forward Network packets (formatted unit of data) containing a given port number, if the port is permitted by the algorithm. The main advantage of a proxy server is its ability to provide Network Address Translation (NAT), which can hide the user's IP address from the Internet, effectively protecting all internal information from the Internet.

Application-level Gateway

An application-level firewall is a third generation firewall where a proxy server operates at the very top of the OSI model, the IP suite application level. A network packet is forwarded only if a connection is established using a known protocol. Application-level gateways are notable for analyzing entire messages rather than individual packets of data when the data are being sent or received.

Browser Choice

Web browser statistics tend to affect the amount a Web browser is exploited. For example, Internet Explorer 6, which used to own a majority of the Web browser market share, is considered extremely insecure because vulnerabilities were exploited due to its former popularity. Since browser choice is now more evenly distributed (Internet Explorer at 28.5%, Firefox at 18.4%, Google Chrome at 40.8%, and so on), vulnerabilities are exploited in many different browsers.

Internet Security Products

Antivirus

Antivirus software and Internet security programs can protect a programmable device from attack by detecting and eliminating viruses; Antivirus software was mainly shareware in the early years of the Internet, but there are now several free security applications on the Internet to choose from for all platforms.

Password Managers

A password manager is a software application that helps a user store and organize passwords. Password managers usually store passwords encrypted, requiring the user to create a master password; a single, ideally very strong password which grants the user access to their entire password database from top to bottom.

Security Suites

So called *security suites* were first offered for sale in 2003 (McAfee) and contain a suite of firewalls, anti-virus, anti-spyware and more. They also offer theft protection, portable storage device safety check, private Internet browsing, cloud anti-spam, a file shredder or make security-related decisions (answering popup windows) and several were free of charge.

Browser Security

Browser security is the application of Internet security to web browsers in order to protect networked data and computer systems from breaches of privacy or malware. Security exploits of browsers often use JavaScript — sometimes with cross-site scripting

(XSS) — sometimes with a secondary payload using Adobe Flash. Security exploits can also take advantage of vulnerabilities (security holes) that are commonly exploited in all browsers (including Mozilla Firefox, Google Chrome, Opera, Microsoft Internet Explorer, and Safari).

Security

Web browsers can be breached in one or more of the following ways:

- Operating system is breached and malware is reading/modifying the browser memory space in privilege mode.

- Operating system has a malware running as a background process, which is reading/modifying the browser memory space in privileged mode.

- Main browser executable can be hacked.

- Browser components may be hacked.

- Browser plugins can be hacked.

- Browser network communications could be intercepted outside the machine.

The browser may not be aware of any of the breaches above and may show user a safe connection is made.

Whenever a browser communicates with a website, the website, as part of that communication, collects some information about the browser (in order to process the formatting of the page to be delivered, if nothing else). If malicious code has been inserted into the website's content, or in a worst-case scenario, if that website has been specifically designed to host malicious code, then vulnerabilities specific to a particular browser can allow this malicious code to run processes within the browser application in unintended ways (and remember, one of the bits of information that a website collects from a browser communication is the browser's identity-allowing specific vulnerabilities to be exploited). Once an attacker is able to run processes on the visitor's machine, then exploiting known security vulnerabilities can allow the attacker to gain privileged access (if the browser isn't already running with privileged access) to the "infected" system in order to perform an even greater variety of malicious processes and activities on the machine or even the victim's whole network.

Breaches of web browser security are usually for the purpose of bypassing protections to display pop-up advertising collecting personally identifiable information (PII) for either Internet marketing or identity theft, website tracking or web analytics about a user against their will using tools such as web bugs, Clickjacking, Likejacking (where Facebook's like button is targeted), HTTP cookies, zombie cookies or Flash cookies (Local

Shared Objects or LSOs); installing adware, viruses, spyware such as Trojan horses (to gain access to users' personal computers via cracking) or other malware including on-line banking theft using man-in-the-browser attacks.

Vulnerabilities in the web browser software itself can be minimized by keeping browser software updated, but will not be sufficient if the underlying operating system is compromised, for example, by a rootkit. Some subcomponents of browsers such as scripting, add-ons, and cookies are particularly vulnerable ("the confused deputy problem") and also need to be addressed.

Following the principle of defence in depth, a fully patched and correctly configured browser may not be sufficient to ensure that browser-related security issues cannot occur. For example, a rootkit can capture keystrokes while someone logs into a banking website, or carry out a man-in-the-middle attack by modifying network traffic to and from a web browser. DNS hijacking or DNS spoofing may be used to return false positives for mistyped website names, or to subvert search results for popular search engines. Malware such as RSPlug simply modifies a system's configuration to point at rogue DNS servers.

Browsers can use more secure methods of network communication to help prevent some of these attacks:

- DNS: DNSSec and DNSCrypt, for example with non-default DNS servers such as Google Public DNS or OpenDNS.

- HTTP: HTTP Secure and SPDY with digitally signed public key certificates or Extended Validation Certificates.

Perimeter defenses, typically through firewalls and the use of filtering proxy servers that block malicious websites and perform antivirus scans of any file downloads, are commonly implemented as a best practice in large organizations to block malicious network traffic before it reaches a browser.

The topic of browser security has grown to the point of spawning the creation of entire organizations, such as The Browser Exploitation Framework Project, creating platforms to collect tools to breach browser security, ostensibly in order to test browsers and network systems for vulnerabilities.

Plugins and Extensions

Although not part of the browser per se, browser plugins and extensions extend the attack surface, exposing vulnerabilities in Adobe Flash Player, Adobe (Acrobat) Reader, Java plugin, and ActiveX that are commonly exploited. Malware may also be implemented as a browser extension, such as a browser helper object in the case of Internet Explorer. Browsers like Google Chrome and Mozilla Firefox can block—or warn users of—insecure plugins.

Flash

An August 2009 study by the Social Science Research Network found that 50% of websites using Flash were also employing flash cookies, yet privacy policies rarely disclosed them, and user controls for privacy preferences were lacking. Most browsers' cache and history delete functions do not affect Flash Player's writing Local Shared Objects to its own cache, and the user community is much less aware of the existence and function of Flash cookies than HTTP cookies. Thus, users having deleted HTTP cookies and purged browser history files and caches may believe that they have purged all tracking data from their computers when in fact Flash browsing history remains. As well as manual removal, the BetterPrivacy addon for Firefox can remove Flash cookies. Adblock Plus can be used to filter out specific threats and Flashblock can be used to give an option before allowing content on otherwise trusted sites.

Charlie Miller recommended "not to install Flash" at the computer security conference CanSecWest. Several other security experts also recommend to either not install Adobe Flash Player or to block it.

Password Security Model

The contents of a web page are arbitrary and controlled by the entity owning the domain named displayed in the address bar. If HTTPS is used, then encryption is used to secure against attackers with access to the network from changing the page contents en route. For normal password usage on the WWW, when the user is confronted by a dialog asking for their password, they are supposed to look at the address bar to determine whether the domain name in the address bar is the correct place to send the password.

An un-compromised browser guarantees that the address bar is correct. This guarantee is one reason why browsers will generally display a warning when entering fullscreen mode, on top of where the address bar would normally be, so that a fullscreen website cannot make a fake browser user interface with a fake address bar.

Privacy

Hardware Browser

There have been attempts to market hardware-based browsers running from non-writable, read-only file systems. Data cannot stored on the device and the media cannot be overwritten, presenting a clean executable each time it loads. The first such device was the ZeusGard Secure Hardware Browser, released in late 2013. The ZeusGard website has not been functional since mid-2016. Another device, the iCloak® Stik from the iCloak website provides a complete Live OS which completely replaces the computer's entire operating system and offers two web browsers from the read-only system. With iCloak they provide the Tor browser for Anonymous browsing as well as a regular Firefox browser for non-anonymous browsing. Any non-secured web traffic (not using https, for example), could still be subject to man-in-the-middle alteration or other network traffic-based manipulations.

LiveCD

LiveCDs, which run an operating system from a non-writable source, typically come with internet browsers as part of their default image. If the original LiveCD image is free of malware, all of the software used, including the internet browser, will load free of malware every time the LiveCD image is booted.

Browser Hardening

Browsing the Internet as a least-privilege user account (i.e. without administrator privileges) limits the ability of a security exploit in a web browser from compromising the whole operating system.

Internet Explorer 4 and later allows the blacklisting and whitelisting of ActiveX controls, add-ons and browser extensions in various ways.

Internet Explorer 7 added "protected mode", a technology that hardens the browser through the application of a security sandboxing feature of Windows Vista called Mandatory Integrity Control. Google Chrome provides a sandbox to limit web page access to the operating system.

Suspected malware sites reported to Google, and confirmed by Google, are flagged as hosting malware in certain browsers.

There are third-party extensions and plugins available to harden even the latest browsers, and some for older browsers and operating systems. Whitelist-based software such as NoScript can block JavaScript and Adobe Flash which is used for most attacks on privacy, allowing users to choose only sites they know are safe - AdBlock Plus also uses whitelist ad filtering rules subscriptions, though both the software itself and the filtering list maintainers have come under controversy for by-default allowing some sites to pass the pre-set filters. The US-CERT recommends to block Flash using NoScript.

Remote Browser Isolation

A relatively new approach (started getting a lot of attention in 2017), known as browser isolation or remote browsing, involves executing browsing sessions in a remote location outside the firewall (e.g., in the DMZ or cloud), within an isolated virtual environment such as a container. The securely rendered web content is streamed back to the local browser in real time, providing a seamless and interactive user experience, while ensuring that any malicious code is fully contained—never making its way onto the endpoint. The entire virtual environment can then be reset to a known good state or discarded altogether at the end of the session.

Best Practice

- Load clean software: Boot from a known clean OS that has a known clean internet browser.

- Prevent attacks via third-party software: Use a hardened internet browser or add-on-free-browsing mode.

- Prevent DNS manipulation: Use trusted and secure DNS.

- Avoid website-based exploits: Employ link-checking browser plug-ins commonly found in internet security software.

- Avoid malicious content: Employ perimeter defenses and anti-malware software.

Trust No One

Trust no one (TNO) is an approach towards Internet and software security issues. In all Internet communication and software packages where some sort of secrecy is needed, usually some sort of encryption is applied. The trust no one approach teaches that no one (but oneself) should be trusted when it comes to the storage of the keys behind the applied encryption technology.

Many encryption technologies rely on the trust of an external party. For instance the security of secure end-to-end SSL connections relies on the trust of a certificate authority (CA).

The trust no one design philosophy requires that the keys for encryption should always be, and stay, in the hands of the user that applies them. This implies that no external party can access the encrypted data (assumed that the encryption is strong enough). It also implies that an external party cannot provide a backup mechanism for password recovery.

Although the philosophy of trust no one at least assures the reliability of the communication of the user that creates it, in real life and in society many communication means rely on a trust relationship between at least two parties.

IP Fragmentation Attack

IP fragmentation is the process of breaking up a single Internet Protocol (IP) datagram into multiple packets of smaller size. Every network link has a characteristic size of messages that may be transmitted, called the maximum transmission unit (MTU).

Part of the TCP/IP suite is the Internet Protocol (IP) which resides at the Internet Layer of this model. IP is responsible for the transmission of packets between network end points. IP includes some features which provide basic measures of fault-tolerance (time to live, checksum), traffic prioritization (type of service) and support for the fragmentation of larger packets into multiple smaller packets (ID field, fragment offset). The support for fragmentation of larger packets provides a protocol allowing routers to fragment a packet into smaller packets when the original packet is too large for the supporting datalink frames. IP fragmentation exploits (attacks) use the fragmentation protocol within IP as an attack vector.

Process

IP datagrams are encapsulated in datalink frames, and, therefore, the link MTU affects larger IP datagrams and forces them to be split into pieces equal to or smaller than the MTU size.

This can be accomplished by several approaches:

- To set the IP datagram size equal or smaller than the directly attached medium and delegate all further fragmentation of datagrams to routers, meaning that routers decide if the current datagram should be re-fragmented or not. This off-loads a lot of work on to routers, and can also result in packets being segmented by several IP routers one after another, resulting in very peculiar fragmentation.

- To preview all links between source and destination and select the smallest MTU in this route, assuming there is a unique route. This way we make sure that the fragmentation is done by the sender, using a packet-size smaller than the selected MTU, and there is no further fragmentation en route. This solution, called Path MTU Discovery, allows a sender to fragment/segment a long Internet packet, rather than relying on routers to perform IP-level fragmentation. This is more efficient and more scalable. It is therefore the recommended method in the current Internet. The problem with this approach is that each packet is routed independently; they may well typically follow the same route, but they may not, and so a probe packet to determine fragmentation may follow a path different from paths taken by later packets.

Three fields in the IP header are used to implement fragmentation and reassembly. The "Identification", "Flags" and "Fragment Offset" fields.

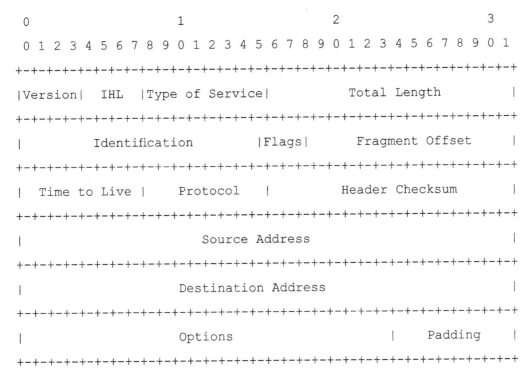

Flags:

A 3 bit field which says if the datagram is a part of a fragmented data frame or not.

Bit 0: reserved, must be zero (unless datagram is adhering to RFC 3514).

Bit 1: (AF) 0 = May Fragment, 1 = Don't Fragment.

Bit 2: (AF) 0 = Last Fragment, 1 = More Fragments.

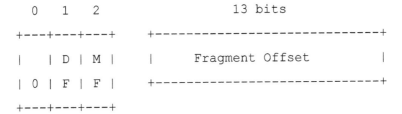

Fragment Offset specifies the fragment's position within the original Datagram, measured in 8-byte units.

Accordingly, every fragment except the last must contain a multiple of 8 bytes of data. It is obvious that Fragment Offset can hold 8192 (2^13) units but the datagram can't have 8192 * 8 = 65536 bytes of data because "Total Length" field of IP header records the total size including the header and data. An IP header is at least 20 bytes long, so the maximum value for "Fragment Offset" is restricted to 8189, which leaves room for 3 bytes in the last fragment.

Because an IP internet can be connectionless, fragments from one datagram may be interleaved with those from another at the destination. The "Identification field" uniquely identifies the fragments of a particular datagram.

The source system sets "Identification" field in each datagram to a unique value for all datagrams which use the same source IP address, destination IP address, and "Protocol" values, for the lifetime of the datagram on the internet. This way the destination can distinguish which incoming fragments belong to a unique datagram and buffer all of them until the last fragment is received. The last fragment sets the "More Fragment" bit to 0 and this tells the receiving station to start reassembling the data if all fragments have been received.

The following is a real-life fragmentation example:

The following was obtained using the Ethereal protocol analyzer to capture ICMP echo request packets. To simulate this open up a terminal and type ping ip_dest -n 1 -l 65000.

The results are as follows:

```
    No. Time          Source              Destination          Protocol Info
      1 0.000000     87.247.163.96           66.94.234.13          ICMP
Echo (ping) request

      2 0.000000     87.247.163.96           66.94.234.13            IP
Fragmented IP protocol (proto=ICMP 0x01, off=1480)

      3 0.002929     87.247.163.96           66.94.234.13            IP
Fragmented IP protocol (proto=ICMP 0x01, off=2960)

      4 6.111328     87.247.163.96           66.94.234.13            IP
Fragmented IP protocol (proto=ICMP 0x01, off=4440)

      5 6.123046     87.247.163.96           66.94.234.13            IP
Fragmented IP protocol (proto=ICMP 0x01, off=5920)

      6 6.130859     87.247.163.96           66.94.234.13            IP
Fragmented IP protocol (proto=ICMP 0x01, off=7400)

      7 6.170898     87.247.163.96           66.94.234.13            IP
Fragmented IP protocol (proto=ICMP 0x01, off=8880)

      8 6.214843     87.247.163.96           66.94.234.13            IP
Fragmented IP protocol (proto=ICMP 0x01, off=10360)

      9 6.239257     87.247.163.96           66.94.234.13            IP
Fragmented IP protocol (proto=ICMP 0x01, off=11840)

     10 6.287109     87.247.163.96           66.94.234.13            IP
Fragmented IP protocol (proto=ICMP 0x01, off=13320)

     11 6.302734     87.247.163.96           66.94.234.13            IP
```

```
Fragmented IP protocol (proto=ICMP 0x01, off=14800)

    12  6.327148      87.247.163.96              66.94.234.13              IP
Fragmented IP protocol (proto=ICMP 0x01, off=16280)

    13  6.371093      87.247.163.96              66.94.234.13              IP
Fragmented IP protocol (proto=ICMP 0x01, off=17760)

    14  6.395507      87.247.163.96              66.94.234.13              IP
Fragmented IP protocol (proto=ICMP 0x01, off=19240)

    15  6.434570      87.247.163.96              66.94.234.13              IP
Fragmented IP protocol (proto=ICMP 0x01, off=20720)

    16  6.455078      87.247.163.96              66.94.234.13              IP
Fragmented IP protocol (proto=ICMP 0x01, off=22200)

    17  6.531250      87.247.163.96              66.94.234.13              IP
Fragmented IP protocol (proto=ICMP 0x01, off=23680)

    18  6.550781      87.247.163.96              66.94.234.13              IP
Fragmented IP protocol (proto=ICMP 0x01, off=25160)

    19  6.575195      87.247.163.96              66.94.234.13              IP
Fragmented IP protocol (proto=ICMP 0x01, off=26640)

    20  6.615234      87.247.163.96              66.94.234.13              IP
Fragmented IP protocol (proto=ICMP 0x01, off=28120)

    21  6.634765      87.247.163.96              66.94.234.13              IP
Fragmented IP protocol (proto=ICMP 0x01, off=29600)

    22  6.659179      87.247.163.96              66.94.234.13              IP
Fragmented IP protocol (proto=ICMP 0x01, off=31080)

    23  6.682617      87.247.163.96              66.94.234.13              IP
Fragmented IP protocol (proto=ICMP 0x01, off=32560)

    24  6.699218      87.247.163.96              66.94.234.13              IP
Fragmented IP protocol (proto=ICMP 0x01, off=34040)

    25  6.743164      87.247.163.96              66.94.234.13              IP
Fragmented IP protocol (proto=ICMP 0x01, off=35520)

    26  6.766601      87.247.163.96              66.94.234.13              IP
Fragmented IP protocol (proto=ICMP 0x01, off=37000)

    27  6.783203      87.247.163.96              66.94.234.13              IP
Fragmented IP protocol (proto=ICMP 0x01, off=38480)

    28  6.806640      87.247.163.96              66.94.234.13              IP
Fragmented IP protocol (proto=ICMP 0x01, off=39960)

    29  6.831054      87.247.163.96              66.94.234.13              IP
Fragmented IP protocol (proto=ICMP 0x01, off=41440)

    30  6.850586      87.247.163.96              66.94.234.13              IP
Fragmented IP protocol (proto=ICMP 0x01, off=42920)

    31  6.899414      87.247.163.96              66.94.234.13              IP
Fragmented IP protocol (proto=ICMP 0x01, off=44400)
```

```
    32  6.915039       87.247.163.96              66.94.234.13            IP
Fragmented IP protocol (proto=ICMP 0x01, off=45880)

    33  6.939453       87.247.163.96              66.94.234.13            IP
Fragmented IP protocol (proto=ICMP 0x01, off=47360)

    34  6.958984       87.247.163.96              66.94.234.13            IP
Fragmented IP protocol (proto=ICMP 0x01, off=48840)

    35  6.983398       87.247.163.96              66.94.234.13            IP
Fragmented IP protocol (proto=ICMP 0x01, off=50320)

    36  7.023437       87.247.163.96              66.94.234.13            IP
Fragmented IP protocol (proto=ICMP 0x01, off=51800)

    37  7.046875       87.247.163.96              66.94.234.13            IP
Fragmented IP protocol (proto=ICMP 0x01, off=53280)

    38  7.067382       87.247.163.96              66.94.234.13            IP
Fragmented IP protocol (proto=ICMP 0x01, off=54760)

    39  7.090820       87.247.163.96              66.94.234.13            IP
Fragmented IP protocol (proto=ICMP 0x01, off=56240)

    40  7.130859       87.247.163.96              66.94.234.13            IP
Fragmented IP protocol (proto=ICMP 0x01, off=57720)

    41  7.151367       87.247.163.96              66.94.234.13            IP
Fragmented IP protocol (proto=ICMP 0x01, off=59200)

    42  7.174804       87.247.163.96              66.94.234.13            IP
Fragmented IP protocol (proto=ICMP 0x01, off=60680)

    43  7.199218       87.247.163.96              66.94.234.13            IP
Fragmented IP protocol (proto=ICMP 0x01, off=62160)

    44  7.214843       87.247.163.96              66.94.234.13            IP
Fragmented IP protocol (proto=ICMP 0x01, off=63640)

    45  7.258789       87.247.163.96              66.94.234.13            IP
Fragmented IP protocol (proto=ICMP 0x01, off=65120)
```

The first packet details:

```
    No.Time          Source                  Destination          Proto-
col Info

     1 0.000000     87.247.163.96            66.94.234.13            ICMP
Echo (ping) request
```

Frame 1 (1514 bytes on wire, 1514 bytes captured) Ethernet II, Src: OmronTat_00:00:00 (00:00:0a:00:00:00), Dst: 40:0f:20:00:0c:00 (40:0f:20:00:0c:00) Internet Protocol, Src: 87.247.163.96 (87.247.163.96), Dst: 66.94.234.13 (66.94.234.13) Internet Control Message Protocol

    Type: 8 (Echo (ping) request)

```
Code: 0

Checksum: 0x6b7d

Identifier: 0x0600

Sequence number: 0x0200

Data (1472 bytes)
```

```
The second packet details:
    No. Time          Source                 Destination         Proto-
col Info

    2 0.000000    87.247.163.96            66.94.234.13           IP
Fragmented IP protocol (proto=ICMP 0x01, off=1480)
```

```
Frame  2  (1514  bytes  on  wire,  1514  bytes  captured)  Ethernet  II,
Src:  OmronTat_00:00:00  (00:00:0a:00:00:00),  Dst:  40:0f:20:00:0c:00
(40:0f:20:00:0c:00)    Internet    Protocol,    Src:    87.247.163.96
(87.247.163.96), Dst: 66.94.234.13 (66.94.234.13) Data (1480 bytes)
```

Note that only the first fragment contains the ICMP header and all remaining fragments are generated without the ICMP header.

Two important points here:

- In some datalink protocols such as Ethernet, only the first fragment contains the full upper layer header, meaning that other fragments look like beheaded datagrams.

- Additional overhead imposed over network because all fragments contains their own IP header. Additional overhead = (number_of_fragments - 1) * (ip_header_len).

Exploits

IP fragment overlapped:

The IP fragment overlapped exploit occurs when two fragments contained within the same IP datagram have offsets that indicate that they overlap each other in positioning within the datagram. This could mean that either fragment A is being completely overwritten by fragment B, or that fragment A is partially being overwritten by fragment B. Some operating systems do not properly handle fragments that overlap in this manner and may throw exceptions or behave in other undesirable ways upon receipt of overlapping fragments. This is the basis for the teardrop attack. Overlapping fragments may also be used in an attempt to bypass Intrusion Detection Systems. In this exploit, part of an attack is sent in fragments along with additional random data; future fragments may overwrite the random data with the remainder of the attack. If the completed datagram is not properly reassembled at the IDS, the attack will go undetected.

IP fragmentation buffer full:

The IP fragmentation buffer full exploit occurs when there is an excessive amount of incomplete fragmented traffic detected on the protected network. This could be due to an excessive number of incomplete fragmented datagrams, a large number of fragments for individual datagrams or a combination of quantity of incomplete datagrams and size/number of fragments in each datagram. This type of traffic is most likely an attempt to bypass security measures or Intrusion Detection Systems by intentional fragmentation of attack activity.

IP fragment overrun:

The IP Fragment Overrun exploit is when a reassembled fragmented datagram exceeds the declared IP data length or the maximum datagram length. By definition, no IP datagram should be larger than 65,535 bytes. Systems that try to process these large datagrams can crash, and can be indicative of a denial of service attempt.

IP fragment too many datagrams:

The Too Many Datagrams exploit is identified by an excessive number of incomplete fragmented datagrams detected on the network. This is usually either a denial of service attack or an attempt to bypass security measures. An example of "Too Many Datagrams", "Incomplete Datagram" and "Fragment Too Small" is the Rose Attack.

IP fragment incomplete datagram:

This exploit occurs when a datagram can not be fully reassembled due to missing data. This can indicate a denial of service attack or an attempt to defeat packet filter security policies.

IP Fragment Too Small:

If an IP fragment is too small it indicates that the fragment is likely intentionally crafted. Any fragment other than the final fragment that is less than 400 bytes could be considered too small. Small fragments may be used in denial of service attacks or in an attempt to bypass security measures or detection.

Fragmentation for Evasion

Network infrastructure equipment such as routers, load-balancers, firewalls and IDS have inconsistent visibility into fragmented packets. For example, a device may subject the initial fragment to rigorous inspection and auditing, but might allow all additional fragments to pass unchecked. Some attacks may use this fact to evade detection by placing incriminating payload data in fragments. Devices operating in "full" proxy mode are generally not susceptible to this subterfuge.

VoIP Vulnerabilities

VoIP is vulnerable to similar types of attacks that Web connection and emails are prone to. VoIP attractiveness, because of its low fixed cost and numerous features, come with some risks that are well known to the developers an are constantly being addressed. But these risks are usually not mentioned to the business which is the most common target.

VoIP also allows the use of fraud and shady practices that most people are not aware of. And while this practices are restricted by most providers, the possibility that someone is using them for his own gain still exists.

Vulnerabilities

Remote Eavesdropping

Unencrypted connections lead to communication and security breaches. Hackers/trackers can eavesdrops on important or private conversations and extract valuable data. The overheard conversations might be sold to or used by competing businesses. The gathered intelligence can also be used as blackmail for personal gain.

Network Attacks

Attacks to the user network, or internet provider can disrupt or even cut the connection. Since VOIP is highly dependent on our internet connection, direct attacks on the internet connection, or provider, are highly effective way of attack. This kind of attacks are targeting office telephony, since mobile internet is harder to interrupt. Also mobile applications not relying on internet connection to make VOIP calls. are immune to such attacks.

Default Security Settings

Hardphones (a.k.a. VoIP phone) are smart devices, they are more a computer than a phone, and as such they need to be well configured. The Chinese manufacturers, in some cases are using default passwords for each of the manufactured devices leading to vulnerabilities.

VoIP over WiFi

VoIP even while VoIP is relatively secure in 2017, it still needs a source of internet, which in most cases is WIFI network. And while a home/office WIFI can be relatively secure, using public or shared networks will further compromise the connection.

VoIP Exploits

VoIP Spam

Voip has its own spam called SPIT (Spam over Internet Telephony). Using the unlimited extensions provided by VOIP PBX capabilities, the spammer can constantly harass his target from different numbers. The process is not hard to automate and can fill the targets voice mail with notifications. The caller can make calls often enough to block the target from getting important incoming calls. This practices can cost a lot to the caller and are rarely used for other than marketing needs.

VoIP Phishing

VOIP users can change their Caller ID (a.k.a. Caller ID spoofing), allowing caller to represent himself as relative, colleague, or part of the family, in order to extract information, money or benefits form the target.

Transport Layer Security

Transport Layer Security (TLS) – and its predecessor, Secure Sockets Layer (SSL), which is now prohibited from use by the Internet Engineering Task Force (IETF) – are cryptographic protocols that provide communications security over a computer network. Several versions of the protocols find widespread use in applications such as web browsing, email, Internet faxing, instant messaging, and voice over IP (VoIP). Websites are able to use TLS to secure all communications between their servers and web browsers.

The TLS protocol aims primarily to provide privacy and data integrity between two communicating computer applications. When secured by TLS, connections between a client and a server have one or more of the following properties:

- The connection is *private* (or *secure*) because symmetric cryptography is used to encrypt the data transmitted. The keys for this symmetric encryption are generated uniquely for each connection and are based on a shared secret negotiated at the start of the session. The server and client negotiate the details of which encryption algorithm and cryptographic keys to use before the first byte of data is transmitted. The negotiation of a shared secret is both secure (the negotiated secret is unavailable to eavesdroppers and cannot be obtained, even by an attacker who places themselves in the middle of the connection) and reliable (no attacker can modify the communications during the negotiation without being detected).

- The identity of the communicating parties can be *authenticated* using public-key cryptography. This authentication can be made optional, but is generally required for at least one of the parties (typically the server).

- The connection ensures *integrity* because each message transmitted includes a message integrity check using a message authentication code to prevent undetected loss or alteration of the data during transmission.

In addition to the properties above, careful configuration of TLS can provide additional privacy-related properties such as forward secrecy, ensuring that any future disclosure of encryption keys cannot be used to decrypt any TLS communications recorded in the past.

TLS supports many different methods for exchanging keys, encrypting data, and authenticating message integrity. As a result, secure configuration of TLS involves many configurable parameters, and not all choices provide all of the privacy-related properties described in the list above.

Attempts have been made to subvert aspects of the communications security that TLS seeks to provide and the protocol has been revised several times to address these security threats. Developers of web browsers have also revised their products to defend against potential security weaknesses after these were discovered.

The TLS protocol comprises two layers: the TLS record and the TLS handshake protocols.

TLS is a proposed Internet Engineering Task Force (IETF) standard, first defined in 1999 and updated in RFC 5246 (August 2008) and RFC 6176 (March 2011). It builds on the earlier SSL specifications (1994, 1995, 1996) developed by Netscape Communications for adding the HTTPS protocol to their Navigator web browser.

Description

Client-server applications use the TLS protocol to communicate across a network in a way designed to prevent eavesdropping and tampering.

Since applications can communicate either with or without TLS (or SSL), it is necessary for the client to indicate to the server the setup of a TLS connection. One of the main ways of achieving this is to use a different port number for TLS connections, for example port 443 for HTTPS. Another mechanism is for the client to make a protocol-specific request to the server to switch the connection to TLS; for example, by making a

STARTTLS request when using the mail and news protocols.

Once the client and server have agreed to use TLS, they negotiate a stateful connection by using a handshaking procedure. The protocols use a handshake with an asymmetric cipher to establish not only cipher settings but also a session-specific shared key with which further communication is encrypted using a symmetric cipher. During this handshake, the client and server agree on various parameters used to establish the connection's security:

- The handshake begins when a client connects to a TLS-enabled server requesting a secure connection and the client presents a list of supported cipher suites (ciphers and hash functions).

- From this list, the server picks a cipher and hash function that it also supports and notifies the client of the decision.

- The server usually then provides identification in the form of a digital certificate. The certificate contains the server name, the trusted certificate authority (CA) that vouches for the authenticity of the certificate, and the server's public encryption key.

- The client confirms the validity of the certificate before proceeding.

- To generate the session keys used for the secure connection, the client either:

  o Encrypts a random number with the server's public key and sends the result to the server (which only the server should be able to decrypt with its private key); both parties then use the random number to generate a unique session key for subsequent encryption and decryption of data during the session.

  o Uses Diffie–Hellman key exchange to securely generate a random and unique session key for encryption and decryption that has the additional property of forward secrecy: if the server's private key is disclosed in future, it cannot be used to decrypt the current session, even if the session is intercepted and recorded by a third party.

This concludes the handshake and begins the secured connection, which is encrypted and decrypted with the session key until the connection closes. If any one of the above steps fails, then the TLS handshake fails and the connection is not created.

TLS and SSL do not fit neatly into any single layer of the OSI model or the TCP/IP model. TLS runs "on top of some reliable transport protocol (e.g., TCP)," which would imply that it is above the transport layer. It serves encryption to higher layers, which is normally the function of the presentation layer. However, applications generally use TLS as if it were a transport layer, even though applications using TLS must actively control initiating TLS handshakes and handling of exchanged authentication certificates.

Digital Certificates

A digital certificate certifies the ownership of a public key by the named subject of the certificate, and indicates certain expected usages of that key. This allows others (relying parties) to rely upon signatures or on assertions made by the private key that corresponds to the certified public key.

Certificate Authorities

TLS typically relies on a set of trusted third-party certificate authorities to establish the authenticity of certificates. Trust is usually anchored in a list of certificates distributed with user agent software, and can be modified by the relying party.

According to Netcraft, who monitors active TLS certificates, the market-leading CA has been Symantec since the beginning of their survey (or VeriSign before the authentication services business unit was purchased by Symantec). Symantec currently accounts for just under a third of all certificates and 44% of the valid certificates used by the 1 million busiest websites, as counted by Netcraft.

As a consequence of choosing X.509 certificates, certificate authorities and a public key infrastructure are necessary to verify the relation between a certificate and its owner, as well as to generate, sign, and administer the validity of certificates. While this can be more convenient than verifying the identities via a web of trust, the 2013 mass surveillance disclosures made it more widely known that certificate authorities are a weak point from a security standpoint, allowing man-in-the-middle attacks (MITM).

Algorithm

Key Exchange or Key Agreement

Before a client and server can begin to exchange information protected by TLS, they must securely exchange or agree upon an encryption key and a cipher to use when encrypting data. Among the methods used for key exchange/agreement are: public and private keys generated with RSA (denoted TLS_RSA in the TLS handshake protocol), Diffie–Hellman (TLS_DH), ephemeral Diffie–Hellman (TLS_DHE), Elliptic Curve Diffie–Hellman (TLS_ECDH), ephemeral Elliptic Curve Diffie–Hellman (TLS_ECDHE), anonymous Diffie–Hellman (TLS_DH_anon), pre-shared key (TLS_PSK) and Secure Remote Password (TLS_SRP).

The TLS_DH_anon and TLS_ECDH_anon key agreement methods do not authenticate the server or the user and hence are rarely used because those are vulnerable to man-in-the-middle attack. Only TLS_DHE and TLS_ECDHE provide forward secrecy.

Public key certificates used during exchange/agreement also vary in the size of the public/private encryption keys used during the exchange and hence the robustness of the security provided. In July 2013, Google announced that it would no longer use 1024 bit public keys and would switch instead to 2048 bit keys to increase the security of the TLS encryption it provides to its users because the encryption strength is directly related to the key size.

Key exchange/agreement and authentication							
Algorithm	SSL 2.0	SSL 3.0	TLS 1.0	TLS 1.1	TLS 1.2	TLS 1.3 (Draft)	Status
RSA	Yes	Yes	Yes	Yes	Yes	No	
DH-RSA	No	Yes	Yes	Yes	Yes	No	
DHE-RSA (forward secrecy)	No	Yes	Yes	Yes	Yes	Yes	
ECDH-RSA	No	No	Yes	Yes	Yes	No	
ECDHE-RSA (forward secrecy)	No	No	Yes	Yes	Yes	Yes	
DH-DSS	No	Yes	Yes	Yes	Yes	No	
DHE-DSS (forward secrecy)	No	Yes	Yes	Yes	Yes	No	
ECDH-ECDSA	No	No	Yes	Yes	Yes	No	
ECDHE-ECDSA (forward secrecy)	No	No	Yes	Yes	Yes	Yes	
PSK	No	No	Yes	Yes	Yes		Defined for TLS 1.2 in RFCs
PSK-RSA	No	No	Yes	Yes	Yes		
DHE-PSK (forward secrecy)	No	No	Yes	Yes	Yes		
ECDHE-PSK (forward secrecy)	No	No	Yes	Yes	Yes		
SRP	No	No	Yes	Yes	Yes		
SRP-DSS	No	No	Yes	Yes	Yes		
SRP-RSA	No	No	Yes	Yes	Yes		
Kerberos	No	No	Yes	Yes	Yes		
DH-ANON (insecure)	No	Yes	Yes	Yes	Yes		
ECDH-ANON (insecure)	No	No	Yes	Yes	Yes		
GOST R 34.10-94 / 34.10-2001	No	No	Yes	Yes	Yes		Proposed in RFC drafts

Cipher

Cipher security against publicly known feasible attacks									
Cipher			**Protocol version**						**Status**
Type	**Algorithm**	**Nominal strength (bits)**	**SSL 2.0**	**SSL 3.0** [n 1][n 2][n 3][n 4]	**TLS 1.0** [n 1][n 3]	**TLS 1.1** [n 1]	**TLS 1.2** [n 1]	**TLS 1.3 (Draft)**	
Block cipher with mode of operation	AES GCM[n 5]	256, 128	N/A	N/A	N/A	N/A	Secure	Secure	Defined for TLS 1.2 in RFCs
	AES CCM[n 5]		N/A	N/A	N/A	N/A	Secure	Secure	
	AES CBC[n 6]		N/A	N/A	Depends on mitigations	Secure	Secure	N/A	
	Camellia GCM[n 5]	256, 128	N/A	N/A	N/A	N/A	Secure	Secure	
	Camellia CBC[n 6]		N/A	N/A	Depends on mitigations	Secure	Secure	N/A	
	ARIA GCM[n 5]	256, 128	N/A	N/A	N/A	N/A	Secure	Secure	
	ARIA CBC[n 6]		N/A	N/A	Depends on mitigations	Secure	Secure	N/A	
	SEED CBC[n 6]	128	N/A	N/A	Depends on mitigations	Secure	Secure	N/A	
	3DES EDE CBC[n 6][n 7]	112[n 8]	Insecure	Insecure	Insecure	Insecure	Insecure	N/A	
	GOST 28147-89 CNT[n 7]	256	N/A	N/A	Insecure	Insecure	Insecure		Defined in RFC 4357
	IDEA CBC[n 6][n 7][n 9]	128	Insecure	Insecure	Insecure	Insecure	N/A	N/A	Removed from TLS 1.2
	DES CBC[n 6][n 7][n 9]	056	Insecure	Insecure	Insecure	Insecure	N/A	N/A	
		040[n 10]	Insecure	Insecure	Insecure	N/A	N/A	N/A	Forbidden in TLS 1.1 and later
	RC2 CBC[n 6][n 7]	040[n 10]	Insecure	Insecure	Insecure	N/A	N/A	N/A	
Stream cipher	ChaCha20-Poly1305[n 5]	256	N/A	N/A	N/A	N/A	Secure	Secure	Defined for TLS 1.2 in RFCs
	RC4[n 11]	128	Insecure	Insecure	Insecure	Insecure	Insecure	N/A	Prohibited in all versions of TLS by RFC 7465
		040[n 10]	Insecure	Insecure	Insecure	N/A	N/A	N/A	
None	Null[n 12]	–	N/A	Insecure	Insecure	Insecure	Insecure	Insecure	Defined for TLS 1.2 in RFCs

Data Integrity

Message authentication code (MAC) is used for data integrity. HMAC is used for CBC mode of block ciphers and stream ciphers. AEAD is used for authenticated encryption such as GCM mode and CCM mode.

Data integrity							
Algorithm	SSL 2.0	SSL 3.0	TLS 1.0	TLS 1.1	TLS 1.2	TLS 1.3 (Draft)	Status
HMAC-MD5	Yes	Yes	Yes	Yes	Yes	No	Defined for TLS 1.2 in RFCs
HMAC-SHA1	No	Yes	Yes	Yes	Yes	No	
HMAC-SHA256/384	No	No	No	No	Yes	No	
AEAD	No	No	No	No	Yes	Yes	
GOST 28147-89 IMIT	No	No	Yes	Yes	Yes		Proposed in RFC drafts
GOST R 34.11-94	No	No	Yes	Yes	Yes		

Security

SSL 2.0

SSL 2.0 is flawed in a variety of ways:

- Identical cryptographic keys are used for message authentication and encryption. (In SSL 3.0, MAC secrets may be larger than encryption keys, so messages can remain tamper resistant even if encryption keys are broken.)

- SSL 2.0 has a weak MAC construction that uses the MD5 hash function with a secret prefix, making it vulnerable to length extension attacks.

- SSL 2.0 does not have any protection for the handshake, meaning a man-in-the-middle downgrade attack can go undetected.

- SSL 2.0 uses the TCP connection close to indicate the end of data. This means that truncation attacks are possible: the attacker simply forges a TCP FIN, leaving the recipient unaware of an illegitimate end of data message (SSL 3.0 fixes this problem by having an explicit closure alert).

- SSL 2.0 assumes a single service and a fixed domain certificate, which clashes with the standard feature of virtual hosting in Web servers. This means that most websites are practically impaired from using SSL.

SSL 2.0 is disabled by default, beginning with Internet Explorer 7, Mozilla Firefox 2, Opera 9.5, and Safari. After it sends a TLS "ClientHello", if Mozilla Firefox finds that the server is unable to complete the handshake, it will attempt to fall back to using SSL 3.0 with an SSL 3.0 "ClientHello" in SSL 2.0 format to maximize the likelihood of successfully handshaking with older servers. Support for SSL 2.0 (and weak 40-bit and 56-bit ciphers) has been removed completely from Opera as of version 10.

SSL 3.0

SSL 3.0 improved upon SSL 2.0 by adding SHA-1–based ciphers and support for certificate authentication.

From a security standpoint, SSL 3.0 should be considered less desirable than TLS 1.0. The SSL 3.0 cipher suites have a weaker key derivation process; half of the master key that is established is fully dependent on the MD5 hash function, which is not resistant to collisions and is, therefore, not considered secure. Under TLS 1.0, the master key that is established depends on both MD5 and SHA-1 so its derivation process is not currently considered weak. It is for this reason that SSL 3.0 implementations cannot be validated under FIPS 140-2.

In October 2014, the vulnerability in the design of SSL 3.0 was reported, which makes CBC mode of operation with SSL 3.0 vulnerable to the padding attack.

TLS

TLS has a variety of security measures:

- Protection against a downgrade of the protocol to a previous (less secure) version or a weaker cipher suite.

- Numbering subsequent Application records with a sequence number and using this sequence number in the message authentication codes (MACs).

- Using a message digest enhanced with a key (so only a key-holder can check the MAC). The HMAC construction used by most TLS cipher suites is specified in RFC 2104 (SSL 3.0 used a different hash-based MAC).

- The message that ends the handshake ("Finished") sends a hash of all the exchanged handshake messages seen by both parties.

- The pseudorandom function splits the input data in half and processes each one with a different hashing algorithm (MD5 and SHA-1), then XORs them together to create the MAC. This provides protection even if one of these algorithms is found to be vulnerable.

Attacks against TLS/SSL

Significant attacks against TLS/SSL are listed below:

Note: In February 2015, IETF issued an informational RFC summarizing the various known attacks against TLS/SSL.

Renegotiation Attack

A vulnerability of the renegotiation procedure was discovered in August 2009 that can lead to plaintext injection attacks against SSL 3.0 and all current versions of TLS. For example, it allows an attacker who can hijack an https connection to splice their own requests into the beginning of the conversation the client has with the web server. The attacker can't actually decrypt the client–server communication, so it is different from a typical man-in-the-middle attack. A short-term fix is for web servers to stop allowing renegotiation, which typically will not require other changes unless client certificate authentication is used. To fix the vulnerability, a renegotiation indication extension was proposed for TLS. It will require the client and server to include and verify information about previous handshakes in any renegotiation handshakes. This extension has become a proposed standard and has been assigned the number RFC 5746. The RFC has been implemented by several libraries.

Downgrade Attacks: FREAK Attack and Logjam Attack

A protocol downgrade attack (also called a version rollback attack) tricks a web server into negotiating connections with previous versions of TLS (such as SSLv2) that have long since been abandoned as insecure.

Previous modifications to the original protocols, like False Start (adopted and enabled by Google Chrome) or Snap Start, reportedly introduced limited TLS protocol downgrade attacks or allowed modifications to the cipher suite list sent by the client to the server. In doing so, an attacker might succeed in influencing the cipher suite selection in an attempt to downgrade the cipher suite negotiated to use either a weaker symmetric encryption algorithm or a weaker key exchange. A paper presented at an ACM conference on computer and communications security in 2012 demonstrated that the False Start extension was at risk: in certain circumstances it could allow an attacker to recover the encryption keys offline and to access the encrypted data.

Encryption downgrade attacks can force servers and clients to negotiate a connection using cryptographically weak keys. In 2014, a man-in-the-middle attack called FREAK was discovered affecting the OpenSSL stack, the default Android web browser, and some Safari browsers. The attack involved tricking servers into negotiating a TLS connection using cryptographically weak 512 bit encryption keys.

Logjam is a security exploit discovered in May 2015 that exploits the option of using legacy "export-grade" 512-bit Diffie–Hellman groups dating back to the 1990s. It forces susceptible servers to downgrade to cryptographically weak 512-bit Diffie–Hellman groups. An attacker can then deduce the keys the client and server determine using the Diffie–Hellman key exchange.

Cross-protocol Attacks: DROWN

The DROWN attack is an exploit that attacks servers supporting contemporary SSL/TLS protocol suites by exploiting their support for the obsolete, insecure, SSLv2 protocol to leverage an attack on connections using up-to-date protocols that would otherwise be secure. DROWN exploits a vulnerability in the protocols used and the configuration of the server, rather than any specific implementation error. Full details of

DROWN were announced in March 2016, together with a patch for the exploit. At that time, more than 81,000 of the top 1 million most popular websites were among the TLS protected websites that were vulnerable to the DROWN attack.

BEAST Attack

On September 23, 2011 researchers Thai Duong and Juliano Rizzo demonstrated a proof of concept called BEAST (Browser Exploit Against SSL/TLS) using a Java applet to violate same origin policy constraints, for a long-known cipher block chaining (CBC) vulnerability in TLS 1.0: an attacker observing 2 consecutive ciphertext blocks C_0, C_1 can test if the plaintext block P_1 is equal to x by choosing the next plaintext block $P_2 = x \wedge C_0 \wedge C_1$; due to how CBC works C_2 will be equal to C_1 if $x = P_1$. Practical exploits had not been previously demonstrated for this vulnerability, which was originally discovered by Phillip Rogaway in 2002. The vulnerability of the attack had been fixed with TLS 1.1 in 2006, but TLS 1.1 had not seen wide adoption prior to this attack demonstration.

RC4 as a stream cipher is immune to BEAST attack. Therefore, RC4 was widely used as a way to mitigate BEAST attack on the server side. However, in 2013, researchers found more weaknesses in RC4. Thereafter enabling RC4 on server side was no longer recommended.

Chrome and Firefox themselves are not vulnerable to BEAST attack, however, Mozilla updated their NSS libraries to mitigate BEAST-like attacks. NSS is used by Mozilla Firefox and Google Chrome to implement SSL. Some web servers that have a broken implementation of the SSL specification may stop working as a result.

Microsoft released Security Bulletin MS12-006 on January 10, 2012, which fixed the BEAST vulnerability by changing the way that the Windows Secure Channel (SChannel) component transmits encrypted network packets from the server end. Users of Internet Explorer (prior to version 11) that run on older versions of Windows (Windows 7, Windows 8 and Windows Server 2008 R2) can restrict use of TLS to 1.1 or higher.

Apple fixed BEAST vulnerability by implementing 1/n-1 split and turning it on by default in OS X Mavericks, released on October 22, 2013.

CRIME and BREACH Attacks

The authors of the BEAST attack are also the creators of the later CRIME attack, which can allow an attacker to recover the content of web cookies when data compression is used along with TLS. When used to recover the content of secret authentication cookies, it allows an attacker to perform session hijacking on an authenticated web session.

While the CRIME attack was presented as a general attack that could work effectively against a large number of protocols, including but not limited to TLS, and application-layer protocols such as SPDY or HTTP, only exploits against TLS and SPDY were demonstrated and largely mitigated in browsers and servers. The CRIME exploit against HTTP compression has not been mitigated at all, even though the authors of CRIME have warned that this vulnerability might be even more widespread than SPDY and TLS compression combined. In 2013 a new instance of the CRIME attack against HTTP compression, dubbed BREACH, was announced. Based on the CRIME attack a BREACH attack can extract login tokens, email addresses or other sensitive information from TLS encrypted web traffic in as little as 30 seconds (depending on the number of bytes to be extracted), provided the attacker tricks the victim into visiting a malicious web link or is able to inject content into valid pages the user is visiting (ex: a wireless network under the control of the attacker). All versions of TLS and SSL are at risk from BREACH regardless of the encryption algorithm or cipher used. Unlike previous instances of CRIME, which can be successfully defended against by turning off TLS compression or SPDY header compression, BREACH exploits HTTP compression which cannot realistically be turned off, as virtually all web servers rely upon it to improve data transmission speeds for users. This is a known limitation of TLS as it is susceptible to chosen-plaintext attack against the application-layer data it was meant to protect.

Timing Attacks on Padding

Earlier TLS versions were vulnerable against the padding oracle attack discovered in 2002. A novel variant, called the Lucky Thirteen attack, was published in 2013.

Some experts also recommended avoiding Triple-DES CBC. Since the last supported ciphers developed to support any program using Windows XP's SSL/TLS library like Internet Explorer on Windows XP are RC4 and Triple-DES, and since RC4 is now deprecated, this makes it difficult to support any version of SSL for any program using this library on XP.

A fix was released as the Encrypt-then-MAC extension to the TLS specification, released as RFC 7366. The Lucky Thirteen attack can be mitigated in TLS 1.2 by using only AES_GCM ciphers; AES_CBC remains vulnerable.

POODLE Attack

On October 14, 2014, Google researchers published a vulnerability in the design of SSL 3.0, which makes CBC mode of operation with SSL 3.0 vulnerable to a padding attack (CVE-2014-3566). They named this attack POODLE (Padding Oracle On Downgraded Legacy Encryption). On average, attackers only need to make 256 SSL 3.0 requests to reveal one byte of encrypted messages.

Although this vulnerability only exists in SSL 3.0 and most clients and servers support TLS 1.0 and above, all major browsers voluntarily downgrade to SSL 3.0 if the handshakes with newer versions of TLS fail unless they provide the option for a user or administrator to disable SSL 3.0 and the user or administrator does so. Therefore, the man-in-the-middle can first conduct a version rollback attack and then exploit this vulnerability.

In general, graceful security degradation for the sake of interoperability is difficult to carry out in a way that cannot be exploited. This is challenging especially in domains where fragmentation is high.

On December 8, 2014, a variant of POODLE was announced that impacts TLS implementations that do not properly enforce padding byte requirements.

RC4 Attacks

Despite the existence of attacks on RC4 that broke its security, cipher suites in SSL and TLS that were based on RC4 were still considered secure prior to 2013 based on the way in which they were used in SSL and TLS. In 2011, the RC4 suite was actually recommended as a work around for the BEAST attack. New forms of attack disclosed in March 2013 conclusively demonstrated the feasibility of breaking RC4 in TLS, suggesting it was not a good workaround for BEAST. An attack scenario was proposed by AlFardan, Bernstein, Paterson, Poettering and Schuldt that used newly discovered statistical biases in the RC4 key table to recover parts of the plaintext with a large number of TLS encryptions. An attack on RC4 in TLS and SSL that requires 13×2^{20} encryptions to break RC4 was unveiled on 8 July 2013 and later described as "feasible" in the accompanying presentation at a USENIX Security Symposium in August 2013. In July 2015, subsequent improvements in the attack make it increasingly practical to defeat the security of RC4-encrypted TLS.

As many modern browsers have been designed to defeat BEAST attacks (except Safari for Mac OS X 10.7 or earlier, for iOS 6 or earlier, and for Windows), RC4 is no longer a good choice for TLS 1.0. The CBC ciphers which were affected by the BEAST attack in the past have become a more popular choice for protection. Mozilla and Microsoft recommend disabling RC4 where possible. RFC 7465 prohibits the use of RC4 cipher suites in all versions of TLS.

On September 1, 2015, Microsoft, Google and Mozilla announced that RC4 cipher suites would be disabled by default in their browsers (Microsoft Edge, Internet Explorer 11 on Windows 7/8.1/10, Firefox, and Chrome) in early 2016.

Truncation Attack

A TLS (logout) truncation attack blocks a victim's account logout requests so that the user unknowingly remains logged into a web service. When the request to sign out is sent, the attacker injects an unencrypted TCP FIN message (no more data from sender) to close the connection. The server therefore doesn't receive the logout request and is unaware of the abnormal termination.

Published in July 2013, the attack causes web services such as Gmail and Hotmail to display a page that informs the user that they have successfully signed-out, while ensuring that the user's browser maintains authorization with the service, allowing an attacker with subsequent access to the browser to access and take over control of the user's logged-in account. The attack does not rely on installing malware on the victim's computer; attackers need only place themselves between the victim and the web server (e.g., by setting up a rogue wireless hotspot). This vulnerability also requires access to the victim's computer. Another possibility is when using FTP the data connection can have a false FIN in the data stream, and if the protocol rules for exchanging close_notify alerts is not adhered to a file can be truncated.

Unholy PAC Attack

This attack, discovered in mid-2016, exploits weaknesses in the Web Proxy Autodiscovery Protocol (WPAD) to expose the URL that a web user is attempting to reach via a TLS-enabled web link. Disclosure of a URL can violate a user's privacy, not only because of the website accessed, but also because URLs are sometimes used to authenticate users. Document sharing services, such as those offered by Google and Dropbox, also work by sending a user a security token that's included in the URL. An attacker who obtains such URLs may be able to gain full access to a victim's account or data.

The exploit works against almost all browsers and operating systems.

Sweet32 Attack

The Sweet32 attack breaks all 64-bit block ciphers used in CBC mode as used in TLS by exploiting a birthday attack and either a man-in-the-middle attack or injection of a malicious JavaScript into a web page. The purpose of the man-in-the-middle attack or the JavaScript injection is to allow the attacker to capture enough traffic to mount a birthday attack.

Implementation Errors: Heartbleed Bug, BERserk Attack, Cloudflare Bug

The Heartbleed bug is a serious vulnerability specific to the implementation of SSL/TLS in the popular OpenSSL cryptographic software library, affecting versions 1.0.1 to 1.0.1f. This weakness, reported in April 2014, allows attackers to steal private keys from servers that should normally be protected. The Heartbleed bug allows anyone on the Internet to read the memory of the systems protected by the vulnerable versions of the OpenSSL software. This compromises the secret private keys associated with the public certificates used to identify the service providers and to encrypt the traffic, the names and passwords of the users and the actual content. This allows attackers to eavesdrop on communications, steal data directly from the services and users and to impersonate services and users. The vulnerability is caused by a buffer over-read bug in the OpenSSL software, rather than a defect in the SSL or TLS protocol specification.

In September 2014, a variant of Daniel Bleichenbacher's PKCS#1 v1.5 RSA Signature Forgery vulnerability was announced by Intel Security Advanced Threat Research. This attack, dubbed BERserk, is a result of incomplete ASN.1 length decoding of public key signatures in some SSL implementations, and allows a man-in-the-middle attack by forging a public key signature.

In February 2015, after media reported the hidden pre-installation of Superfish adware on some Lenovo notebooks, a researcher found a trusted root certificate on affected Lenovo machines to be insecure, as the keys could easily be accessed using the company name, Komodia, as a passphrase. The Komodia library was designed to intercept client-side TLS/SSL traffic for parental control and surveillance, but it was also used in numerous adware programs, including Superfish, that were often surreptitiously installed unbeknownst to the computer user. In turn, these potentially unwanted programs installed the corrupt root certificate, allowing attackers to completely control web traffic and confirm false websites as authentic.

In May 2016, it was reported that dozens of Danish HTTPS-protected websites belonging to Visa Inc. were vulnerable to attacks allowing hackers to inject malicious code and forged content into the browsers of visitors. The attacks worked because the TLS implementation used on the affected servers incorrectly reused random numbers (nonces) that are intended be used only once, ensuring that each TLS handshake is unique.

In February 2017, an implementation error caused by a single mistyped character in code used to parse HTML created a buffer overflow error on Cloudflare servers. Similar in its effects to the Heartbleed bug discovered in 2014, this overflow error, widely known as Cloudbleed, allowed unauthorized third parties to read data in the memory of programs running on the servers—data that should otherwise have been protected by TLS.

Survey of Websites Vulnerable to Attacks

As of October 2016, Trustworthy Internet Movement estimate the ratio of websites that are vulnerable to TLS attacks.

Survey of the TLS vulnerabilities of the most popular websites				
Attacks	Security			
	Insecure	Depends	Secure	Other
Renegotiation attack	1.2% (−0.1%) support insecure renegotiation	0.4% (±0.0%) support both	96.2% (+0.1%) support secure renegotiation	2.2% (±0.0%) no support

	<0.1% (±0.0%) support only RC4 suites	6.0% (−0.3%) support RC4 suites used with modern browsers	28.5% (−0.7%) support some RC4 suites	65.5% (+1.0%) no support	N/A
RC4 attacks					
CRIME attack	2.4% (−0.1%) vulnerable		N/A	N/A	N/A
Heartbleed	0.1% (±0.0%) vulnerable		N/A	N/A	N/A
ChangeCipherSpec injection attack	0.8% (±0.0%) vulnerable and exploitable		4.7% (−0.2%) vulnerable, not exploit- able	92.6% (+0.4%) not vulnerable	1.9% (+0.1%) un- known
POODLE attack against TLS (Original POODLE against SSL 3.0 is not included)	2.1% (−0.1%) vulnerable and exploitable		N/A	97.1% (+0.2%) not vulnerable	0.8% (−0.1%) un- known
Protocol downgrade	23.2% (−0.4%) TLS_FALLBACK_SCSV not supported		N/A	67.6% (+0.7%) TLS_FALLBACK_ SCSV supported	9.1% (−0.4%) un- known

Forward Secrecy

Forward secrecy is a property of cryptographic systems which ensures that a session key derived from a set of public and private keys will not be compromised if one of the private keys is compromised in the future. Without forward secrecy, if the server's private key is compromised, not only will all future TLS-encrypted sessions using that server certificate be compromised, but also any past sessions that used it as well (provided of course that these past sessions were intercepted and stored at the time of transmission). An implementation of TLS can provide forward secrecy by requiring the use of ephemeral Diffie–Hellman key exchange to establish session keys, and some notable TLS implementations do so exclusively: e.g., Gmail and other Google HTTPS services that use OpenSSL. However, many clients and servers supporting TLS (including browsers and web servers) are not configured to implement such restrictions. In practice, unless a web service uses Diffie–Hellman key exchange to implement forward secrecy, all of the encrypted web traffic to and from that service can be decrypted by a third party if it obtains the server's master (private) key; e.g., by means of a court order.

Even where Diffie–Hellman key exchange is implemented, server-side session management mechanisms can impact forward secrecy. The use of TLS session tickets (a TLS extension) causes the session to be protected by AES128-CBC-SHA256 regardless of any other negotiated TLS parameters, including forward secrecy ciphersuites, and the long-lived TLS session ticket keys defeat the attempt to implement forward secrecy.

Stanford University research in 2014 also found that of 473,802 TLS servers surveyed, 82.9% of the servers deploying ephemeral Diffie–Hellman (DHE) key exchange to support forward secrecy were using weak Diffie–Hellman parameters. These weak parameter choices could potentially compromise the effectiveness of the forward secrecy that the servers sought to provide.

Since late 2011, Google has provided forward secrecy with TLS by default to users of its Gmail service, along with Google Docs and encrypted search among other services. Since November 2013, Twitter has provided forward secrecy with TLS to users of its service. As of June 2016, 51.9% of TLS-enabled websites are configured to use cipher suites that provide forward secrecy to modern web browsers.

Dealing with Man-in-the-middle Attacks

Certificate Pinning

One way to detect and block many kinds of man-in-the-middle attacks is "certificate pinning", sometimes called "SSL pinning", but more accurately called "public key pinning". A client that does key pinning adds an extra step beyond the normal X.509 certificate validation: After obtaining the server's certificate in the standard way, the client checks the public key(s) in the server's certificate chain against a set of (hashes of) public keys for the server name. Typically the public key hashes are bundled with the application. For example, Google Chrome includes public key hashes for the *.google.com certificate that detected fraudulent certificates in 2011. (Chromium does not enforce the hardcoded key pins.) Since then, Mozilla has introduced public key pinning to its Firefox browser.

In other systems the client hopes that the first time it obtains a server's certificate it is trustworthy and stores it; during later sessions with that server, the client checks the server's certificate against the stored certificate to guard against later MITM attacks.

Perspectives Project

The Perspectives Project operates network notaries that clients can use to detect if a site's certificate has changed. By their nature, man-in-the-middle attacks place the attacker between the destination and a single specific target. As such, Perspectives would warn the target that the certificate delivered to the web browser does not match the certificate seen from other perspectives – the perspectives of other users in different times and places. Use of network notaries from a multitude of perspectives makes it possible for a target to detect an attack even if a certificate appears to be completely valid. Other projects, such as the EFF's SSL Observatory, also make use of notaries or similar reporters in discovering man-in-the-middle attacks.

DNSChain

DNSChain relies on the security that blockchains provide to distribute public keys. It uses one pin to secure the connection to the DNSChain server itself, after which all other public keys (that are stored in a block chain) become accessible over a secure channel.

Protocol Details

The TLS protocol exchanges *records*—which encapsulate the data to be exchanged in a specific format. Each record can be compressed, padded, appended with a message authentication code (MAC), or encrypted, all depending on the state of the connection. Each record has a *content type* field that designates the type of data encapsulated, a length field and a TLS version field. The data encapsulated may be control or procedural messages of the TLS itself, or simply the application data needed to be transferred by TLS. The specifications (cipher suite, keys etc.) required to exchange application data by TLS, are agreed upon in the "TLS handshake" between the client requesting the data and the server responding to requests. The protocol therefore defines both the structure of payloads transferred in TLS and the procedure to establish and monitor the transfer.

TLS Handshake

When the connection starts, the record encapsulates a "control" protocol—the handshake messaging protocol (*content type* 22). This protocol is used to exchange all the information required by both sides for the exchange of the actual application data by TLS. It defines the format of messages and the order of their exchange. These may vary according to the demands of the client and server—i.e., there are several possible procedures to set up the connection. This initial exchange results in a successful TLS connection (both parties ready to transfer application data with TLS) or an alert message.

Basic TLS Handshake

A typical connection example follows, illustrating a handshake where the server (but not the client) is authenticated by its certificate:

1. Negotiation phase:

    o A client sends a ClientHello message specifying the highest TLS protocol version it supports, a random number, a list of suggested cipher suites and suggested compression methods. If the client is attempting to perform a resumed handshake, it may send a *session ID*. If the client can use Application-Layer Protocol Negotiation, it may include a list of supported application protocols, such as HTTP/2.

    o The server responds with a ServerHello message, containing the chosen protocol version, a random number, CipherSuite and compression method from the choices offered by the client. To confirm or allow resumed handshakes the server may send a *session ID*. The chosen protocol version should be the highest that both the client and server support. For example, if the client supports TLS version 1.1 and the server supports version 1.2, version 1.1 should be selected; version 1.2 should not be selected.

o   The server sends its Certificate message (depending on the selected cipher suite, this may be omitted by the server).

o   The server sends its ServerKeyExchange message (depending on the selected cipher suite, this may be omitted by the server). This message is sent for all DHE and DH_anon ciphersuites.

o   The server sends a ServerHelloDone message, indicating it is done with handshake negotiation.

o   The client responds with a ClientKeyExchange message, which may contain a *PreMasterSecret*, public key, or nothing. (Again, this depends on the selected cipher.) This *PreMasterSecret* is encrypted using the public key of the server certificate.

o   The client and server then use the random numbers and *PreMasterSecret* to compute a common secret, called the "master secret". All other key data for this connection is derived from this master secret (and the client- and server-generated random values), which is passed through a carefully designed pseudorandom function.

2.   The client now sends a ChangeCipherSpec record, essentially telling the server, "Everything I tell you from now on will be authenticated (and encrypted if encryption parameters were present in the server certificate)." The ChangeCipherSpec is itself a record-level protocol with content type of 20.

o   Finally, the client sends an authenticated and encrypted Finished message, containing a hash and MAC over the previous handshake messages.

o   The server will attempt to decrypt the client's *Finished* message and verify the hash and MAC. If the decryption or verification fails, the handshake is considered to have failed and the connection should be torn down.

3.   Finally, the server sends a ChangeCipherSpec, telling the client, "Everything I tell you from now on will be authenticated (and encrypted, if encryption was negotiated)."

o   The server sends its authenticated and encrypted Finished message.

o   The client performs the same decryption and verification procedure as the server did in the previous step.

4. Application phase: at this point, the "handshake" is complete and the application protocol is enabled, with content type of 23. Application messages exchanged between client and server will also be authenticated and optionally encrypted exactly like in their *Finished* message. Otherwise, the content type will return 25 and the client will not authenticate.

Client-authenticated TLS Handshake

The following *full* example shows a client being authenticated (in addition to the server as in the example above) via TLS using certificates exchanged between both peers.

1. Negotiation Phase:

   o A client sends a ClientHello message specifying the highest TLS protocol version it supports, a random number, a list of suggested cipher suites and compression methods.

   o The server responds with a ServerHello message, containing the chosen protocol version, a random number, cipher suite and compression method from the choices offered by the client. The server may also send a *session id* as part of the message to perform a resumed handshake.

   o The server sends its Certificate message (depending on the selected cipher suite, this may be omitted by the server).

   o The server sends its ServerKeyExchange message (depending on the selected cipher suite, this may be omitted by the server). This message is sent for all DHE and DH_anon ciphersuites.

   o The server requests a certificate from the client, so that the connection can be mutually authenticated, using a CertificateRequest message.

   o The server sends a ServerHelloDone message, indicating it is done with handshake negotiation.

   o The client responds with a Certificate message, which contains the client's certificate.

   o The client sends a ClientKeyExchange message, which may contain a *PreMasterSecret*, public key, or nothing. (Again, this depends on the selected cipher.) This *PreMasterSecret* is encrypted using the public key of the server certificate.

   o The client sends a CertificateVerify message, which is a signature over the previous handshake messages using the client's certificate's private key. This signature can be verified by using the client's certificate's public key.

This lets the server know that the client has access to the private key of the certificate and thus owns the certificate.

- o The client and server then use the random numbers and *PreMasterSecret* to compute a common secret, called the "master secret". All other key data for this connection is derived from this master secret (and the client- and server-generated random values), which is passed through a carefully designed pseudorandom function.

2. The client now sends a ChangeCipherSpec record, essentially telling the server, "Everything I tell you from now on will be authenticated (and encrypted if encryption was negotiated). " The ChangeCipherSpec is itself a record-level protocol and has type 20 and not 22.

- o Finally, the client sends an encrypted Finished message, containing a hash and MAC over the previous handshake messages.

- o The server will attempt to decrypt the client's *Finished* message and verify the hash and MAC. If the decryption or verification fails, the handshake is considered to have failed and the connection should be torn down.

3. Finally, the server sends a ChangeCipherSpec, telling the client, "Everything I tell you from now on will be authenticated (and encrypted if encryption was negotiated)."

- o The server sends its own encrypted Finished message.

- o The client performs the same decryption and verification procedure as the server did in the previous step.

4. Application phase: at this point, the "handshake" is complete and the application protocol is enabled, with content type of 23. Application messages exchanged between client and server will also be encrypted exactly like in their *Finished* message.

Resumed TLS Handshake

Public key operations (e.g., RSA) are relatively expensive in terms of computational power. TLS provides a secure shortcut in the handshake mechanism to avoid these operations: resumed sessions. Resumed sessions are implemented using session IDs or session tickets.

Apart from the performance benefit, resumed sessions can also be used for single sign-on, as it guarantees that both the original session and any resumed session originate from the same client. This is of particular importance for the FTP over TLS/SSL protocol, which would otherwise suffer from a man-in-the-middle attack in which an attacker could intercept the contents of the secondary data connections.

Session IDs

In an ordinary *full* handshake, the server sends a *session id* as part of the ServerHello message. The client associates this *session id* with the server's IP address and TCP port, so that when the client connects again to that server, it can use the *session id* to shortcut the handshake. In the server, the *session id* maps to the cryptographic parameters previously negotiated, specifically the "master secret". Both sides must have the same "master secret" or the resumed handshake will fail (this prevents an eavesdropper from using a *session id*). The random data in the ClientHello and ServerHello messages virtually guarantee that the generated connection keys will be different from in the previous connection. In the RFCs, this type of handshake is called an *abbreviated* handshake. It is also described in the literature as a *restart* handshake.

1. Negotiation phase:

   ○ A client sends a ClientHello message specifying the highest TLS protocol version it supports, a random number, a list of suggested cipher suites and compression methods. Included in the message is the *session id* from the previous TLS connection.

   ○ The server responds with a ServerHello message, containing the chosen protocol version, a random number, cipher suite and compression method from the choices offered by the client. If the server recognizes the *session id* sent by the client, it responds with the same *session id*. The client uses this to recognize that a resumed handshake is being performed. If the server does not recognize the *session id* sent by the client, it sends a different value for its *session id*. This tells the client that a resumed handshake will not be performed. At this point, both the client and server have the "master secret" and random data to generate the key data to be used for this connection.

2. The server now sends a ChangeCipherSpec record, essentially telling the client, "Everything I tell you from now on will be encrypted." The ChangeCipherSpec is itself a record-level protocol and has type 20 and not 22.

   ○ Finally, the server sends an encrypted Finished message, containing a hash and MAC over the previous handshake messages.

   ○ The client will attempt to decrypt the server's *Finished* message and verify the hash and MAC. If the decryption or verification fails, the handshake is considered to have failed and the connection should be torn down.

3. Finally, the client sends a ChangeCipherSpec, telling the server, "Everything I tell you from now on will be encrypted."

   ○ The client sends its own encrypted Finished message.

- The server performs the same decryption and verification procedure as the client did in the previous step.

4. Application phase: at this point, the "handshake" is complete and the application protocol is enabled, with content type of 23. Application messages exchanged between client and server will also be encrypted exactly like in their *Finished* message.

Session Tickets

RFC 5077 extends TLS via use of session tickets, instead of session IDs. It defines a way to resume a TLS session without requiring that session-specific state is stored at the TLS server.

When using session tickets, the TLS server stores its session-specific state in a session ticket and sends the session ticket to the TLS client for storing. The client resumes a TLS session by sending the session ticket to the server, and the server resumes the TLS session according to the session-specific state in the ticket. The session ticket is encrypted and authenticated by the server, and the server verifies its validity before using its contents.

One particular weakness of this method with OpenSSL is that it always limits encryption and authentication security of the transmitted TLS session ticket to AES128-CBC-SHA256, no matter what other TLS parameters were negotiated for the actual TLS session. This means that the state information (the TLS session ticket) is not as well protected as the TLS session itself. Of particular concern is OpenSSL's storage of the keys in an application-wide context (SSL_CTX), i.e. for the life of the application, and not allowing for re-keying of the AES128-CBC-SHA256 TLS session tickets without resetting the application-wide OpenSSL context (which is uncommon, error-prone and often requires manual administrative intervention).

TLS Record

This is the general format of all TLS records.

+	Byte +0	Byte +1	Byte +2	Byte +3
Byte 0	Content type			
Bytes 1..4	Version		Length	
	(Major)	*(Minor)*	*(bits 15..8)*	*(bits 7..0)*
Bytes 5..(m−1)	Protocol message(s)			
Bytes m..(p−1)	MAC (optional)			
Bytes p..(q−1)	Padding (block ciphers only)			

Content type:

This field identifies the Record Layer Protocol Type contained in this Record.

Content types		
Hex	Dec	Type
0x14	20	ChangeCipherSpec
0x15	21	Alert
0x16	22	Handshake
0x17	23	Application
0x18	24	Heartbeat

Legacy Version:

This field identifies the major and minor version of TLS for the contained message. For a ClientHello message, this need not be the *highest* version supported by the client.

Versions		
Major version	Minor version	Version type
3	0	SSL 3.0
3	1	TLS 1.0
3	2	TLS 1.1
3	3	TLS 1.2

Length:

The length of "protocol message(s)", "MAC" and "padding" fields combined (i.e. $q-5$), not to exceed 2^{14} bytes (16 KiB).

Protocol message(s):

One or more messages identified by the Protocol field. Note that this field may be encrypted depending on the state of the connection.

MAC and padding:

A message authentication code computed over the "protocol message(s)" field, with additional key material included. Note that this field may be encrypted, or not included entirely, depending on the state of the connection.

No "MAC" or "padding" fields can be present at end of TLS records before all cipher algorithms and parameters have been negotiated and handshaked and then confirmed by sending a CipherStateChange record for signalling that these parameters will take effect in all further records sent by the same peer.

Handshake Protocol

Most messages exchanged during the setup of the TLS session are based on this record, unless an error or warning occurs and needs to be signaled by an Alert protocol record, or the encryption mode of the session is modified by another record.

+	Byte +0	Byte +1	Byte +2	Byte +3
Byte 0	22			
Bytes 1..4	Version		Length	
	(Major)	*(Minor)*	*(bits 15..8)*	*(bits 7..0)*
Bytes 5..8	Message type	Handshake message data length		
		(bits 23..16)	*(bits 15..8)*	*(bits 7..0)*
Bytes 9..(n−1)	Handshake message data			
Bytes n..(n+3)	Message type	Handshake message data length		
		(bits 23..16)	*(bits 15..8)*	*(bits 7..0)*
Bytes (n+4)..	Handshake message data			

Message type:

    This field identifies the handshake message type.

Message types	
Code	Description
0	HelloRequest
1	ClientHello
2	ServerHello
4	NewSessionTicket
11	Certificate
12	ServerKeyExchange
13	CertificateRequest
14	ServerHelloDone
15	CertificateVerify
16	ClientKeyExchange
20	Finished

Handshake message data length:

    This is a 3-byte field indicating the length of the handshake data, not including the header.

Note that multiple handshake messages may be combined within one record.

Alert Protocol

This record should normally not be sent during normal handshaking or application exchanges. However, this message can be sent at any time during the handshake and up to the closure of the session. If this is used to signal a fatal error, the session will be closed immediately after sending this record, so this record is used to give a reason for this closure. If the alert level is flagged as a warning, the remote can decide to close the session if it decides that the session is not reliable enough for its needs (before doing so, the remote may also send its own signal).

+	Byte +0	Byte +1	Byte +2	Byte +3
Byte 0	21			
Bytes 1..4	Version		Length	
	(Major)	*(Minor)*	0	2
Bytes 5..6	Level	Description		
Bytes 7..(p−1)	MAC (optional)			
Bytes p..(q−1)	Padding (block ciphers only)			

Level:

> This field identifies the level of alert. If the level is fatal, the sender should close the session immediately. Otherwise, the recipient may decide to terminate the session itself, by sending its own fatal alert and closing the session itself immediately after sending it. The use of Alert records is optional, however if it is missing before the session closure, the session may be resumed automatically (with its handshakes).

> Normal closure of a session after termination of the transported application should preferably be alerted with at least the *Close notify* Alert type (with a simple warning level) to prevent such automatic resume of a new session. Signalling explicitly the normal closure of a secure session before effectively closing its transport layer is useful to prevent or detect attacks (like attempts to truncate the securely transported data, if it intrinsically does not have a predetermined length or duration that the recipient of the secured data may expect).

Alert level types		
Code	Level type	Connection state
1	warning	connection or security may be unstable.
2	fatal	connection or security may be compromised, or an unrecoverable error has occurred.

Description:

This field identifies which type of alert is being sent.

Alert description types			
Code	Description	Level types	Note
0	Close notify	warning/fatal	
10	Unexpected message	fatal	
20	Bad record MAC	fatal	Possibly a bad SSL implementation, or payload has been tampered with e.g. FTP firewall rule on FTPS server.
21	Decryption failed	fatal	TLS only, reserved
22	Record overflow	fatal	TLS only
30	Decompression failure	fatal	
40	Handshake failure	fatal	
41	No certificate	warning/fatal	SSL 3.0 only, reserved
42	Bad certificate	warning/fatal	
43	Unsupported certificate	warning/fatal	e.g. certificate has only Server authentication usage enabled and is presented as a client certificate
44	Certificate revoked	warning/fatal	
45	Certificate expired	warning/fatal	Check server certificate expire also check no certificate in the chain presented has expired
46	Certificate unknown	warning/fatal	
47	Illegal parameter	fatal	
48	Unknown CA (Certificate authority)	fatal	TLS only
49	Access denied	fatal	TLS only – e.g. no client certificate has been presented (TLS: Blank certificate message or SSLv3: No Certificate alert), but server is configured to require one.
50	Decode error	fatal	TLS only
51	Decrypt error	warning/fatal	TLS only
60	Export restriction	fatal	TLS only, reserved
70	Protocol version	fatal	TLS only
71	Insufficient security	fatal	TLS only
80	Internal error	fatal	TLS only
86	Inappropriate Fallback	fatal	TLS only
90	User canceled	fatal	TLS only
100	No renegotiation	warning	TLS only
110	Unsupported extension	warning	TLS only
111	Certificate unobtainable	warning	TLS only
112	Unrecognized name	warning/fatal	TLS only; client's Server Name Indicator specified a hostname not supported by the server

113	Bad certificate status response	fatal	TLS only
114	Bad certificate hash value	fatal	TLS only
115	Unknown PSK identity (used in TLS-PSK and TLS-SRP)	fatal	TLS only
120	No Application Protocol	fatal	TLS only, client's ALPN did not contain any server-supported protocols

Change Cipher Spec protocol

+	Byte +0	Byte +1	Byte +2	Byte +3
Byte 0	20			
Bytes 1..4	Version		Length	
	(Major)	*(Minor)*	0	1
Byte 5	CCS protocol type			

CCS protocol type:

> Currently only 1.

Application protocol

+	Byte +0	Byte +1	Byte +2	Byte +3
Byte 0	23			
Bytes 1..4	Version		Length	
	(Major)	*(Minor)*	*(bits 15..8)*	*(bits 7..0)*
Bytes 5..(m−1)	Application data			
Bytes m..(p−1)	MAC (optional)			
Bytes p..(q−1)	Padding (block ciphers only)			

Length:

> Length of application data (excluding the protocol header and including the MAC and padding trailers).

MAC:

> 20 bytes for the SHA-1-based HMAC, 16 bytes for the MD5-based HMAC.

Padding:

> Variable length; last byte contains the padding length.

Support for Name-based Virtual Servers

From the application protocol point of view, TLS belongs to a lower layer, although the TCP/IP model is too coarse to show it. This means that the TLS handshake is usually (except in the STARTTLS case) performed before the application protocol can start. In the name-based virtual server feature being provided by the application layer, all co-hosted virtual servers share the same certificate because the server has to select and send a certificate immediately after the ClientHello message. This is a big problem in hosting environments because it means either sharing the same certificate among all customers or using a different IP address for each of them.

There are two known workarounds provided by X.509:

- If all virtual servers belong to the same domain, a wildcard certificate can be used. Besides the loose host name selection that might be a problem or not, there is no common agreement about how to match wildcard certificates. Different rules are applied depending on the application protocol or software used.

- Add every virtual host name in the subjectAltName extension. The major problem being that the certificate needs to be reissued whenever a new virtual server is added.

To provide the server name, RFC 4366 Transport Layer Security (TLS) Extensions allow clients to include a Server Name Indication extension (SNI) in the extended ClientHello message. This extension hints the server immediately which name the client wishes to connect to, so the server can select the appropriate certificate to send to the clients.

RFC 2817, also documents a method to implement name-based virtual hosting by upgrading HTTP to TLS via an HTTP/1.1 Upgrade header. Normally this is to securely implement HTTP over TLS within the main "http" URI scheme (which avoids forking the URI space and reduces the number of used ports), however, few implementations currently support this.

Standards

Primary Standards

The current approved version of TLS is version 1.2, which is specified in:

- RFC 5246: "The Transport Layer Security (TLS) Protocol Version 1.2".

The current standard replaces these former versions, which are now considered obsolete:

- RFC 2246: "The TLS Protocol Version 1.0".

- RFC 4346: "The Transport Layer Security (TLS) Protocol Version 1.1".

As well as the never standardized SSL 2.0 and 3.0, which are considered obsolete:

- Internet Draft (1995), SSL Version 2.0.

- RFC 6101: "The Secure Sockets Layer (SSL) Protocol Version 3.0".

Extensions

Other RFCs subsequently extended TLS.

Extensions to TLS 1.0 include:

- RFC 2595: "Using TLS with IMAP, POP3 and ACAP". Specifies an extension to the IMAP, POP3 and ACAP services that allow the server and client to use transport-layer security to provide private, authenticated communication over the Internet.

- RFC 2712: "Addition of Kerberos Cipher Suites to Transport Layer Security (TLS)". The 40-bit cipher suites defined in this memo appear only for the purpose of documenting the fact that those cipher suite codes have already been assigned.

- RFC 2817: "Upgrading to TLS Within HTTP/1.1", explains how to use the Upgrade mechanism in HTTP/1.1 to initiate Transport Layer Security (TLS) over an existing TCP connection. This allows unsecured and secured HTTP traffic to share the same *well known* port (in this case, http: at 80 rather than https: at 443).

- RFC 2818: "HTTP Over TLS", distinguishes secured traffic from insecure traffic by the use of a different 'server port'.

- RFC 3207: "SMTP Service Extension for Secure SMTP over Transport Layer Security". Specifies an extension to the SMTP service that allows an SMTP server and client to use transport-layer security to provide private, authenticated communication over the Internet.

- RFC 3268: "AES Ciphersuites for TLS". Adds Advanced Encryption Standard (AES) cipher suites to the previously existing symmetric ciphers.

- RFC 3546: "Transport Layer Security (TLS) Extensions", adds a mechanism for negotiating protocol extensions during session initialisation and defines some extensions. Made obsolete by RFC 4366.

- RFC 3749: "Transport Layer Security Protocol Compression Methods", specifies the framework for compression methods and the DEFLATE compression method.

- RFC 3943: "Transport Layer Security (TLS) Protocol Compression Using Lempel-Ziv-Stac (LZS)".

- RFC 4132: "Addition of Camellia Cipher Suites to Transport Layer Security (TLS)".

- RFC 4162: "Addition of SEED Cipher Suites to Transport Layer Security (TLS)".

- RFC 4217: "Securing FTP with TLS".

- RFC 4279: "Pre-Shared Key Ciphersuites for Transport Layer Security (TLS)", adds three sets of new cipher suites for the TLS protocol to support authentication based on pre-shared keys.

Extensions to TLS 1.1 include:

- RFC 4347: "Datagram Transport Layer Security" specifies a TLS variant that works over datagram protocols (such as UDP).

- RFC 4366: "Transport Layer Security (TLS) Extensions" describes both a set of specific extensions and a generic extension mechanism.

- RFC 4492: "Elliptic Curve Cryptography (ECC) Cipher Suites for Transport Layer Security (TLS)".

- RFC 4680: "TLS Handshake Message for Supplemental Data".

- RFC 4681: "TLS User Mapping Extension".

- RFC 4785: "Pre-Shared Key (PSK) Ciphersuites with NULL Encryption for Transport Layer Security (TLS)".

- RFC 5054: "Using the Secure Remote Password (SRP) Protocol for TLS Authentication". Defines the TLS-SRP ciphersuites.

- RFC 5077: "Transport Layer Security (TLS) Session Resumption without Server-Side State".

- RFC 5081: "Using OpenPGP Keys for Transport Layer Security (TLS) Authentication", obsoleted by RFC 6091.

Extensions to TLS 1.2 include:

- RFC 5288: "AES Galois Counter Mode (GCM) Cipher Suites for TLS".

- RFC 5289: "TLS Elliptic Curve Cipher Suites with SHA-256/384 and AES Galois Counter Mode (GCM)".

- RFC 5746: "Transport Layer Security (TLS) Renegotiation Indication Extension".

- RFC 5878: "Transport Layer Security (TLS) Authorization Extensions".

- RFC 5932: "Camellia Cipher Suites for TLS".

- RFC 6066: "Transport Layer Security (TLS) Extensions: Extension Definitions", includes Server Name Indication and OCSP stapling.

- RFC 6091: "Using OpenPGP Keys for Transport Layer Security (TLS) Authentication".

- RFC 6176: "Prohibiting Secure Sockets Layer (SSL) Version 2.0".

- RFC 6209: "Addition of the ARIA Cipher Suites to Transport Layer Security (TLS)".

- RFC 6347: "Datagram Transport Layer Security Version 1.2".

- RFC 6367: "Addition of the Camellia Cipher Suites to Transport Layer Security (TLS)".

- RFC 6460: "Suite B Profile for Transport Layer Security (TLS)".

- RFC 6655: "AES-CCM Cipher Suites for Transport Layer Security (TLS)".

- RFC 7027: "Elliptic Curve Cryptography (ECC) Brainpool Curves for Transport Layer Security (TLS)".

- RFC 7251: "AES-CCM Elliptic Curve Cryptography (ECC) Cipher Suites for TLS".

- RFC 7301: "Transport Layer Security (TLS) Application-Layer Protocol Negotiation Extension".

- RFC 7366: "Encrypt-then-MAC for Transport Layer Security (TLS) and Datagram Transport Layer Security (DTLS)".

- RFC 7465: "Prohibiting RC4 Cipher Suites".

- RFC 7507: "TLS Fallback Signaling Cipher Suite Value (SCSV) for Preventing Protocol Downgrade Attacks".

- RFC 7568: "Deprecating Secure Sockets Layer Version 3.0".

- RFC 7627: "Transport Layer Security (TLS) Session Hash and Extended Master Secret Extension".

- RFC 7685: "A Transport Layer Security (TLS) ClientHello Padding Extension".

Encapsulations of TLS include:

- RFC 5216: "The EAP-TLS Authentication Protocol".

Informational RFCs

- RFC 7457: "Summarizing Known Attacks on Transport Layer Security (TLS) and Datagram TLS (DTLS)".

- RFC 7525: "Recommendations for Secure Use of Transport Layer Security (TLS) and Datagram Transport Layer Security (DTLS)".

References

- Boudriga, Noureddine (2010). Security of mobile communications. Boca Raton: CRC Press. pp. 32–33. ISBN 0849379423

- Chang, Rocky (October 2002). "Defending Against Flooding-Based Distributed Denial-of-Service Attacks: A Tutorial". IEEE Communications Magazine. 40 (10): 42–43. doi:10.1109/mcom.2002.1039856

- Conway, Richard (204). Code Hacking: A Developer's Guide to Network Security. Hingham, Massachusetts: Charles River Media. p. 281. ISBN 1-58450-314-9

- Abdullah A. Mohamed, «Design Intrusion Detection System Based On Image Block Matching», International Journal of Computer and Communication Engineering, IACSIT Press, Vol. 2, No. 5, September 2013

- McGraw, Gary (May 2007). "Silver Bullet Talks with Becky Bace" (PDF). IEEE Security & Privacy Magazine. 5 (3): 6–9. doi:10.1109/MSP.2007.70. Retrieved 18 April 2017

- Proceedings of National Conference on Recent Developments in Computing and Its Applications, August 12–13, 2009. I.K. International Pvt. Ltd. 2009-01-01. Retrieved 2014-04-22

Permissions

Index

CPSIA information can be obtained
at www.ICGtesting.com
Printed in the USA
LVHW061634090222
710692LV00006B/486